The Life of the Rev. Freeborn Garrettson

REV. FREEBORN GARRETTSON.
Aged 73

THE LIFE

1899.

REV. FREEBORN GARRETTSON.
Aged 73

THE LIFE

OF THE

REV. FREEBORN GARRETTSON;

COMPILED FROM

HIS PRINTED AND MANUSCRIPT

JOURNALS,

AND OTHER AUTHENTIC DOCUMENTS.

BY NATHAN BANGS, D. D.

"And they that be wise shall shine as the brightness of the firmament; and they that turn many to righteousness, as the stars for ever and ever." Daniel xii. 3.

NEW-YORK,

PUBLISHED BY J. EMORY AND B. WAUGH, AT THE CONFERENCE OFFICE, 14 CROSBY-STREET.

J. Collord, Printer.

1832.

DEDICATION.

TO MRS. CATHARINE GARRETTSON.

Madam,—To whom can I so appropriately dedicate this account of one endeared to you by so many ties, as to yourself, who for so long a time knew and appreciated his worth, enjoyed his society, and now so seriously mourn your loss? May that benignant Being, who so mercifully supported and directed your late excellent and venerable husband through a long life, and finally gave him such a complete victory over death, spread around you the wing of his mercy, and safely conduct you to "glory and immortality."

With Christian affection,
I am your humble servant,
NATHAN BANGS.

New-York, August 1, 1829.

PREFACE.

Very soon after the death of Mr. Garrettson it was made known to me by the bereaved widow, that he had expressed a desire that herself and daughter and myself should take the charge of his papers, and make such a disposition of them as we might consider to be fit and right.

After taking a cursory survey of them, it was resolved that Mrs. Garrettson and her daughter should first examine them, make such alterations or emendations as they might think expedient, and transmit them to me to be prepared for publication in the manner I might judge most suitable and proper.

Whatever reluctance I might feel to undertake a task so delicate, I could not refuse to comply with a request coming from one to whom I felt myself under many obligations for numerous tokens of his friendship, backed as it was by the wishes of his bereaved widow and daughter, and more especially as he had, previously to his death, frequently suggested the same thing to me.

It is generally known that Mr. Garrettson published an account of his experience and travels in the year 1791. This account embraces a period of about thirty-nine years of his natural life, and sixteen of his spiritual pilgrimage. To this printed journal he had appended several manuscript notes. These, which appear to have been written near the close of his life, give a more detailed account of some of the incidents glanced at in his printed journal. They have been carefully examined, and such parts of them as were considered most important, either to throw additional light on his history, or to make the incidents more interesting and useful, have been incorporated in the present memoir.

The original manuscript journal of his travels in Nova Scotia, and in some parts of the United States after his return from that province, was likewise consulted, and collated with the printed journal as far as it extended, with some letters from his friends in that country, his correspondence with Mr. Wesley, Dr. Coke, Mr. Asbury, and others, together with some anecdotes furnished by his pious daughter. From these documents several extracts have been made, some entire letters inserted, and after collating his printed and manuscript journals, it was found expedient, in order to make the narrative the more complete, to weave the two together.

During some periods of his life, Mr. Garrettson, it appears, either made no record of his exercises and labours, or did not preserve it. These chasms have been filled up either from the records of the church, from information furnished by a member of the family, or from my own recollection.

In giving an account of his early experience, and some of the first years of his labours in the "ministry of reconciliation," I thought it most advisable to give it chiefly in his own words, as thereby the genuine sentiments of his heart, the exercises of his mind, and the blessing of God upon his labours, would be the more accurately and forcibly expressed,—reserving to myself, however, the privilege of adding a word or sentence to make the sense clearer, and substituting one word for another, without either altering the meaning or changing the style.

From the month of March, 1824, to June, 1826, he kept a very regular account of the manner in which he employed his time. That the reader might see the influence of pure religion on the heart and conduct of a man who had been for so many years devoted to the service of God, and who expected so soon to appear in the presence of his Judge, I have made copious extracts from this part of his journal; and I humbly trust that they will tend to make that religion which shone so steadily and brightly in the life of Mr. Garrettson, appear above all other things the most desirable and necessary.

For the account of his remaining days, of his last sickness, and of his death, I am indebted partly to information received from Mrs. Garrettson and other friends who attended him in those solemn moments, and partly to my own knowledge.

These are the materials from which the following memoir has been compiled. It has been my endeavour to furnish the reader with a faithful narration of the incidents of his life, and of the various transactions in which he was engaged, as well as to exhibit an exact portraiture of Mr. Garrettson both in his private exercises and public labours. Though the critical reader will doubtless discover many defects, it is hoped not more than may find a reasonable apology from the circumstances under which I have performed my task. Other duties have had an imperious claim on my time and attention, and necessarily prevented my bestowing that labour on the work which otherwise I might have done.

I have only to say in conclusion, that should the reader find his faith in God confirmed, his love to Him and desire to be more entirely devoted to His service increased by reading this narration of the many instances of the displays of Divine providence and grace in behalf of a fellow being,—as I cannot but think will be the case,—he will add another testimony in favour of the utility of Christian biography, and the writer will feel that he has "not laboured in vain, nor spent his strength for naught," in furnishing to the surviving friends of Mr. Garrettson, and to the church generally, this imperfect account of his experience and labours, and of his triumphant entry into the world of spirits.   N. BANGS.

New-York, August 1, 1829.

CONTENTS.

INTRODUCTION, ... Page 5—16

CHAPTER I.
His ancestors—Childhood—Education—First Methodist preachers—His brother John—Illness—Death of his father—False security—His awakening and conversion, ... 17—31

CHAPTER II.
His happiness in God—Endures severe temptations—Frees his slaves—Reflections on slavery—Attends a class meeting—Declares what God had done for him—First speaks in public—Suffers persecution—Holds evening meetings, and God blesses his labours—Conversation with the parish priest—Strong exercises respecting becoming a travelling preacher—Makes the trial—Then tempted to desist—Makes trial of his gift again, . 31—47

CHAPTER III.
Commences a regular travelling preacher—Severely exercised—Much assisted—Holds a watch night—Goes to Fairfax circuit—Preaches in the parish church—Great manifestation of the power of God—Attacked by a Presbyterian minister on the doctrine of perfection—Farewell sermon—Lodges with a Quaker—Attends conference, . . 47—53

CHAPTER IV.
Deer creek conference—Goes to Brunswick circuit, Virginia—Happy seasons in preaching on the way—Arrives on his circuit, and finds a lively people—An officer interrogates him on the subject of fighting—Confidence in God increased—Great consolation in preaching—Tempting offers, which he resists—Whites and blacks much affected—Refuses the state oath—Escapes a threatened imprisonment—Goes to North Carolina—Reflections on Christian perfection—Experiences perfect love, and preaches this doctrine—Narrowly escapes being shot, ... 53—62

CHAPTER V.
From the conference in Leesburg, goes to the Peninsula, Md.—Persecution against the Methodists—Its causes—Perseveres in his work—Beaten and bruised—Blessed effects of this opposition in his own soul—Preaches the word with great effect—Enters the state of Delaware, and preaches the word with great success—Goes to Kent Island—Death of his brother John—Remarkable instance of conversion—Meets with opposition at Dover, but succeeds in preaching—Rescues a man who was attempting to hang himself—Conversion of an old persecutor—Not an enthusiast—Sinners flock to Christ—Delivered from the hand of the civil officer—Preaches and forms a society in Quantico—Vindicates infant baptism—Opposition meetings unsuccessful—Good effects of the gospel—Providential interview with a strange woman—Work of God greatly prospers—Remarks on silent meetings—Great inward conflicts—Remarkable answer to prayer—The arm of the Lord made bare in the conversion of souls—The wicked persecute—Escapes unhurt—Silences an ignorant disputant—And escapes imprisonment, 62—100

CONTENTS.

CHAPTER VI.

Leaves the Peninsula, and at the request of Mr. Asbury goes to Philadelphia—Society there in a depressed state—British army had just left the city—Citizens returned to their employments—Success in New-Jersey—Conversion of an old man—Remarkable account of a young woman, 100—104

CHAPTER VII.

Returns to the Peninsula—Introduction of Methodism into Dorset county—Peculiar exercises, and happy deliverance—Escapes an attempt to take his life—Taken by a mob—Imprisonment of J. Hartley—Maltreated and imprisoned—Happy in his own soul—Is set at liberty—Strange visions of the night, ... 104—117

CHAPTER VIII.

Disputes respecting the ordinances—Mistakes corrected—Breach healed, and harmony restored—Mr. Asbury's account of this affair—Goes to Baltimore—Thence to the Peninsula—Singular dream, . 118—123

CHAPTER IX.

Goes to Little York—Curious account of the conversion of a man and his wife—Effects thereof on the people—Goes to Colchester—Curious account of a deluded woman—Persecution rages—Visits a distressed man—Opposed by some soldiers who were quartered in the town—Powerful effects of the word preached—Attends conference in Baltimore where unanimity prevails—Great distress in Virginia—Rev. Mr. Jarret friendly to the Methodists, ... 124—133

CHAPTER X.

Travels extensively through Virginia and North Carolina—Political difficulties—Goes to Little York—Preaches in the fields—Preaches on the doctrine of perfection—Remarkable dream—Remarks on infant baptism—Greatly encouraged to persevere—Visits and rejoices with his old friends—Mourns over the stupidity of the people—Attends conference in Baltimore—Account of a blind man—Interesting account of a young female—Attends to the people of colour—Conversion of a great opposer—Meets Dr. Coke—Reflections on Mr. Wesley's plan for the organization of a church—Goes to call a conference of the preachers at Baltimore, . . 133—146

CHAPTER XI.

State of the societies at the conclusion of the war—Destitute of the ordinances—Mr. Wesley solicited to supply this deficiency—Finally consents—Ordains Dr. Coke, who arrives in America, in company with Richard Whatcoat and Thomas Vasey—Christmas conference—Mr. Asbury ordained a superintendent, and Mr. Garrettson and others, elders—He volunteers for Nova Scotia—Pastoral letters—Embarks for Halifax—Stormy passage—Kindly received at Halifax, preaches and forms a society—Makes a tour into the country, and preaches with success—Account of the Allenites—Letter to Mr. Wesley—Mr. Wesley's answer—Visits Liverpool—Society doubled by his labours—Commencement of Methodism in Liverpool—Visits Shelburne—Kindly treated by the rector of the parish—Society increases amidst opposition—Returns to Liverpool—Thence to Halifax—Correspondence with Mr. Wesley, Dr. Coke, and Bishop Asbury—Anecdotes and reflections—Leaves Nova Scotia for Boston—Origin of Methodism in Boston—Mr. Garrettson preaches there—Passes thence to Providence—Newport—New-York—Philadelphia—to Baltimore, and attends conference, 147—182

CHAPTER XII.

Attends conference in Baltimore—Elected superintendent of the societies in British America—Strong solicitations to accept the office—Reasons for declining—Appointed to the Peninsula—Contrast between the present and former state of the people here—Methodism generally prosperous—But some delusions—Their cause—Closes his labours in this place, . 183—189

CHAPTER XIII.

Proposes visiting New-England—Stops in New-York—Takes charge of the northern district—Enters on his work with twelve young preachers under his oversight—General state of the country—Correspondence with Mr. Wesley—Second tour through his district—Death of Mr. Cook—Curious conversation—Origin of Methodism in Ashgrove—Dangerously wounded—Commencement of Methodism on Long Island—Mr. Garrettson visits there—Obstacles to the progress of truth—Attends the first council in Baltimore—Journal of a tour through a part of New-England to Boston—Attends conference in New-York—Comparative view of the work in this part of the country, ... 189—219

CHAPTER XIV.

End of the printed journal—Division of his district—Visits Albany—Meets with Bishop Asbury—Attends conference—His testimony of Bishop Asbury's excellences—Account of the Shakers—Tour into the new settlements—State of the country—Work of God revives—Providential escape from danger—Visits the eastern part of his district—Meets Bishop Asbury, and converses with him on church government—Attends general conference in Baltimore—Mr. O'Kelly's division—Its effects—Visits his friends in Maryland—Returns to New-York—Passes through his district—His marriage, 220—234

CHAPTER XV.

Mr. Garrettson stationed in Philadelphia—On the New-York district—Settles his family in Rhinebeck—Prosecutes his labours—Erects a house—Goodness of God displayed towards him—Situation of his mansion—His cares multiply—Dedicates his new house to the Lord—Several stations he filled—In 1809 visits his old friends at the south—His account of this tour—Remarkable preservation—Visits Baltimore, Washington city, and various places on the Peninsula of Md.—Attends camp meetings, &c, 234—253

CHAPTER XVI.

Appointed to the New-York district—Some account of his duties—His sermon on the union of fear, hope, and love—General conference in 1808—Attends the first delegated conference in 1812—His views on some parts of our ecclesiastical economy—Appointed a conference missionary—His letter to the Rev. Lyman Beecher—State of that controversy—Mr. Garrettson's views of the subject—His charity sermon—Not pleased with being returned a supernumerary—Domestic enjoyments—Makes a journey to Albany, Schenectady, Troy, &c—Returns home—Solemn reflections—Makes another

xii   CONTENTS.

southern tour—Visits New-York, Trenton, Burlington, Philadelphia, Wilmington, Abington, and his native place—Reflections on the state of the people—Goes to Baltimore, and participates in a revival of the work of God in that city—Returns to Rhinebeck, ... 253—268

CHAPTER XVII.

Attends the New-York conference—Secession of a number from the church in New-York—His feelings in relation to that unhappy affair—Makes a short tour to the north—Thence to the eastward—Passes through New-York—Thence on to Middletown, Conn.—Thence to New-London, where he enjoys much peace—Visits Norwich and preaches—Conversation with a pious lady—Revival of religion—Grieved with beholding the ravages of Socinianism—Goes to Providence, R. I., and preaches—Probable check to the Socinian heresy—Visits Boston and Lynn—Origin of Methodism in Dorchester, Mass.—Visits Cambridge—Returns to Hartford—Thence to Rhinebeck—Domestic felicity—Makes a second tour—Affliction—Reflections thereon—Ardent desire for the salvation of souls—Returns through New-York city to Rhinebeck—Revival of religion there—Attends conference, . 269—279

CHAPTER XVIII.

Mr. Garrettson holds on his way—Engaged in building a house of worship at Rhinebeck—Sets off to attend general conference—Last visit to his native place—Some of the transactions of the conference—English delegates—Friendly intercourse and correspondence between the English and American conferences—His views on some points of church government—Attends the New-York conference—Makes a western tour—Reflections—Novatian schism—Testimony against sabbath breaking—Solemn reflections—Attends a camp meeting—Retires to his mansion—Private meditations—Visits some of his old friends in Westchester county—Notice of Governor Jay—Death of Mrs. Carpenter—Her character—Visits Kingston—Death and character of Mr. Sands—Death of Mr. C—— S—— Death of old friends in New-York—Reflections on a call to the ministry—Death and character of Mrs. Suckley—Visits Philadelphia—His zeal for missions—Deadness to the world—Attends the New-York conference—Preaches and publishes his semi-centennial sermon—Extracts from the sermon—Returns to Rhinebeck—Last entry in his journal, ... 280—313

CHAPTER XIX.

Continued a conference missionary—Instance of his affection—His last letter to Mrs. Garrettson—Attends conference at Troy—His health and activity—Presentiment of his approaching dissolution—Visits New-York—His last sermon—His sickness, and death—His remains taken to Rhinebeck, and buried—His death a loss to the church—General outlines of his character—Simplicity his distinguishing feature—This gave him success in his ministry—Inspired him with persevering zeal—Induced him to forsake all for Christ's sake—Gave him liberal views—Attached him to his brethren—It shone in domestic life—In the order of his household, his hospitality, his placability, and in the pulpit—His perseverance—Veneration for the sacred Scriptures—Dependence on Divine aid—Variety and usefulness of his preaching—Infirmities common to man—His unblemished reputation for nearly fifty-two years—Was the oldest Methodist travelling preacher—Concluding remark, ... 313—336

INTRODUCTION.

Mr. Garrettson was among the earliest Methodist preachers that were raised up in America. Being active and zealous from the commencement of his ministerial career, his life and labours are intimately connected with the rise and progress of Methodism in this country, and his name will therefore ever be associated with those self denying men who were instrumental in beginning and carrying forward that blessed work of God which has since spread so rapidly and extensively over this continent. On this account, it may not be amiss to introduce him to the notice of the reader by a sketch of the commencement of the work in this country.

The first Methodist society in America was formed in the city of New-York, in the year 1766, by a few emigrants from Ireland. About the same time, however, that Mr. Philip Embury and his associates were laying the foundation for such permanent good in this city, a similar society was formed in Frederick county, Maryland, through the instrumentality of Mr. Strawbridge, another local preacher from Ireland.

Those obscure emigrants, having been connected with the Methodists in their own country, and having tasted of the comforts of religion, not finding on their arrival here spiritual associates with whom they could "take sweet counsel," were induced to assemble by themselves in a private room. Here, by the earnest entreaties of Mrs. Hick, a pious matron, Mr. Embury very reluctantly commenced preaching the doctrines of the gospel as taught by the Rev. John Wesley, and God blessed his labours. Some, indeed, have denominated Captain Webb the founder of Methodism in America. This I believe to be a mistake. Though he might have been in America before Mr. Embury and his associates arrived, we have no authentic account of his preaching, much less of his attempting to form a society, until after Mr. Embury began in New-York. To ascertain the truth in respect to whom this honour belongs, the writer took much pains some years since by conversing with several of the aged members of the society, all of whom have since been called to their reward in heaven, who distinctly remembered the first rise of the society, and took a grateful delight in rehearsing the circumstances attending its formation and progress.

But though Capt. Webb, who was a converted soldier attached to the British army, which was at that time stationed in Albany, may not be considered the founder of Methodism in this country, he was one of its most zealous and successful promoters. Hearing of the society in New-York, and of the difficulties with which they had to contend, he came to their assistance, introduced himself to Mr. Embury, and appeared before the assembly in his military costume as a preacher of righteousness. To behold a military officer in the character of an ambassador of Jesus Christ was a matter of no small surprise to the citizens who attended the meetings: but when they heard his addresses in the name of his divine Master, coming, as they did, warm from a heart inflamed with the love of God, their curiosity was exchanged for a conviction of the truth, and a surrender of the heart to God.

In consequence of an increased attention to the word preached by Mr. Embury and Capt. Webb, the room in which they assembled became too small. They therefore hired a rigging loft in William-street, which they fitted up for a place of worship. Here they continued for a time to build "each other up in their most holy faith." While Mr. Embury remained in the city, working with his hands for a living, and preaching to the people on sabbath, attending prayer meetings, &c, Capt. Webb made excursions upon Long Island, where he preached Jesus Christ unto the people with peculiar energy and effect.

It was not long, however, before the rigging loft in William-street was found too small to accommodate all who wished to assemble with them. To remedy this inconvenience, they began to think seriously about building a chapel. To this undertaking, however, there were many difficulties. The members of the society were mostly poor, few in number, and but little known among the wealthy and influential portion of the citizens. Being encouraged, however, by the exhortations of Mrs. Hick, a woman of deep piety and great intrepidity of mind, they made an effort to erect a house for the Lord. Meeting with more favour than they had anticipated, they finally succeeded in purchasing some lots in John-street, on which they built a house, 60 feet by 42, in the year 1768, calling it, in honour of the founder of Methodism, WESLEY CHAPEL. While this house was in progress, T. T., in behalf of the society, addressed the following letter to Mr. Wesley:

"New-York, 11th April, 1768.

"REV. AND VERY DEAR SIR,—I intended writing to you for several weeks past; but a few of us had a very material transaction in view. I therefore postponed writing, until I could give you a particular account thereof: this was the purchasing of ground for building a preaching house upon, which, by the blessing of God, we have now concluded. But before I proceed, I shall give you a short account of the state of religion in this city. By the best intelligence I can collect, there was little either of the form or power of it, until Mr. Whitefield came over thirty years ago; and even after his first and second visits, there appeared but little fruit of his labours. But during his visit fourteen or fifteen years ago, there was a considerable shaking among the dry bones. Divers were savingly converted; and this work was much increased in his last journey about fourteen years since, when his words were really like a hammer and like a fire. Most part of the adults were stirred up: great numbers pricked to the heart, and by a judgment of charity, several found peace and joy in believing. The consequence of this work was, churches were crowded, and subscriptions raised for building new ones. Mr.

Whitefield's example provoked most of the ministers to a much greater degree of earnestness. And by the multitudes of people, old and young, rich and poor, flocking to the churches, religion became an honourable profession. There was now no outward cross to be taken up therein. Nay, a person who could not speak about the grace of God, and the new birth, was esteemed unfit for genteel company. But in awhile, instead of pressing forward, and growing in grace, (as he exhorted them,) the generality were pleading for the remains of sin, and the necessity of being in darkness. They esteemed their opinions as the very essentials of Christianity, and regarded not holiness either of heart or life.

"The above appears to me to be a genuine account of the state of religion in New-York eighteen months ago, when it pleased God to rouse up Mr. Embury to employ his talent (which for several years had been hid as it were in a napkin) by calling sinners to repentance, and exhorting believers to let their light shine before men. He spoke at first only in his own house. A few were soon collected together and joined into a little society, chiefly his own countrymen, Irish Germans. In about three months after, brother White and brother Souse from Dublin, joined them. They then rented an empty room in their neighbourhood, which was in the most infamous street in the city, adjoining the barracks. For some time few thought it worth their while to hear: but God so ordered it by his providence, that about fourteen months ago captain Webb, barrack master at Albany, (who was converted three years since at Bristol,) found them out, and preached in his regimentals. The novelty of a man preaching in a scarlet coat, soon brought greater numbers to hear than the room could contain. But his doctrines were quite new to the hearers; for he told them point blank, 'that all their knowledge and religion were not worth a rush, unless their sins were forgiven, and they had 'the witness of God's Spirit with theirs, that they were the children of God."

This strange doctrine, with some peculiarities in his person, made him soon taken notice of; and obliged the little society to look out for a larger house to preach in. They soon found a place that had been built for a rigging house, 60 feet in length and 18 in breadth.

"About this period Mr. Webb, whose wife's relations lived at Jamaica, Long Island, took a house in that neighbourhood, and began to preach in his own house, and several other places on Long Island. Within six months, about twenty-four persons received justifying grace, nearly half of them whites,—the rest negroes. While Mr. Webb was (to borrow his own phrase) 'felling trees on Long Island,' brother Embury was exhorting all who attended on Thursday evenings, and Sundays, morning and evening, at the rigging house, to flee from the wrath to come. His hearers began to increase, and some gave heed to his report, about the time the gracious providence of God brought me safe to New-York, after a very favourable passage of six weeks from Plymouth. It was the 26th day of October last, when I arrived, recommended to a person for lodging; I inquired of my host (who was a very religious man) if any Methodists were in New-York; he answered, that there was one Captain Webb, a strange sort of man, who lived on Long Island, and who sometimes preached at one Embury's, at the rigging house. In a few days I found out Embury. I soon found of what spirit he was, and that he was personally acquainted with you, and your doctrines, and that he had been a helper in Ireland. He had formed two classes, one of the men, and the other of the women, but had never met the society apart from the congregation, although there were six or seven men, and as many women, who had a clear sense of their acceptance in the beloved.

"You will not wonder at my being agreeably surprised in meeting with a few here, who have been and desire again to be in connexion with you. God only knows the weight of affliction I felt on leaving my native country. But I have reason now to conclude God intended all for my good. Ever since I left London, my load has been removed, and I have found a cheerfulness in being banished from all near and dear to me, and I made a new covenant with my God, that I would go to the utmost parts of the earth, provided he would raise up a people, with whom I might join in his praise. On the great deep I found a more earnest desire to be united with the people of God than ever before. I made a resolution that God's people should be my people, and their God my God: and bless his holy name, I have since experienced more heartfelt happiness than ever I thought it possible to have on this side eternity. All anxious care about my dear wife and children is taken away. I cannot assist them, but I daily and hourly commend them to God in prayer, and I know he hears my prayers, by an answer of love in my heart. I find power daily to devote myself unto him; and I find power also to overcome sin. If any uneasiness at all affects me, it is because I can speak so little of so good a God.

"Mr. Embury lately has been more zealous than formerly; the consequence of which is, that he is more lively in preaching; and his gifts as well as graces are much increased. Great numbers of serious persons came to hear God's word as for their lives; and their numbers increased so fast, that our house for six weeks past would not contain half the people.

"We had some consultations how to remedy this inconvenience, and Mr. Embury proposed renting a small lot of ground for twenty-one years, and to exert our utmost endeavours to build a wooden tabernacle; a piece of ground was proposed; the ground rent was agreed for, and the lease was to be executed in a few days. We, however, in the mean time, had two several days for fasting and prayer, for the direction of God and his blessing on our proceedings; and providence opened such a door as we had no expectation of. A young man, a sincere Christian, and constant hearer, though not joined in society, not giving any thing towards this house, offered ten pounds to buy a lot of ground, went of his own accord to a lady who had two lots to sell, on one of which there is a house that rents for eighteen pounds per annum. He found the purchase money of the two lots was six hundred pounds, which she was willing should remain in the purchasers' possession, on good security. We called once more on God for his direction, and resolved to purchase the whole. There are eight of us who are joint purchasers: among whom Mr. Webb and Mr. Lupton are men of property. I was determined the house should be on the same footing as the orphan house at New-Castle, and others in England: but as we were ignorant how to draw the deeds, we purchased for us and our heirs, until a copy of the writing is sent us from England, which we desire may be sent by the first opportunity.

"Before we began to talk of building, the devil and his children were very peaceable: but since this affair took place, many ministers have cursed us in the name of the Lord, and laboured with all their might to stop their congregations from assisting us. But he that sitteth in the highest laughed them to scorn. Many have broken through and given their friendly assistance. We have collected above one hundred pounds more than our own contributions; and have reason to hope in the whole we shall have two hundred pounds: but the house will cost us four hundred pounds more, so that unless God is pleased to raise up friends we shall yet be at a loss. I believe Mr. Webb and Mr. Lupton will borrow or advance two hundred pounds, rather than the building should not go forward; but the interest of money here is a great burden—being seven per cent. Some of our brethren proposed writing to you for a collection in England: but I was averse to this, as I well know our friends there are over burdened already. Yet so far I would earnestly beg: if you would intimate our circumstances to particular persons of ability, perhaps God would open their hearts to assist this infant society, and contribute to the first preaching house on the original Methodist plan in all America, (excepting Mr. Whitefield's orphan house in Georgia;) but I shall write no more on this subject.

"There is another point far more material, and in which I must importune your assistance, not only in my own name, but also in the name of the whole society. We want an able and experienced preacher; one who has both gifts and grace necessary for the work. God has not, indeed, despised the day of small things. There is a real work of grace begun in many hearts, by the preaching of Mr. Webb and Mr. Embury; but although they are both useful, and their hearts in the work, they want many qualifications for such an undertaking; and the progress of the gospel here depends much upon the qualifications of preachers.

"In regard to a preacher, if possible we must have a man of wisdom, of sound faith, and a good disciplinarian: one whose heart and soul are in the work; and I doubt not but by the goodness of God such a flame would be soon kindled, as would never stop until it reached the great South sea. We may make many shifts to evade temporal inconveniences; but we cannot purchase such a preacher as I have described. Dear sir, I entreat you for the good of thousands, to use your utmost endeavours to send one over. I would advise him to take shipping at Boston, Liverpool, or Dublin, in the month of July or early in August; by embarking at this season he will have fine weather in his passage, and probably arrive here in the month of September. He will see before winter what progress the gospel has made.

"With respect to money for the payment of the preacher's passage over, if they could not procure it, we would sell our coats and shirts to procure it for them.

"I most earnestly beg an interest in your prayers, and trust you and many of our brethren will not forget the church in this wilderness.

"I remain with sincere esteem, rev. and dear sir,

"Your very affectionate brother and servant,
"T. T."

In answer to the earnest request contained in this letter, Mr. Wesley sent over Messrs. Boardman and Pilmoor, and £50 sterling, as a "token of brotherly love." They were cordially received by the people here, and soon much encouraged in their work, as the following letter from Mr. Pilmoor will fully show:

"Philadelphia, Oct. 31, 1769.

"Rev. sir,—By the blessing of God we are safely arrived here, after a tedious passage of nine weeks. We were not a little surprised to find Capt. Webb in town, and a society of about one hundred members, who desire to be in close connexion with you. 'This is the Lord's doing, and it is marvellous in our eyes.'

"I have preached several times, and the people flock to hear in multitudes. Sunday evening I went out upon the common. I had the stage appointed for the horse race for my pulpit, and I think between four and five thousand hearers, who heard with attention still as night. 'Blessed be God for field preaching. When I began to talk of preaching at five o'clock in the morning, the people thought it would not answer in America; however, I resolved to try, and I had a very good congregation.

"Here seems to be a great and effectual door opening in this country, and I hope many souls will be gathered in. The people in general like to hear the word, and seem to have ideas of salvation by grace."

After continuing a short time in Philadelphia, Mr. Pilmoor made an excursion to Maryland, where he found Mr. Strawbridge, and preached with some success. He likewise visited some parts of Virginia and North Carolina; and witnessing the happy effects of his labours in the awakening of sinners, he formed some societies. In all places which he visited, he found people eager to hear the word, and kind to those who came to preach it. From hence he returned to Philadelphia, and soon came to New-York, while Mr. Boardman went to Philadelphia; thus commencing, in the early stage of their labours, a regular change from place to place. The society in New-York, under the labours of Mr. Embury and Capt. Webb, was in a flourishing state on the arrival of Mr. Boardman, whose godly simplicity and evangelical preaching were made a peculiar blessing to many. In this prosperous state of the society, Mr. Pilmoor entered upon his charge over them. As he thought it most prudent to make a fair trial before he transmitted his account of the state of things to Mr. Wesley, he deferred writing until April 24, 1770, on which day he wrote the following letter:—

"Our house contains about seventeen hundred hearers. About a third part of those who attend get in; the rest are glad to hear without. There appears such a willingness in the Americans to hear the word, as I never saw before. They have no preaching in some of the back settlements. I doubt not but an effectual door will be opened among them! O! may the Most High now give his Son the heathen for his inheritance. The number of the blacks that attend the preaching affects me much."

From these representations of the state and disposition of the people in America, Mr. Wesley was induced to concert measures to send them over more labourers. Accordingly the next year, 1771, Mr. Francis Asbury and Mr. Richard Wright, who volunteered their services, were dismissed under the blessing of God for the help of their brethren in America. They set sail from Bristol, Sept. 2, 1771, and landed in Philadelphia the 24th of Oct. following. They were received with great cordiality, "the people hardly knowing," says Mr. Asbury, "how to show their love sufficiently, bidding us welcome with fervent affection, and receiving us as the angels of God."

According to a notice in Mr. Asbury's Journal, vol. iii, p. 109, it appears that when he arrived in this country, he found three hundred Methodists in New-York, two hundred and fifty in Philadelphia, and a few in New-Jersey, probably in all about six hundred. Those in Maryland do not appear to be included in this number. On the arrival of Mr. Asbury, he very properly judged that they could not expect a general spread of the work of God, unless they extended themselves into the country towns and villages. He accordingly led the way, by which the prospects of usefulness opened before them in every direction.

By the faithful exertions of Mr. Asbury and those who were associated with him, the work of God extended among the people, and it was soon perceived that more help was much needed to supply the calls of the people. Indeed the people in many places, particularly in the middle and southern provinces—for so these United States were then called, being a part of the British dominions—were but poorly supplied with the word and ordinances of Christ, and pure religion was generally at a very low ebb. A taste for experimental religion had, it is true, been created in some hearts, by the powerful preaching of the celebrated Whitefield, who, some time previously to the arrival of the Methodist missionaries, had travelled through the country, and preached with his usual zeal and success. The fields, however, at this time, "were ripe for the harvest;" and a faithful account of the state of affairs here being transmitted to Mr. Wesley, in 1773 Messrs. Thomas Rankin and George Shadford volunteered their services and came over to the continent: and the following year Messrs. James Dempster and Martin Rodda were added to the number.

To Mr. Rankin Mr. Wesley committed the general superintendency of the work, and he called the first regular conference in the city of Philadelphia, in the month of June, 1773.* At this conference there were returned on the minutes 10 travelling preachers, and 1160 members of society. From the printed minutes of the conference for 1774, it appears there were 14 preachers who commenced their itinerant labours in America, viz. William Watters, Abraham Whiteworth, Joseph Yearbry, Philip Gatch, Philip Ebert, William Duke, John Wade, Daniel Ruff, Edward Drumgole, Isaac Rollins, Robert Lindsay, Samuel Spragg, Richard Webster, John King; and three English preachers, viz. Thomas Rankin, Francis Asbury, and George Shadford. The numbers in society this year were 2073. Mr. Boardman, who was a man deeply devoted to God, and a sound able minister of Jesus Christ, and Mr. Pilmoor, it appears had both returned to England.

From the above list of preachers it will be perceived that the Lord of the harvest had raised up labourers in this country to cultivate his field.

This sketch brings us down to the year 1775, at which time, according to the printed minutes, there were 19 preachers stationed, and 3148 members in society. It was during this year that Mr. Freeborn Garrettson, who is to be the subject of the following memoir, was brought to the saving knowledge of the truth, and commenced his ministerial labours. I shall therefore close this introduction by remarking that the above short account of the commencement of Methodism in this country, compared with what it now is, shows by what feeble and comparatively inefficient means, God often accomplishes His work in the souls of men; and that all this is done according to an inspired declaration, that "no man should glory in man, but he that glorieth must glory in the Lord."

* This date corresponds with that in the printed minutes; but according to Mr. Asbury's Journal, this conference was held July 14, 1773, and Mr. Drew, in his Life of Dr. Coke, agrees with Mr. Asbury in an extract from Mr. Rankin.

THE LIFE
OF THE
REV. FREEBORN GARRETTSON.

CHAPTER I.

His ancestors—Childhood—Education—First Methodist preachers—His brother John—Illness—Death of his father—False security—His awakening and conversion.

Mr. Garrettson was born in the state of Maryland, August 15, in the year 1752. His parents were members of the Church of England, and educated their children in the same faith. His grandfather was an emigrant from Great Britain, and was among the first settlers in the province of Maryland, on the west side of the Chesapeake bay, near the mouth of the Susquehannah river. Being surrounded with the aborigines of the country, his situation was so perilous that he found himself compelled to go armed by day and night. The place where he first settled is still designated by his name, and is the residence of a branch of the family.

Mr. Garrettson's father was a man of moral character, and esteemed by his neighbours as a good Christian. His mother truly feared the Lord, having been enlightened under the ministrations of some of the followers of the Rev. George Whitefield, who itinerated so largely and preached so successfully through the country. Though she did not connect herself with these people, she had frequent intercourse with them, and "I have," says Mr. Garrettson, "frequently heard her speak of their piety with tears." He adds, "Those blessed men of God, the Tennants, in their itinerating tours, often preached through those parts, and their labours were blessed to many."

The following is the account which Mr. Garrettson gives of his early childhood: "I was," as my parents informed me, "from my infancy prone to pride, self will, and stubbornness. As far as I know of any one predominant principle of my nature, it was a love of freedom and independence. I could easily be led, but it seemed morally impossible to drive me. When I was at school, if ever I got into a difficulty with any of my school mates, it was in consequence of my taking part with some poor children, who I thought were not treated kindly. With such it was a pleasure with me to divide my morsel." "It would be well," he adds, "for parents to be acquainted with the native genius of their children, and to educate them accordingly. Had this been the case with me, perhaps I might have engaged in the work for which I was designed, under more favourable auspices, as it respects education." These reflections are certainly founded in the nature of things, and should be heeded, as far as practicable, by every parent. The following account shows the benign influence which parental example and admonitions have on young and tender minds.

"I was very early taught the Lord's prayer, creed, and ten commandments, together with the catechism of the church of England; and was in early life restrained by my tender parents from open sin. It pleased the Lord to remove my dear mother into eternity when I was young. But I shall never forget the admonitions which she gave me. One Lord's day, when I was about seven years of age, my mother was retired, (I was sitting by her side,) and while she was reading the two last chapters of the Revelation, when she came to the place where it speaks of the tree and water of life, she made a full stop, and with eyes uplifted to heaven, and tears flowing down, "O!" said she, "that I may be happy enough to eat of that fruit, and drink of that water in my heavenly Father's kingdom!" I believe the blessed Spirit was with her, and I felt the divine operations: but I knew him not; for we lived in a dark time. One day when I was about nine years of age, as I was walking alone in the field, it was strongly impressed on my mind, as if I had heard a voice, "Ask, and it shall be given you." I was immediately desirous to know what it meant, and it occurred to my mind, that this was a scriptural promise. But I, having no ideas of spiritual things, immediately ran to the house and told my elder brother it was revealed to me that I should be very rich. Shortly after this, I was by myself and it was suggested to me, "Do you know what a saint is?" I paused a while in my mind, and answered, there are no saints in this our day on earth. The suggestion continued, "A saint is one that is wholly given up to God." And immediately in idea, I saw such a person who appeared the most beautiful of any I had ever beheld. I was affected, and prayed to the Lord to make me a saint, and it was strongly impressed upon my mind that I should be one; and a spirit of joy sprung up within me; but I had no one to open to me the way of salvation.

"Some time after this, great afflictions befell my father's family: first a sister, then my mother, and then two servants were removed into eternity. The ninth day of my sister's illness, she asked for nourishment, and ate heartily for one in her low state. After she had done she desired to be raised in the bed; I am, said she, about to leave the world. The family were called together by her request, and were in a flood of tears: "Weep not for me," said she, "for I am not afraid to die. I am going to my Jesus, who will do more for me than any of you can do." I believe her soul was happy. And the affecting exhortation which she gave will never be forgotten by me. When almost spent, she desired to be laid down, bidding all farewell; and within a few minutes, with a smiling countenance, she bid the world adieu. From her infancy her conscientiousness and uprightness were noticed by all who knew her. It was not common to find her on the Lord's day without a Bible; her old uncle, who was a communicant in the church, used to say, "Sally lives as she would wish to die." From this time a melancholy gloom hung over me, and I frequently went alone to weep. I felt that I wanted something, but what it was I knew not; for I had none to take me by the hand and lead me into the narrow path. I know the blessed Spirit often strove with me, so that I have been melted into tenderness; but I knew not the way of salvation. About this time I bought myself a pocket Testament, frequently withdrew to read it; and was much affected with the sufferings of our blessed Lord. Our unhappy minister was a stranger to God, and the most of his flock, I fear, were in the way to ruin.

When I was about twelve years of age I was removed to another school, where after a time I threw off all seriousness and became as wild as the rest of my young play mates. The most of my school hours, after I turned fourteen, were taken up in branches of the mathematics and book keeping, and the intervals of my time, in the study of astronomy. I have often continued alone in the study of this till after midnight without a serious thought of God, or my eternal welfare. Between the seventeenth and eighteenth years of my age I left school and began to think of living in the world. But alas! I was careless, and carnal, though what the world calls a moral youth. I was fond of pleasure, and loved this world more than God. O! what reason have I to praise God for his goodness, in pursuing me with the overtures of mercy."

The following account of the introduction of Methodism into this country, taken principally from manuscript notes which Mr. Garrettson had written to his printed journal, corresponds with what has already been said on this subject in the introduction:

"About this time there began to be much said about the people called Methodists in Baltimore county where I then lived. The following is the manner in which these people commenced their work of love in this country: Mr. Strawbridge, a local preacher from Ireland, came to this province and settled at Pipe creek, in Maryland, and Mr. Williams, another Irish local preacher, came over. These two men travelled, and preached considerably, and did much good. Mr. Strawbridge raised a society at Pipe creek. About the same time Mr. Embury, a local preacher from Ireland, came over and settled in New-York, and raised a society. All this was before Mr. Wesley sent any regular travelling preacher to this country. Mr. Strawbridge came to the house of a gentleman near where I lived to stay all night; I had never heard him preach, but as I had a great desire to be in company with a person who had caused so much talk in the country, I went over and sat and heard him converse till nearly midnight, and when I retired, it was with these thoughts, I have never spent a few hours so agreeably in my life. He spent most of the time in explaining Scripture and in giving interesting anecdotes, and perhaps one of them would do to relate here: 'A congregation came together at a certain place, and a gentleman who was hearing thought the preacher had directed his whole sermon to him, and retired home after service in disgust. However, he concluded he would hear him once more, and hide himself behind the people so that the preacher should not see him: it was the old story; his character was delineated—he retired dejected, but concluded, possibly the preacher saw me, and I will try him once more: he did so, and hid himself behind a door. The preacher happened to take his text from Isaiah, 'And a man shall be as a hiding place,' &c. In the midst of the sermon the preacher cried out, Sinner, come from your scouting hole! The poor fellow came forward, looked the preacher in the face, and said, you are a wizzard, and the devil is in you; I will hear you no more."

At the time of which we are now speaking there were

several zealous itinerants circulating through the country, who had been instrumental in the conversion of souls, and in establishing societies.

"Many went out to hear them, and I among the rest, but the place was so crowded I could not get into the house: but from what I could understand, I thought they preached the truth, and did by no means dare to join with the multitude in persecuting them; but thought I would let them alone, and keep close to my own church. O! those soul damning sins, pride and unbelief, which kept me from God and his people!

"Blessed be God, it was not long after that his Holy Spirit began again to work powerfully with me. One day as I was riding home, I met a young man who had been hearing the Methodists, and had got his heart touched under the word. He stopped me in the road, and began to talk so sweetly about Jesus and his people, and recommended him to me in such a winning manner, that I was deeply convinced there was a reality in that religion, and that it was time for me to think seriously on the subject.

"Not many days had passed before a little book fell into my hands, called Russel's Seven Sermons. By this book I was advised to make as exact an estimate of all my sins as possible; I did so, and found they were numerous, for I began to see myself in the gospel glass; and many were the tears I shed over this book. I promised an amendment of life; but my repentance was too much like the early dew. The way of salvation was not open to me, and there was an unwillingness in me to submit. But as my blessed Lord was not willing that I should perish, his good Spirit still strove with me. One day as I was passing over a rapid stream, a log on which I had frequently gone gave way, and I was near being swept down the stream; after struggling a while I got out, though much wounded among the sharp rocks. This query struck my mind with great weight, 'What would have become of your soul, had you been drowned?' I wept bitterly, and prayed to the Lord under a sense of my guilt. Still my stubborn heart was not willing to submit, though I began to carry a little hell in my bosom.

"In May, 1772, as I was riding out one afternoon, I went down a descent over a large broad rock; my horse stumbled and threw me; and with the fall on the rock, and the horse blundering over me, I was beaten out of my senses. I was alone, and how long I laid I know not; but when I had in some measure recovered, I found myself on my knees, with my hands and eyes raised to heaven, crying to God for mercy. It came strongly into my mind that had I then been taken into the other world, I should have dropped into hell. I felt my misery, and praised God, as well as I knew how, for my deliverance; and before I moved from the place I promised to serve him all the days of my life. But before I arose from my knees, all my pain of body was removed, and I felt nearly as well as ever I did in my life. I also felt the drawing of God's Spirit, and in a measure saw a beauty in Jesus; but I did not know that my sins were forgiven; neither was the plan of salvation clearly open to me; but I went on my way determined, by grace, to be a follower of Christ. All the Antinomians in the world could not make me believe, that a man cannot feel sweet drawings before he experiences justification.

"I now procured a collection of the best religious books that I could; among which were the writings of Mr. Hervey, The Travels of True Godliness, and Alleine's Alarm to the Unconverted; for as yet I had not seen any of Mr. Wesley's publications, nor conversed on religious subjects with any of the Methodists, except the one above mentioned.

"As I lived a retired life, I frequently read, prayed, and wept till after midnight; and often withdrew to the woods and other private places for prayer. In some measure my name was already cast out as evil, though I was ashamed to let any one know the exercises of my mind, or that I used secret prayer: and in order to conceal it when in company, I have frequently grieved the blessed Spirit, by joining in trifling conversation; for I was much afraid of being thought a hypocrite. The Holy Spirit still pursued me, and I attended strictly to the duties of the family over which I was placed. I had as yet heard very few Methodist sermons; and the devil strove very hard to keep me from going among those people. Some time after, my late well tried friend and brother, Mr. Francis Asbury, came to our country: I went to hear him one evening at R. W.'s. The place was crowded, but I got to the door and sat down. He had not preached long before I sensibly felt the word, and his doctrine seemed as salve to a festering wound. I heard him with delight, and bathed in tears could have remained there till the rising of the sun, the time passed so sweetly away; I was delightfully drawn, and was greatly astonished to find a person go on so fluently without his sermon before him. I suppose hundreds of thoughts passed through my mind. But I returned home with gladness, fully persuaded that he was a servant of God, and that he preached in a way I had not heard before. I followed him to another preaching place, and fixing my attentive eye upon him, I found him to be a workman that need not be ashamed, rightly dividing the word. He began to wind about me in such a manner that I found my sins in clusters, as it were, around me: and the law in its purity, probing to the very bottom, and discovering the defects of my heart. I was ready to cry out, "How does this stranger know me so well!" After sermon was ended, I wished not to speak to any one, but returned home with my mind very solemnly affected.

"Methodism at this time began in some measure to spread; for the blessed God touched the hearts of several young men, converted their souls, and called them to preach, which appeared to be a new thing in our country. Among the first were W. Watters, R. Webster, two brothers by the name of Rollins, and several others who began to exhort; they were zealous, their labours were blessed, and persecution arose: the cry began to be, enthusiasm—false prophets. Indeed, though I was under conviction, and had felt the drawings of the Spirit, I had my fears that matters were going too far, though I did not dare open my mouth against the work.

"My father began to be troubled about me, and came to see me. We sat up talking till nearly midnight. 'I have no objection,' said he, 'to your being religious; but why would you turn from the church?' I replied, I have no intention to leave the church, but whenever persons become serious, they are called Methodists, and their names are cast out as evil. After we parted I found great tenderness of heart, and shed many tears in private, and many promises occurred to my mind. I loved the Methodists, and yet the enemy of my soul kept me at a distance from them. Unbelief and pride deprived me of the comforts of assurance.

"In April, 1773, my brother John was taken dangerously ill, so that his life was despaired of. One Lord's day many of our relations and friends came to see him, expecting every minute that he would breathe his last. I was greatly concerned on account of his soul, which seemed to be just launching into eternity, and I feared that he was unprepared. I went round to the back part of the bed, and kneeling down, I prayed earnestly to the Lord to have mercy on his soul. After I had done praying I perceived his lips were moving, but could not hear a word that he spoke, till I put my ear close to his mouth, (apparently he was just going,) and heard him say, "Lord, thou knowest I am unprepared to die, have mercy on me, and raise me up, and give me a longer space, and I will serve thee; thy Spirit has often strove with me, but I have rejected thee," &c. Thus did he plead with the Lord for a considerable time. He knew, and so did I, the moment of time when the Lord answered prayer, and granted him a longer space. Immediately I rose from my knees, and told the waiting company they need not be uneasy, for the Lord would raise him again; instantly the disorder turned, he fell into a doze, and within a few days was able to walk about his room. After his recovery, I conversed with him on the subject, and he told me that he saw death approaching, that he was summoned to appear in the world of spirits, and that hell was his doom. I knew, said he, when a reprieve in answer to prayer was sent, the blow averted, and the tender thread lengthened, on condition that I would give the remainder of my days to the Lord. A few years after he was really changed in heart; he lived two years and eight months happy in the service of God, and died a witness of perfect love.

"About this time the Lord laid me under his afflicting hand, and I was brought nigh unto death. During the time of my illness, I was in a very strange way; I lay on my bed singing praises to God without any dread of death; I felt my mind easy; I thought if I was removed I should go to heaven; I was willing to die; I did not know my sins were forgiven; but I felt a strong hope, though I was not fully acquainted with the plan of salvation. Who can tell what state my soul was in? I was a good Churchman,* but a poor Methodist. Blessed be the name of the Lord! He delights not in the death of a sinner, for he raised me up again; but still the enemy of my soul strove to keep me from among God's dear despised children.

"The August following, it pleased the Lord to take my father into eternity;—surely it was painful to lose the tenderest of parents. From my earliest knowledge of his family, consisting of about twenty in number, I do not

* Religion in the Church of England was at this time at a very low ebb in Maryland.

remember ever to have heard an oath sworn either by white or black; and it was a rare thing for him to correct either children or servants, though still there was a trembling at his word. I frequently visited him in the time of his illness, (for he had a long and tedious sickness,) and he seemed very fond of my company: I have reason to believe he went happy out of this dangerous world. Being now left in the entire charge of a family, and the settlement of my father's business mostly devolving on me, I was surrounded with many cares and troubles, which were no help to the affairs of my salvation. The devil strove hard to drive away all my good desires, but still I attended constantly to my secret devotions, though at times cold enough. It was not long after the death of my father that I had a particular interview with the new parish minister, who was a very clever man, of a moral character, and much respected in the place. I was a constant attendant on his ministry, and frequently conversed with him on divine subjects. He told me the Methodists carried matters too far, that a man could not know his sins were forgiven, and that all we might expect in this life was a hope springing from an upright life. This doctrine exactly tallied with my experience, and was food for my fallen nature. I soon fully agreed with him in sentiment, and plead that no man could know his sins forgiven in this world. The grand enemy began now to exercise my mind in another way; namely, to seek a literary qualification for the ministry in the church. This hung upon me for a considerable time; and I applied myself to reading and study for that purpose, often consulting my new counsellor. The Spirit of the Lord at times strove very powerfully, and I was frequently afraid that all was not well with me, especially when I was under Methodist preaching. To these people I was drawn: but it was like death to me; for I thought I had rather serve God in any way than among them; while at the same time something within would tell me they were right. Being amazingly agitated in mind, I at length came to this conclusion, to give up my former pursuits bend my mind to the improvement of my worldly property, and serve God in a private manner. I now sat out in full pursuit of business, with an expectation of accumulating the riches of the world.

"During the time of my self-secure state, I had the form of godliness, attended the Church constantly, and sometimes went to hear the Methodists: I fasted once a week, prayed frequently every day in secret places, endeavoured to attend strictly to the sabbath, often reproved open sin, and denied myself of what the world calls pleasure. I was so fast set in my way, that I thought I should certainly go to heaven; and if at any time I was overtaken by sin, I would endeavour to mend my pace and pray more frequently. I cannot say I was always without doubts; for often, under Methodist preaching, my poor foundation would shake, especially under the preaching of dear brother George Shadford, and I would scarcely recover my hope for many days; then I would be tempted to think they were a deluded people, and I would go among them no more: but still I was drawn again and again. I stood in a manner between the children of God and the world. When I was with the people of God I would endeavour to confute them; and when I was among their enemies, I plead their cause.

"One day, being at a distance from home, I met with a zealous Methodist exhorter. He asked me if I was born again? I told him I had a hope that I was. Do you know, said he, that your sins are forgiven? No, replied I, neither do I expect that knowledge in this world. I perceive, said he, that you are in the broad road to hell, and if you die in this state you will be damned. The Scripture, said I, tells us that the tree is known by its fruit; and our Lord likewise condemns rash judgment. What have you seen or known of my life that induced you to judge me in such a manner? I pity you, said I, and turned my back on him.

But I could not easily forget the words of that pious young man, for they were as spears running through me.

"In this state I continued till June, 1775. The blessed morning I shall never forget! In the night I went to bed as usual, and slept till day break: just as I awoke, I was alarmed by an awful voice, 'Awake, sinner, for you are not prepared to die.' This was as strongly impressed on my mind, as if it had been a human voice as loud as thunder. I was instantly smitten with conviction in a manner I had not been before. I started from my pillow, and cried out, Lord, have mercy on my soul! As it was about the commencement of the late unhappy war, and there was to be a general review that day near my house, I had promised myself much satisfaction; for I was a professed friend to the American cause: however, instead of giving my attendance, I passed the morning in solitude; and in the afternoon went out and heard a Methodist sermon. In sorrow I went, and in sorrow returned; and in sorrow the night passed away. None but those that have experienced the like exercises, can form an idea of what I underwent for several days.

"The enmity of my heart seemed to rise higher and higher. On the Tuesday following in the afternoon I heard Mr. Daniel Ruff preach; and was so oppressed that I was scarcely able to support my burden. After preaching I called in with D. R. at Mrs. G——'s, and stayed till about nine o'clock. On my way home, being much distressed, I alighted from my horse in a lonely wood, and bowed my knees before the Lord; I sensibly felt two spirits striving with me. The good Spirit set forth to my inmost mind the beauties of religion; and I seemed almost ready to lay hold on my Saviour. O unbelief, soul damning sin! it kept me from my Jesus. Then would the enemy rise up on the other hand, and dress religion in as odious a garb as possible; yea, he seemed in a moment of time, to set the world and the things of it in the most brilliant colours before me; telling me, all these things should be mine if I would give up my false notions and serve him. His temptations of a truth might be compared to a sweeping rain. I continued on my knees a considerable time, and at last began to give way to the reasoning of the enemy. My tender feelings abated, and my tears were gone; my heart was hard, but I continued on my knees in a kind of meditation; and at length addressed my Maker thus: Lord, spare me one year more, and by that time I can put my worldly affairs in such a train that I can serve thee. I seemed as if I felt the two spirits with me. The answer was, 'Now is the accepted time.' I then plead for six months, but was denied—one month, no—I then asked for one week, the answer was, 'This is the time.' For some time the devil was silent, till I was denied one week in his service; then it was he shot a powerful dart. 'The God,' said he, 'you are attempting to serve is a hard Master; and I would have you to desist from your endeavour.' Carnal people know very little of this kind of exercise: but it was as perceptible to me, as if I had been conversing with two persons face to face. As soon as this powerful temptation came, I felt my heart rise sensibly (I do not say with enmity) against my Maker, and immediately I arose from my knees with these words, 'I will take my own time, and then I will serve thee.' I mounted my horse with a hard unbelieving heart, unwilling to submit to Jesus. O what a good God had I to deal with! I might in justice have been sent to hell.

"I had not rode a quarter of a mile, before the Lord met me powerfully with these words, 'These three years have I come seeking fruit on this fig tree; and find none.' And then the following words were added, 'I have come once more to offer you life and salvation, and it is the last time: choose, or refuse.' I was instantly surrounded with a divine power: heaven and hell were disclosed to my view, and life and death were set before me. I do believe if I had rejected this call, mercy would have been for ever taken from me. Man hath power to choose or refuse in religious matters; otherwise God could have no reasonable service from his creatures. I knew the very instant when I submitted to the Lord, and was willing that Christ should reign over me: I likewise knew the two sins which I parted with last, pride and unbelief. I threw the reins of my bridle on my horse's neck, and putting my hands together, cried out, Lord, I submit. I was less than nothing in my own sight; and was now, for the first time, reconciled to the justice of God. The enmity of my heart was slain—the plan of salvation was open to me—I saw a beauty in the perfections of the Deity, and felt that power of faith and love that I had ever been a stranger to before."

CHAPTER II.

His happiness in God—Endures severe temptations—Frees his slaves—Reflections on slavery—Attends a class meeting—Declares what God had done for him—First speaks in public—Suffers persecution—Holds evening meetings, and God blesses his labours—Conversation with the parish priest—Strong exercises respecting becoming a travelling preacher—Makes the trial—Then tempted to desist—Makes trial of his gift again.

"After I found this pearl of great price, my soul was so exceedingly happy, that I seemed as if I wanted to take wing and fly away to heaven. Although alone in an unfrequented wood, I was constrained to sound forth the praise of my Redeemer. I thought I should not be ashamed to publish it to the ends of the earth. As I drew near to the house the servants heard me, and came to meet me at the gate in great surprise. The stars seemed as so many seraphs going forth in their Maker's praise. I called the family together for prayer, but my prayer was turned into praise.

"About midnight I laid down to rest; but my soul was

so happy in God I scarcely wished for sleep; however, at length my eyes were closed; but behold! about day break, I awoke, and was strongly tempted by the devil, 'O!' said the adversary, 'where is your religion now? It was only a dream.' I started from my pillow—I remembered the time and place where I received the blessing: and was enabled to repel that temptation. Again said he, 'It is all a delusion.' This assault pained me to the heart. Not feeling as I had done, I began to conclude perhaps it might be so, and betook myself to the fields and woods under deep distress. I frequently bowed my knees before the Lord; and blessed be his adorable name, about nine in the morning my beloved Master visited my heart with his love. And I think I received as great a manifestation as at the first. This visit was attended with an impression to go to such a place, and declare to all who might be there, what great things the Lord had done for me. I went to the house, got my horse, and set out. When I arrived at the place, I found a Methodist preacher and several of my acquaintance; and it was strongly impressed on my mind to deliver my message. I sat down among them, but the cross was too heavy. I sat hours and grieved the blessed Spirit till I was brought under heavy trials; yea, deep distress of soul; and in that way I returned home.

"For the good of others, I shall speak of a few days' exercise on this occasion. The blessed Redeemer left me, or rather hid his face from me: and I had to wade through deep waters. I fasted and prayed till I was almost reduced to a skeleton; but did not open my mouth to any one. I was sinking into desperation.—O! how powerfully was I harassed by the devil, day and night! The Saturday following I was walking through the fields; all nature was clothed with beauty and verdure; but I could discover no charms in aught around me; I was under the deepest exercises of mind, and severely tempted of the devil. 'Ah,' suggested he, 'where is your God now?' He thrust atheism and deism against me; and thus suggested to my mind, 'You see you have been deluded; and if you will now take my advice, you will deny every pretension to this religion. The Methodists are a set of enthusiasts, and you have now a proof of this.' Then with what splendour was the world exhibited to my imagination: 'All these things,' suggested he, 'will I give you if you will deny that God you have been attempting to serve, and pray to him no more.' I was sunk as low as I could possibly be; for my mind was encompassed with darkness, and the most severe distress. I was afraid my lips would be forced open to deny the God who made me. Glory, glory to my Lord! who again gave me a view of an opening eternity, and a sense of his dread majesty; the sight of which brought me into the dust, prostrate with my face to the ground, where I lay for a considerable time with language similar to this, if I perish, it shall be at thy feet, crying for mercy. Thus I lay till I recovered a gleam of hope that I should be saved at last.

"I arose from the earth and advancing towards the house in deep thought, I came to this conclusion, that I would exclude myself from the society of men, and live in a cell upon bread and water, mourning out my days for having grieved my Lord. I went into my room and sat in one position till nine o'clock. I then threw myself on the bed, and slept till morning. Although it was the Lord's day, I did not intend to go to any place of worship; neither did I desire to see any person, but wished to pass my time away in total solitude. I continued reading the Bible till eight, and then under a sense of duty, called the family together for prayer. As I stood with a book in my hand, in the act of giving out a hymn, this thought powerfully struck my mind, 'It is not right for you to keep your fellow creatures in bondage; you must let the oppressed go free.' I knew it to be that same blessed voice which had spoken to me before—till then I had never suspected that the practice of slave keeping was wrong; I had not read a book on the subject, nor been told so by any—I paused a minute, and then replied, 'Lord, the oppressed shall go free.' And I was as clear of them in my mind, as if I had never owned one. I told them they did not belong to me, and that I did not desire their services without making them a compensation: I was now at liberty to proceed in worship. After singing I kneeled to pray. Had I the tongue of an angel, I could not fully describe what I felt; all my dejection and that melancholy gloom which preyed upon me vanished in a moment, a divine sweetness ran through my whole frame.*

* In how many instances in the course of our experience is the truth of the declaration of Solomon demonstrated—"A man's heart deviseth his way; but the Lord directeth his steps." Such is our short-sightedness that we should often seek death in the error of our ways, did not our heavenly Father frustrate our designs and lead us in a way which we knew not. These remarks were suggested by the following reflections found in a manuscript note to his printed journal, which appears to have been written but a short time before his death:

"I have since clearly seen the goodness of God in preparing me for future usefulness: I was a babe, and knew very little of the insinuations of our powerful foe. I shall always have an aversion to the practice of holding our fellow creatures in abject slavery. It was the blessed God that taught me the rights of man. I can now tell the present and rising generation that their privileges are very great; formerly in this country darkness was all around, and now gospel light breaks forth from every direction. Formerly the unregenerate were in ignorance; but now they have no cloak for their sins. The magnitude of a crime depends greatly upon the light we sin against. I shall not soon forget my solitary wanderings in search of a suitable place where I could be excluded from the world. My plan seemed to be, to sell my property and put it to use, and have one person employed that I could confide in, to bring me, and do for me, what was really necessary. I had opened my mind to no one. When the blessed God brought me through these trials, all my schemes were afloat, and I was far from desiring to hide myself in a corner."

"I had now no desire to confine myself to a cell, but wished to spread my Redeemer's glory to the ends of the world. I bless the Lord for leading me safely through such fiery trials! My late affliction of mind was for my good. It was God, not man, that taught me the impropriety of holding slaves: and I shall never be able to praise him enough for it. My very heart has bled, since that, for slave holders, especially those who make a profession of religion; for I believe it to be a crying sin. In the forenoon I attended Church, but I could not find what I wanted. In the afternoon I went to hear the Methodists; and something told me, 'These are the people.' I was so happy in the time of preaching, that I could conceal it no longer; so I determined to choose God's people for my people, and returned home rejoicing.

"A few days after, I attended a class meeting on Deer creek, for the first time, and was convinced it was a prudential institution; and my heart was more than ever united to this community. I told brother H. a pious man, what the Lord had done for me. I now began again to be pressed in spirit to visit my friends and neighbours; and especially some particular families who lay with weight on my mind. The first visit I made, the man of the house was much enraged against me; but my Lord gave me one or two of his children. Shortly after I visited another family; and the master was brought to cry for mercy, on his knees before the Lord. The third was nearly twenty miles off: I seemed to go with confidence, and got there a little before night: I told him what God had done for me, and desired he would send out and call in the neighbours, and I would pray with and for them. The person did so, and after prayer I was obliged, for the first time, to open my mouth by way of exhortation; and the Lord filled it, and sent his arrows to the hearts of three sinners, one of whom slept very little that night; and another followed me nearly sixteen miles the next day.

"Shortly after I was brought into gospel liberty, I thought it my duty to open religious meetings in several places, principally at my own house, and at the house of my brother John, where a blessed work of God broke out, and I took down the names of those who were awakened and converted and who expressed a wish to unite together. Though I had not yet joined the Methodists, I was considerably acquainted with them, had read some of Mr. Wesley's writings, and saw clearly that religious people ought to unite together. I formed a society of about thirty which I generally met weekly, and several of them were happy in God. I invited Mr. Rodda, a Methodist preacher with whom I had met, to come and preach a sermon; he did, and after preaching I told him there was a people prepared for him, that I thought him more capable of taking care of them than myself, and that if he would take them in, and give them regular preaching, I would deliver them up to his charge, which he accordingly did. The next day he told me I must travel with him, which I did for about nine days; he preached and I exhorted after him. I then told him I must return home; when he asked why, I replied that I was not disposed to be a travelling preacher. It was now the enemy suggested that there was no other way for me to prevent or get clear of those itinerating impressions but to alter my condition in life. The thought was so pleasing, that I employed carpenters to put an addition to my house. I received a letter from Mr. Rodda to meet him in Baltimore; I did so, and after staying with him a few days, he told me that he wanted to stay in town a few weeks, and he wished I would take his circuit, and he would meet me at such a place. I attended every appointment for which I engaged, and we had precious seasons; but instead of meeting Mr. R. at the appointed place, I cut across, and started for home; I had about fifty miles to go. I called at the house of a pious old gentleman for some refreshments; he looked me in the face and said.

are you the young man that was with Mr. R. I told him I was. Where are you going, said he: home I replied. What are you going home for? I do not intend to be a travelling preacher, I replied. From every thing that I can understand, said he, God has called you to that work, and if you reject that call he will pursue you. I replied, I cannot help it, I do not intend to be a travelling preacher.

"I again attended class for the second time at Mr. D's; and as they had not heard what had happened to me, some of them were fearful that I had come in to spy out their liberties. I arose from my seat, and, for the first time among the Methodists, publicly declared what the Lord had done for me. A divine kindling ran through the whole house; and we had a blessed meeting. The leader offered to give up his paper to me; but I refused, saying, I would visit them as often as I could; and so returned home praising God.

"I felt an impression to go to that brother I have before mentioned, who was raised from the jaws of death: he was in a seeking way; but did not profess the faith of assurance I begged of him to call a meeting in his own house, and I found great freedom to speak, and appointed another meeting; about forty people gathered; and while I was speaking, the power of the Lord came down in a wonderful manner: nearly half the poor sinners that were present were struck to the floor, and cried for mercy to such a degree that they were heard at a great distance. After the meeting was over, many continued crying for mercy.

"The next morning a gentleman who lived not far off, came to the house to beat me: soon after he entered he began to swear, affirming I would spoil all his negroes. I told him if he did not leave off swearing, God would send his soul to hell. He replied, 'If I said that again, he would level me to the floor.' I assured him I would reprove him whenever he took the Lord's name in vain. He then rose up and struck me on the side of the face, and repeated his blows. There were five of us in the house, my brother, his overseer, myself, and two enemies. I was afraid we should have had a general battle. My brother was only awakened; his overseer had no religion, beyond a zeal for the truth, and such a love for my brother and myself, that he would almost have lain down his life for us. My mind was perfectly calm and my soul so happy that I scarcely felt his blows. I saw the Lord's hand in my preservation; for though he was in so violent a rage, I had not been exhorting many minutes (with tears) before he was as quiet as a lamb: and he and his man, bidding us good morning, went away. Dear man! not long after he was taken into an awful eternity.

"I now began to hold evening meetings in different places, several times in a week: and united those who were awakened into a kind of society; and several, I trust, were happily united to Jesus. O! what sweet times I used to have. Frequently we have continued singing, praying, and praising God till after midnight. Many of my relations expressed great sorrow for me; but glory to God! I delighted in the cross of my Saviour. I was assaulted by many inward conflicts from the devil and the corruptions of my own heart; but Jesus was precious to me.

"I had an appointment one Lord's day, but before I got there a company of belial's children gathered to prevent the meeting; but blessed be God, I was enabled to speak boldly; and although some raged and threatened me, my faith was so strong I did not believe they could hurt me. I shall never forget that day; it was a time of rejoicing to my poor soul! O that I may always give glory to my Lord!

"I was determined I would have nothing to do with the unhappy war; it was contrary to my mind, and grievous to my conscience, to have any hand in shedding human blood. Accordingly I was brought before the officers at a general muster, because I refused to meet, as usual, to learn the art of war. The general officer called me aside, we sat down together, and he asked me why I refused to muster as I used to do. I told him that a recital of the great things God had lately done for me would, perhaps, be the best answer I could give him. I then in a plain manner related to him my experience, and the happy state of my mind. Moreover, I told him that it was useless for me to learn a trade which I never intended to follow, and assured him, that it was not from any disaffection to my country's cause, but conscience, and a conviction that there was a greater work for me to engage in. My experience seemed to take some hold on his mind, and he said he did not blame me at all, but he was sorry to lose me from the company, and he could not exempt me; so I was called before the company, and I sat on my horse and exhorted more than a thousand people, whilst the tears flowed down my cheeks: however a court marshal sat on my case, and laid a fine of twelve dollars and a half yearly, but they never called for the fine, and I have never since been troubled with their military works.

"It was impressed on my mind to have some conversation with Mr. W——, the minister of our parish. He had been the means of keeping me from God and his people for a long time. We had a long discourse in the vestry chamber, before the vestry: where I told him what God had done for me. He desired to know who gave me authority to hold meetings in his parish? I told him I did not do it either for money or honour; that while there were sinners in his parish, and the Lord pressed it on my mind, I should call them to repentance. 'You have no right to do it,' said he, 'unless you are ordained.' The love of God constraineth me, said I, and I must open my mouth in his cause. Having tasted his goodness, I have a longing desire that my neighbours should be made happy too. After a conversation of nearly two hours on the new birth, finding his mind disturbed, I told him in a plain manner what I thought of his doctrine, and what effect it formerly had on me, and so our meeting ended. After I withdrew to my home, being young in the way, very few to strengthen and many to weaken my hands, I was sorely tempted of Satan to give up my confidence in the Lord. Under heavy affliction of mind I withdrew, and wrestled in prayer till the Lord visited me and dispersed every doubt and every fear; giving me these words for my comfort, 'Fear not, I am with you, and will support you under all your trials.' O what consolatory streams flowed into my heart! and how was I strengthened and enabled to rejoice in the Lord!"

Mr. Garrettson observes that he has been thus particular in relating the exercises of his mind for the benefit of young preachers who may hereafter be induced to engage in the same work. And is it to be wondered at that the grand adversary of souls should thrust so sore at him who became an instrument of so great injury to his tyrannical kingdom? Perhaps it is not too much to say that of all the Methodist preachers raised up in that day, there were none more devoted to the work, more zealous and useful, than the subject of this memoir. Being at the same time young in Christian experience, not having many examples before him of those similarly situated, he had not the many helps which are now generally afforded to young ministers of the gospel by the conversation and counsel of the aged and deeply experienced.

What reason have we of the present generation of preachers, as well as the more private Christians, to be thankful to God for the various helps with which we are favoured. The experience of our fathers instructs us; their example stimulates us; and the truths they delivered guide us safely on in our perilous course: while, if we imitate their example in their entire devotion to the cause of their divine Master, no doubt but we shall participate in their reward.

Notwithstanding the natural aversion which it is appasent Mr. Garrettson felt to enter the field of itinerant labour, the evident tokens of divine approbation which attended the commencement of his efforts, tended to remove his scruples, until his opposition was entirely subdued by the perpetual and powerfully inward calls of the Holy Spirit to this work. Call not this enthusiasm. The sequel of his life, so abundant in labours, so rich in success, refutes the slander, and confirms the assumption that he was called of God and set apart by the Holy Ghost for the work of the ministry. It was from a consciousness of this call that Mr. Garrettson was enabled to go forward, and willingly devote himself to this labour; and which so fortified his soul against the assaults of temptation, that though he had to struggle hard, he finally overcame them all. Hence also arose that sweet peace of mind of which he so often speaks, notwithstanding the violence of his inward conflicts. To have " fightings without and fears within," is perfectly consistent with a consciousness of the favour of God, and is therefore common to the experience of all true Christians, and more especially to Christian ministers. Hence he says:

"I found great liberty of speech, and the word was blessed to many souls, for the Lord greatly assisted me, and I had sweet refreshing seasons. O how happy might I have been, had I guarded against my powerful adversary! but I had not been on the circuit more than fifteen days, before I gave way to his suggestions, and concluding that I was not called to this work, I left the circuit under deep dejection and returned home, determined I would never attempt it again: It was suggested that the more I went among the Methodists, particularly the preachers, the more my mind would be distressed about travelling. I was still willing to speak occasionally about home; but to go through the world, I knew not where, was a burden, as I thought, too heavy for me to endure.

"'Tis not in my power to give a full account of my exercises from the fall till the following spring. It may, however, be necessary to touch on a few particulars; for about four months I spent my time in prayer, reading, and such like exercises, except when I was from home, at preaching, or holding meetings myself. The idea of travelling, and preaching the gospel was continually held up to my view. Frequently when riding, or walking, I was drawn out on divine subjects, and at times the Bible seemed all open to me: it was not uncommon for me to preach in my sleep. One night the whole world of sinners seemed to be exhibited as it were in the air, suspended by a slender thread, and the dismal pit beneath them. I saw them careless and unconcerned, in all kinds of ungodly practices, as secure as if in no sort of danger: in my sleep I began to cry aloud to convince them of their danger, till I aroused my brother, who then awoke me: I was sitting up in my bed, trembling, and as wet with sweat as if I had been dipped in a river. Although I lived so abstemiously, I had very little happiness, except at those times when I felt a degree of willingness to labour for my Lord. I have frequently stood astonished, wept and mourned in secret before the Lord, and entreated him to send some one else, that was more sensible and capable than myself: looking around in my mind and nominating such and such persons, whom I conceived to be more fit for the ministry; saying, how can it be, that such an unworthy, ignorant being should be set apart for so great a work? When on my way to my occasional appointments, I would promise in my mind, that if the Lord attended his word with great power, I would consent to give up and labour for him. And at such times I have had great displays of the goodness of God, and have seen sinners weeping all around; but although my mind at those seasons was resolved, unbelief would again assault and overpower me.

"In the month of March my conflicts were so great I

almost sunk under them. The ungodly amongst my acquaintances knew not what was the matter with me: some would ask if I was sick, for I was much worn away. Others would say behind my back, he will come to nothing. I believe I had a more severe travail of soul before I submitted to be an itinerant preacher, than I had gone through for justifying grace. One day being almost weary of life, and under deep dejection, I thought if the Lord would manifest his will, I would through grace obey. I was next led to inquire how I was to expect this desired favour. I kneeled down by the bed, and prayed to the Lord, by some means or other, to make a discovery to me, in the clearest manner, of what he would have me to do. I arose from my knees without any particular answer, much burdened and greatly distressed. I threw myself on the bed again, and in less than two minutes I was in a sound sleep. I dreamed I saw the devil come in at the door, and advance towards me; I thought a good angel came and spake to me saying, 'Will you go and preach the gospel?' I replied, 'I am unworthy, I cannot go:' Instantly the devil laid hold of my hand, and I began to struggle to get from him; I saw but one way that I could escape, and that was a very narrow one. The good angel said to me, 'There is a dispensation of the gospel committed to you, and wo unto you, if you preach not the gospel.' I struggled for some time to get from him, but in vain: at length I cried out, 'Lord, send by whom thou wilt; I am willing to go and preach thy gospel.' No sooner had I thus submitted, than I saw the devil fly as it were through the end of the house in a flame of fire. I awoke; immediately every cloud was dispersed, and my soul was enraptured with the love of my Saviour. I wanted now to converse with some experienced person on the subject; my way now appeared so open, I thought I should never have any more doubts to contend with. I believe it was the next day, I received a letter from brother D. R., desiring me to come and take the circuit a few weeks while he went to Philadelphia. I had no doubt but the Lord directed him to write thus. Before the day arrived that I was to set off, the enemy strove again to prevent me; telling me I was deluded, that it was only my own fancy, or the vanity of my own heart. After I set out I was pursued to that degree, I was ready to desire my horse might throw me, and put an end to my life; or maim me so that I might not be able to go on. In the evening I got to brother D. R.'s, in Cecil, where he had an appointment for me; but my exercises were so severe that I could say but little. The next day he left me, and I concluded to go on the circuit. Of all creatures in the world, I have the greatest reason to be thankful to the Lord, for his tender care of me, a poor weak rebel against him. At the first and second places to which I went, the Lord was powerfully present; and I believe good was done. I was now quite willing to be an exhorter; but thought I would not take a text; I had not, however, travelled far before I had a text suggested to me, and I refused, till my gift of exhortation was almost taken away; and my mind was amazingly distressed again.

"One sabbath I came to a place near Choptank bridge, where I again refused to give out a text, and it pleased the Lord to hide his face, so that I was unable to speak with any degree of freedom. I went to my afternoon's appointment very low both in mind and body, having taken very little refreshment for several days. I determined if a text opened to me, I would give it out boldly, and trust in the Lord. It was so, and I gave out, "Behold the man." I shall never forget the afternoon; it was a time of power to me and many others; the whole Bible seemed open to me. The next day I went to my appointment, with some willingness to be a preacher. I gave out this text, "The great day of his wrath is come, and who shall be able to stand." I endeavoured to show, as I could, how awful that day would be; who would, and who would not be able to stand, with the consequences to each class. The power of God in a very remarkable manner came down among the people, and hardened sinners were brought to cry for mercy. When almost spent, I stopt; but the people continued praying. O, it was a memorable season! my soul was happy, and my heart humbled. I was now willing to be a preacher, and thought, surely I shall never doubt again.

"When brother D. R. returned, he took the circuit, and I went out to open a new one. As I passed along through Tuckeyhoe Neck, I called at a house and asked the woman if she wanted to hear the word of the Lord preached; if she did, to send and call in her neighbours; she did so, and I found great freedom. I gave out that I would preach again the next day. The man of the house was an officer of rank, and it being a day of general mustering, he marched up all the company, and I spoke to hundreds with freedom; many tears were shed, and several convicted, one of whom has since become a preacher. I continued several days in the Neck, and my labours were attended with success.*

"I again met brother D. R. in Cecil county, where we had a quarterly meeting, and from thence we set out for Hartford. He solicited me not to fail attending the Baltimore Conference. On the Lord's day following, an ap-

---

* "After I left brother Ruff, I was wandering along in search of an opening for the word, in deep thought and prayer, that my way might be prosperous. I came opposite a gate, the impression was sudden—turn in, this is the place where you are to begin. It was the house of Rev. E. Cooper's mother, and the officer was his step father. Ezekiel was about thirteen years of age, and as he has since informed me, he received a divine touch which he never lost, and some years after, he was happily brought out to testify of the forgiving love of Jesus, was called to the work of the ministry, and to eminent usefulness in the church of God. There is great cause of thankfulness for my feeble efforts in this little excursion."

pointment was made for me to preach in my native place; a multitude gathered, among whom were many of my old friends and relations, which made the cross very heavy. I gave out my old text, 'The great day of his wrath is come, and who shall be able to stand?' Just as I had entered on the subject, I fainted under the cross, and fell to the ground, (I was preaching under the trees,) where I lay till water was brought and thrown on me, when I immediately recovered and was enabled to rise. I then proceeded, the subject opened to me, and we had a solemn season. Tongue cannot express or pen describe what I felt. Some of the careless ones said, 'He is not able to stand.' It seemed as if I could have lain down my life for my relatives and neighbours, had it been required. Thanks be to God, I trust some good was done. The next day I was most severely pursued by the enemy of souls. I was young, and very feeble both in body and mind, and greatly feared lest I should fall under the hand of my powerful foe; but the blessed God had an eye upon me for good. On Monday I had a severe conflict about attending the conference. The exercise of my mind was too great for my emaciated frame. I betook myself to my bed and lay till twelve o'clock, then rose up and set off. I got into Baltimore about sunset. The conference was to begin the next day: I attended, passed through an examination, was admitted on trial, and my name was, for the first time, classed among the Methodists; and I received of Mr. Rankin a written license. My mind continued so agitated, for I still felt an unwillingness to be a travelling preacher, that after I went from the preaching house to dinner, I again fainted under my burden, and sunk to the floor. When I recovered I found myself in an upper chamber on the bed, surrounded by several preachers; I asked, 'where I had been,' as I seemed to be lost to all things below, appearing to have been in a place from whence I did not desire to return. The brethren joined in prayer, and my soul was so happy, while every thing wore so pleasing an aspect, that the preachers appeared to me more like angels than men. And I have praised the Lord ever since, that, though unworthy of a seat among them, I was ever united to this happy family."

CHAPTER III.

Commences a regular travelling preacher—Severely exercised—Much assisted—Holds a watch night—Goes to Fairfax circuit—Preaches in the parish church—Great manifestation of the power of God—Attacked by a Presbyterian minister on the doctrine of perfection—Farewell sermon—Lodges with a Quaker—Attends conference.

"I was appointed to travel in the Frederick circuit with Mr. Rodda, and as the conference ended on Friday, I set out, arrived at Mr. W——n's, and the next day got into my circuit. I preached on the Lord's day with very little freedom or happiness to my own soul, the enemy still pursuing me with his fiery darts. At times I had sweet communion with my blessed Lord; but a consciousness of my weakness and inability for the great work in which I had engaged, caused my hands to hang down. I was a young soldier, and knew but little about exercising the Christian armour. The goodness of God was great to me, in opening the hearts of the people to receive and bear with my weaknesses.

One day on my way to my appointment my difficulties appeared so great, that I turned my horse, three different times, towards home. I was in a solitary wood, entirely alone; I wept, I mourned, and prayed at the feet of my Lord, and was finally encouraged to go forward, and a sweet and powerful meeting we had. Sometimes when I have been at the appointed place, and the people assembling, I have been tempted to hide myself, or wish that I was sick; at other times I have envied the happiness of crawling insects on the face of the earth; and I have constantly found that the greater cross it was to speak for God, the greater was the blessing, both to myself and the people. In these cases I seldom opened my mouth to speak in public but the power of the Lord was sensibly felt. My Bible, at particular times, would appear so small that I could not find a text. I remember one day, a congregation was gathered, and I was alone, under deep exercise; and it appeared as if there was not one verse in the Bible that I could speak on: all on a sudden whilst I was on my knees before the Lord, the following text was powerfully applied: 'The Spirit of the Lord God is upon me, because he hath anointed me to preach glad tidings to the meek, to bind up the broken hearted, to proclaim liberty to the captives, and the opening of the prison to them that are bound,' Isa. lxi, 1. I immediately met the assembly, and after singing and prayer, gave out the text, and the power of God descended in an extraordinary manner. Previously to this the people were so hardened that we had only four members in that place; but before I left the house, twenty, who seemed to be that day broken in heart, were added to the society. We continued singing and praying till nearly sunset, and there appeared to be very few in the congregation whose hearts were not touched; my voice being almost lost in the cries of the distressed. O blessed be God! this was a day of marrow and fat things to my poor heart.

"Some time after I was requested to appoint a watch-night, to which I consented. Mr. R. was displeased that I had not consulted him; but I was innocent, knowing very little of the discipline. Many people came together, and many of the children of the devil were angry and stoned the house; but the Lord was powerfully present. His people had a little paradise; and I trust there were several new-born souls, and some poor sinners brought to tremble.

"I continued six months in this circuit, and blessed be God! many were added to the society; his children much quickened; and many happily brought into the kingdom of grace. My heart was closely united to the people, and they were remarkably kind to me. I thought it a great favour to be received as a preacher: and I verily believe the Lord inclined the hearts of the people to overlook my many weaknesses and want of knowledge; and for the sake of his dear Son in a small measure owned my efforts.

"I think it was in November I was sent to Fairfax circuit, where I staid three months. I had many happy moments, and preached the gospel with freedom. I cannot say I met with much success, neither was I so powerfully harrassed by temptations. I was now better acquainted with Satan's devices; and I trust, had a more steady confidence in my blessed Saviour. I began to preach the word more freely, and was not so easily shaken with respect to my call to the ministry. I was now entirely willing to be a travelling preacher: and blessed be God! he gave me favour in the sight of the people.

"As there were many doors open for us in New Virginia, and several small societies formed, Mr. Rodda thought it expedient to send me into those parts of the country; and blessed be my God! I found a willingness to go any where, and to do any thing that would be of the least service to the church of God. I bless and praise the Lord for his goodness to me during my stay in that part of his vineyard, for he wonderfully enlarged my desires after him; he increased my gifts, and opened the hearts and houses of the people to receive his servant and his word. Many were added to the society.

"I visited Shepherd's town, lying high up on the Potowmac river. On the Lord's day I attended the church, and heard their minister preach on 'Keep holy the sabbath day.' Though he was a man slow of speech, I think his discourse took up only fifteen minutes. He said there was no harm in civil amusements on a week day; but they ought to refrain from them on the sabbath. I had no doubt but his discourse was his own composition. I do not remember a word about the fall of man, faith, or repentance. I asked liberty, and went up into the pulpit after him, and gave out, 'How shall we escape if we neglect so great salvation?' Heb. ii, 3. After I had done, one of his hearers asked him what he thought of the doctrine the stranger had delivered? Why, said he, he seems to bring Scripture to prove it; it may be so, but if it is, I know nothing of it.

"I preached every other Sunday in the church during my stay in this new circuit; and the fourth sermon there were as many people as could crowd into the building. There was a great agitation among the congregation, and the word took such effect on the heart of a woman that she cried aloud for mercy. The people being unacquainted with such things, strove to get out; but the aisle, and every place were so crowded, that they could not, unless those at the doors had first given way. In a few minutes the Lord set her soul at liberty. She clapped her hands in an ecstacy of joy, praised the Lord, and then quietly sat down. The whole congregation seemed to be lost in amazement, and the divine presence appeared to run through the whole house: most of the people were melted into tears. The Presbyterian minister was among the crowd, and most of his congregation came to hear what the babbler had to say. This man with his deacon I met on the road a few days after. 'I was hearing you preach,' said he, 'and I did not like your doctrine.' What was your objection, said I. 'Why it was a volley of stuff.' Well, I replied, if the Lord makes use of it to bring souls to himself, I wish to be thankful and satisfied. 'You preach perfection,' said he, 'and that I do not believe to be attainable in this life.' Then, said I, you do not hold with the doctrine of our Lord and his apostles; our Lord says, 'Be ye perfect even as your Father in heaven is perfect,' and the apostle says, 'The blood of Christ cleanseth from all sin.' When are we to be made perfect? 'Not till death,' said he. Our Lord, said I, 'came to destroy the works of the devil;' and do you suppose he will call death to his assistance? Death in Scripture is called the last enemy, and we learn, that as death leaves us judgment will find us; and that there is no knowledge or work in the grave. And if we die in our sins where the Lord is we cannot come: I want to know how death is to bring this about. 'Why,' said he, 'at the article of death, sin is done away, and not till then.' The Papists say, we must be refined by the fire of purgatory: the Universalists, that the last farthing will be paid in hell; and you say, nay, death will do it: but we profess to hold with the Holy Scriptures, which say, that 'his name shall be called Jesus, for he shall save his people from their sins.' Do you not, said I, believe that the Lord is able to wash and cleanse the soul from all sin one minute before death? To this he agreed. And if a minute, why not a day, a month, yea, why not seven years? The apostle saith, 'Behold, now is the accepted time! behold, now is the day of salvation!' How dare any man limit the holy one of Israel. 'I have done with you,' cried he and his deacon, and so saying turned they their backs upon me.*

* "I shall here observe, that many things were said on both sides, which I penned in my daily journal; the substance of which I gave to the public, and I have since examined my daily journal, and I am assured of the correctness of what was said. But I have to say, we were both beginners in the great work of the ministry, and probably a few years' longer experience, and we should have been capable of handling the controversy more profitably. God alone is absolutely perfect. Among finite intelligences perfection can only be in degrees. Angels are perfect in their measure. Adam in paradise was perfect in his measure. Christians may be perfect in their measure, and what we call Christian perfection, is a high degree of piety—to love God with every power of the soul, and to be saved from all sin, properly so called.

"A few evenings after, I preached near his house, and he and his deacon were present again; a precious season we had; a great shaking among sinners, and I expect the heart of the minister was also softened. He came to me after sermon and asked my pardon if he had said any thing amiss.

"Glory to God, he enabled me to travel largely through that country, to preach one, two, three, and sometimes four sermons a day. The last sermon I preached was from 'Finally, brethren, farewell,' &c. This was a time not soon to be forgotten. A large congregation seemed to drink in every word; such attention was given, and so much of the divine presence felt, that I continued nearly three hours, and then the people hung around me in such a manner that I could scarcely get from them, begging me with tears not to leave them."

Thus ended the labours of this man of God in that part of the country for this conference year. And who that reads the preceding account of his travels, his mode of life, his indefatigable labours to promulgate the gospel of the grace of God, and witnesses at the same time the astonishing effects of his ministrations, but must *glorify God in him?* To young preachers of the gospel in particular, this narrative of the manner in which Mr. Garrettson was called forth into the gospel field, and the various exercises of his mind, as well as the encouragement afforded him by the Head of the church, must be peculiarly interesting and profitable. How different the school in which his mind was disciplined to "the obedience of Christ" and prepared to become a competent and an efficient "minister of the New Testament" from that in which many are fitted by the art and device of men! The instrument

---

"The apostle Paul describes it, 'to be enlightened, to taste the heavenly gift, to partake of the Holy Ghost, to taste the good word of God, and the powers of the world to come.' 'The blood of Christ cleanses from all sin.'"

was fitted for its work, and its effect was powerfully felt wherever it operated.

After lodging and praying with a Quaker family " whose hearts the Lord touched," Mr. Garrettson attended a quarterly meeting at Fairfax with Mr. Rankin, and then went to the conference which was held at Deer creek.

CHAPTER IV.

Deer creek Conference—Goes to Brunswick circuit, Virginia—Happy seasons in preaching on the way—Arrives on his circuit, and finds a lively people—An officer interrogates him on the subject of fighting—Confidence in God increased—Great consolation in preaching—Tempting offers, which he resists—Whites and blacks much affected—Refuses the state oath—Escapes a threatened imprisonment—Goes to North Carolina—Reflections on Christian perfection—Experiences perfect love, and preaches this doctrine—Narrowly escapes being shot.

"Our conference this year began at Deer creek the 20th of May, 1777, and continued till the Friday following. I was greatly refreshed among the servants of God; some of whom I have never seen since, nor shall again on this side of eternity.

"My appointment was in Virginia, in what was called Brunswick circuit, with brother W. and brother T. After spending a few days among my relations and old friends, on Monday I set out for my circuit, and on Tuesday met the preachers at brother M——r's in Fairfax: and the next morning we set out in company on our way. My appointment was much to my mind, and I had a lively hope that my Lord would be with me, and bless my weak endeavours to promote his cause.

"We travelled several days before we met any Methodists; but the Lord befriended us, for we had happy times together; and had an opportunity of preaching several sermons before we reached our circuit: we had a sweet season at the house of a good old man; and I think we were providentially sent thither, not only for the benefit of the family, but likewise of many others.

"June the 4th I parted with my company, and thanks be to God, my soul was refreshed as with new wine. The same day I was brought to the house of a kind widow, who sent out and called a company together. There was a young growing society in this neighbourhood. I preached from 'Fear not, little flock,' &c, Luke xii, 32. From what I could understand they had seldom had such a time of refreshing. I could say it is good for me to be here. My confidence still grew stronger with respect to my call to the ministry.

"On the 5th of June I got into my circuit, and on Saturday the 7th, began my ministry among a lively people. I was attacked by an officer who wanted to know my mind respecting fighting. I told him God had taught me better than to use carnal weapons against the lives of human creatures. He intimated something about stopping me. I told him I was not afraid of man—that if he did not learn to fight with other weapons he would go to hell.

"On Sunday the 8th of June, I preached at brother I——'s to many serious people. While I was pointing out the gospel salvation there was a shout in the camp of Israel; and after the meeting ended there was a rejoicing among God's people. I met the society, and was more than ever confirmed in my belief that the Lord had sent me into that part of the vineyard. I there met with a black boy who was happy in the Lord; and I thought he exceeded all the youths I had ever seen for a gift and power in prayer.

"Monday, June the 9th, I preached a few miles off, from these words, 'Loose him and let him go.' There were as many people as the house could contain. After preaching nearly two hours, the cries of the assembly were so great that I desisted. The people continued together a long time after, and I doubt not but several were set at liberty. O Jesus! thou still increasest my faith; thou givest me lively sensations of thy pardoning love; and I feel that thou hast called me to the ministry of thy blessed word. At this meeting we were so wonderfully drawn out that we knew not when to part, having seldom felt the like. The next day I had great freedom to preach, and one soul was born of God.

"Thursday, June 12th, I found liberty in preaching at Dr. C——r's to an attentive, solemn congregation. I rode to Col. Taylor's and met brother F. P. We held a watch night, and I think I never had more freedom to speak. The word was blessed to the colonel and his family, and they treated me ever after more like a son than a stranger; yea, I may say, more like an angel than a poor clod of earth. And I, on my part, shall ever respect them for their kindness to me.

"The next day I again crossed the Roanoke river, and had great liberty to preach from these words, 'For lo, the winter is past, the rain is over and gone, the flowers appear on the earth, the time of the singing of birds is come, and the voice of the turtle is heard in the land,' &c. After this, we had a love feast, and many spoke freely of the goodness of God. In this place the people wanted to gain me with their kindness; but I refused their obliging offers, being convinced I should do more good in wandering up and down the earth without any incumbrances; and as for riches, I had enough to serve my purposes. The temptation was considerable, and pleasing to nature. Vain world, away with your flattery! I could rejoice in my God, with the testimony of a good conscience, knowing that the oblation was made for the good of Christ's church which he purchased with his own blood. It was no time to think of houses and lands, &c. I passed on, rejoicing in God my Saviour, and was greatly encouraged in the blessed work. But halcyon days did not always attend me. I again experienced the severe buffettings of Satan; but my exercises proved a blessing to me, for my soul was humbled, and I was made in a measure sensible of the need of a deeper work of grace in my heart before I could be completely happy.

"Sunday, June 22d, in Roanoke chapel I preached to about five hundred whites, and almost as many blacks who stood without. I found freedom of mind, and many tears were shed by both white and black. The next day while I was preaching a funeral sermon we had much of the divine presence. In this way I continued around the circuit till the quarterly meeting, which was held in August, at Maberry's chapel. The Lord was with me, blest my endeavours, and increased my love to him and his people. In this circuit I conversed with some deeply experienced Christians, and by their humble walk and heavenly conversation, I was much stirred up to seek a deeper work of grace; especially by the experience of sister B———. I believed there was such a thing as perfect love to be attained in this world; and I likewise knew I was not in possession of it: I saw a beauty in the doctrine, and preached it, but it was at a distance.

"About this time the state oath began to be administered, and was universally complied with, both by preachers and people where I was; but I could by no means be subject to my rulers in this respect, as it touched my conscience towards God: so I was informed I must either leave the state, take the oath, or go to jail. I told those who came to tender the oath to me, that I professed myself a friend to my country: that I would do nothing willingly or knowingly to the prejudice of it: that if they required it, I would give them good security of my friendly behaviour during my stay in the state. 'But why,' said they, 'will you not take the oath?' 'I think,' said I, 'the oath is too binding on my conscience; moreover, I never swore an oath in my life: and ministers of the gospel have enough to do in their sphere. I want, in all things, to keep a conscience void of offence, to walk in the safest way, and to do all the good I can in bringing sinners to God.'

"We began to labour under heavy political trials, as it was a little after the commencement of what we call the revolutionary war, and indeed the clash of arms was a new thing in our country, especially such powerful blows from an over grown mother, who wanted to keep her children under subjection, in matters wherein they thought they were capable of judging for themselves. It might be asked why did you not comply with the law? From reading, my own reflection, and the teachings of the good Spirit, I was drawn quite away from a belief in the lawfulness of shedding human blood under the gospel dispensation, or at most it must be in an extreme case, touching which, at that time my mind was in doubt. Again, I thought the test oath was worded in such a way, as to bind me to take arms whenever called on, and I felt no disposition to use carnal weapons.

"Many of my friends endeavoured to persuade me to comply: alleging that I might be more useful among the people: but it was to no purpose. The rulers said, 'You must leave the state.' This I cannot do, for first, the conference appointed me to labour in this state: and in the second place, I am confident that my appointment is approved of by my heavenly Father; and therefore, I dare not leave the state. 'Then,' said they, 'you must go to prison.' That matter, I replied, I leave to the God of Daniel; assured he is able to defend my cause, whether in or out of jail.

"The many taials I had on this occasion drove me nearer to God, and as many thought that every sermon would be my last, more attended than otherwise would, and I found much freedom to preach the word, and good was done.

"At a certain place several of the rulers bound them-

selves to put me to jail, when I came that way again : my
friends persuaded me to decline going *there;* but I told
them I could not be clear if I distrusted so good a God.
Before I came round to that place, the Lord laid his afflicting hand on some of those ruling men who had threatened
to imprison me; so that when I went there, several of
them had already made their exit into eternity! and another was lying at the point of death. I preached with
much freedom, but though I had been chased for several
months, there was none to lay the hand of violence upon
me. The persecution from this quarter entirely subsided
during my stay in the state. In this circuit I met with a
number of inward and outward trials; but 1 bless God,
that he ever sent me into this part of his vineyard : so
that I can truly say, that the life and conversation of many
of my worthy friends, (some of whom were older in the
grace of God than myself,) were made a great blessing to
me. O! how shall I make suitable returns to my God
for the thousands of his favours.

"In September I went to North Carolina, to travel
Roanoke circuit, and was sweetly drawn out in the glorious work, though my exercises were very great, particularly respecting slavery.* Many times did my heart ache

---

* The question of slavery becomes more and more perplexing in
these United States. It is an evil more easily deplored than extir-
pated. Though it is cause for much gratitude that by the influence
of the gospel many of the slaves are made better, and their masters
have become more humane in their treatment of their slaves, all
seem to agree that it is an evil much to be deprecated. It seems
indeed like an inveterate disease of the body, the pains of which are
sensibly felt, though not easily removed. What effect it may ultimately have on the body politic time alone must and will develope.

In the present state of things in the southern states it seems un-
available to contend for emancipation. The best, I think, which
can be done to meliorate their condition is to bring, as far as possible, all, both master and servant, under the influence of that immuta-
ble law, binding on all human beings, namely, to do to others as we
would they should do unto us in like circumstances. Let slaves

on account of the slaves in this part of the country, and many tears did I shed, both in Virginia and Carolina, while exhibiting a crucified Jesus to their view; and I bless God that my labours were not in vain among them. I endeavoured frequently to inculcate the doctrine of freedom in a private way, and this procured me the ill will of some, who were in that unmerciful practice. I would often set apart times to preach to the blacks, and adapt my discourse to them alone; and precious moments have I had. While many of their sable faces were bedewed with tears, their withered hands of faith were stretched out, and their precious souls made white in the blood of the Lamb. The suffering of these poor out casts of men, through the blessing of God, drove them near to the Lord, and many of them were truly happy.

"Respecting Christian perfection, I believed such a thing to be attainable in this life; I therefore, both in public and private, contended for it and had often felt the need of it in my own soul: but I never had such a view of it in my life as while in this circuit. The Lord, in a very powerful and sudden manner, gave me to see and feel the need of this blessed work. Every heart corruption was discovered to me by the blessed Spirit, at the house of that dear afflicted mother in Israel Mrs. Y. I have had many sweet moments with that precious family; but she has since gone to Abraham's bosom. This discovery was made to me while I was alone in the preachers' room. I expected in a few moments to be in eternity; and the cry of my heart was, Lord save me from inbred sin. The purity of God, heaven, and the law, with the impurity of my heart, were so disclosed to my view, that I was humbled in the very dust; and expected never to enter into

and masters be instructed in this great principle and act under its authority, and it shall ultimately work the entire destruction of slavery itself.—EDITOR.

the kingdom of heaven without a greater likeness to my blessed Lord. I rejoiced that the cold hand of death was not upon me. For more than a week an earnest struggle continued in my heart for all the mind which was in Christ. My appointments were made, or I am apprehensive I should have declined preaching so pure a gospel, till the heart corruptions which I felt were washed away. The enemy strove very hard to rob me of my confidence; but although I was at times brought very low, yet I did not let go my hold of the dear Redeemer, the witness of my justification, &c.

"One day I went to my appointment, and while the people were gathering, I withdrew about a quarter of a mile from the house and wrestled with the Lord in prayer: I thought I could not meet the congregation, unless I was delivered from my inbred sins. However, after the people had waited about an hour, I went to the house, but my struggle seemed to be at the height. I thought I would pray with the people and dismiss them. After prayer my Lord gave me this text, 'Blessed are the pure in heart, for they shall see God.' Never had I such freedom before that time, to describe, 1st, the impurity of the heart: 2dly, how it is to be purified: and 3dly, the blessing resulting therefrom—That they shall see God. While I was speaking of the travail of a soul for purity, all my inward distress vanished; and I felt a little heaven on earth. I know that the Lord deepened his work; but I did not claim the witness of 'perfect love;' yet my soul was happy from day to day.

"From this time I began to preach the doctrine of Christian perfection more than ever; the plan seemed as clear to me as the noon day sun. Many were convinced of the need of perfect love; and some were brought into the possession of it.* The word of the Lord prospered

* What is this perfection? It is not the perfection of God, or angels, nor the perfection of Adam in paradise, but it is Christian

in the circuit; and some of the children of Belial were stirred up to persecute. One day a very wicked man came into the house while I was preaching; he supposed my discourse pointed at him; and stood for a considerable time, swelling, and threatening in his heart that he would haul me down and beat me. But before the sermon was ended, he gave heed to the things delivered, and a spirit of conviction took hold of his heart: before he left the house he professed justifying faith; and I trust became a changed man.

"I then went to the house of a Christian man, whose brother who lived next door was a violent persecutor. While I was at family prayer in the evening, he ran over with a loaded gun, and stood with it presented for a considerable time, but had not power to draw the trigger. A few days after, he was in a rage with his brother on account of his receiving the preacher, shot at him, and slightly wounded his body. I was very thankful I escaped him.

"In this circuit there was a blessed gathering of souls into the fold of Christ, many were convinced and converted, and at the spring quarterly meeting we had some lively witnesses of perfect love; others were greatly moved to seek after that deep work of grace. Glory to God! I can say I had many blessed, happy moments while travelling the Virginia and Carolina forests, endeavouring to gather poor lost souls to the Redeemer's fold.

"I have often thought that the consolations afforded me were an ample compensation for all the difficulties and

---

perfection. It consists in the extirpation of all sin, in having the powers and affections of the heart purified, and the whole soul filled with divine love. 2d, How is this blessing to be attained? As we are justified by faith, so are we sanctified by faith. 1. We are convinced of the need of it. 2. In general there is a sweet distress, but no guilt or condemnation. 3. We must by faith receive the promises. Repentance disclaims all help in man. Faith lays claim to all the help in Christ. Repentance says, I can do nothing. Faith says, *Through Christ Jesus strengthening me I can do all things.*

trials I met with, in wandering up and down in an ill natured world. And I often reflect and bewail my backwardness, when I first entered so unwillingly as a labourer into my Lord's vineyard. But now, thanks to his dear name, I go willingly; and desire cheerfully to obey all his commandments, and do all the little good I can to promote his honour and glory.

"In May, I left the people to whom I found myself closely united, and in whose sight the Lord gave me great favour, and set out for the Leesburg conference."

CHAPTER V.

From the conference in Leesburg, goes to the Peninsula, Md.—Persecution against the Methodists—Its causes—Perseveres in his work—Beaten and bruised—Blessed effects of this opposition in his own soul—Preaches the word with great effect—Enters the state of Delaware, and preaches the word with great success—Goes to Kent Island—Death of his brother John—Remarkable instance of conversion—Meets with opposition at Dover, but succeeds in preaching—Rescues a man who was attempting to hang himself—Conversion of an old persecutor—Not an enthusiast—Sinners flock to Christ—Delivered from the hand of the civil officer—Preaches and forms a society in Quantico—Vindicates infant baptism—Opposition meetings unsuccessful—Good effects of the gospel—Providential interview with a strange woman—Work of God greatly prospers—Remarks on silent meetings—Great inward conflicts—Remarkable answer to prayer—The arm of the Lord made bare in the conversion of souls—The wicked persecuts—Escapes unhurt—Silences an ignorant disputant—And escapes imprisonment.

"We had a comfortable conference in Leesburg, and May 20, 1778, I set out for my destined place. After preaching a few sermons, and visiting my old friends and relations, on the 30th of May I crossed the Chesapeake; and in the evening had a delightful opportunity of pressing the necessity of holiness on the minds of many. Blessed be God! there was a shout in the camp among our blessed Saviour's despised followers; and I have no doubt but that the Lord directed my lot into this part of the work.

"On Sunday I spoke in Kent preaching house with much liberty; and we had a sweet refreshing season. This was the first Methodist preaching house that was built on this shore. In the evening I was much drawn out in prayer and self examination; and felt the sweet beams of the blessed Spirit, and experienced the bliss of prayer, with a comfortable hope that my Lord had deepened his work of grace in my heart. Four preachers were appointed by conference for the Peninsula—Brothers H., L., C., and myself. The enemy of souls had stirred up a great persecution against the Methodists. Brother H. was taken by the rulers, and put in confinement. Brother L. thought it his duty to return to Virginia. And poor brother C. was too unwell to travel much: so that for a considerable time I was left almost alone."

This was a season peculiarly trying to the Methodist preachers. War knows no mercy; and the mere circumstance that the first Methodist preachers were from England, under the direction of Mr. Wesley, whose loyalty to his king and country led him to speak and write against the proceedings of the American provinces, was enough of itself to excite suspicions in the ruling party here against the preachers. The fact, also, as stated by Mr. Garrettson, that most of those who had joined the societies, and especially the preachers, were from principle averse to war, which led them to refuse to bear arms in their country's defence, tended to strengthen the suspicion, and of course to provoke opposition against them. But the following facts, which are recorded in the manuscript notes to the printed journal by Mr. Garrettson, show that some imprudences on the part of those whose example should have been of a different character, evinced that these suspicions were not without a foundation.

"To human appearance," says Mr. Garrettson, "our prospects were gloomy." In this place what was called a tory company embodied themselves, and a backslidden Methodist by the name of Chancey Clowe, who was once thought to be a pious man, of considerable note in the society, laid aside his religion, and began to raise a company with a view to make his way through the country to the Chesapeake to join the British, whose fleet at that time lay in the Chesapeake bay. He succeeded in raising about 300 men. He did much mischief before he was detected and his plans frustrated. It was not, however, before some blood was shed, that this mob was dispersed, and the leaders brought to justice. His excellency, Cesar Rodney, at that time governor of the state, was friendly to religion. Our enemies were assiduous in their endeavours to prejudice his mind against us; inculcating the idea that we were tories, and ought to be crushed as a body. He insisted on knowing how many of these insurrectionists there were of each denomination, and when they found there were only two Methodists among them, the governor's remarks made our enemies look small before the court. They were all pardoned except C. Clowe, the leader, who was hung. This happened in the Peninsula, a tract of country lying between the Chesapeake and Delaware bays, comprehending a part of Maryland, part of Virginia, and the whole of the Delaware state.

While these things were transacting among this class of people, Mr. Rodda, one of the British preachers, no doubt thinking he was doing God service, was spreading on his circuit the king's proclamation, and acting in several respects unbecoming the character of either a Christian or minister. He fled, however, to the bay, and employed a slave or slaves to take him to the British fleet, and thus just escaped with his life. The truth of history requires this record. As Philadelphia was at this time in possession of the British, he was taken there, and from thence to his native land; and so we got clear of a backslidden preacher.

"In the midst of these and many more troubles which might be mentioned, God enabled me to go forward through good and evil report, and he stood by me; and thanks to his blessed name, he fulfilled his promise, and I went on without fear."

The above circumstances, however, as related by Mr. Garrettson, had a very deleterious effect upon the tranquillity of the societies, as they tended very much to stir up the spirit of persecution against the Methodists. At such times when men's spirits are excited, they are not very accurate in distinguishing between the innocent and guilty: though the conduct of these few ought not to have implicated the whole body, yet it served as a pretence for those who wished for an excuse to reproach pure religion. "Hence," Mr. Garrettson observes, "it was soon circulated through the country that the Methodists were enemies to the American cause: and were embodying themselves to meet the English army. A short time before this, the English preachers had embarked for Europe; and the conduct of Mr. R., as before mentioned, had been very injurious to the persecuted flock. During this time, Mr. Asbury found an asylum at the house of good old Judge White, and I believe none but the Lord and himself knew what he suffered for nearly twelve months. We have since seen the hand of the Lord in his preservation.

"My exercises of mind were very great, and my friends in Kent, on every side, entreated me to remain with them and not to travel at large at the hazard of my life. I was ready at first to consent, but had not remained more than a week among them, when my spirit was stirred within me, and I cried earnestly to the Lord to know his will. I felt an impulse to go, believing that God would stand by me, and defend my cause. And I received such a deep sense of God in my heart, and such precious promises of his parental care over me, that I took leave of my Kent friends, and sat out without any dread of my worst enemies. I then travelled largely through the country, preaching once, twice, three, and sometimes four times a day, to listening multitudes bathed in tears.

"I shall not soon forget the 24th of June, 1778. O what a wringing of hands among sinners, and crying for mercy! God's people praising him from a sense of his divine presence. O how did my heart rejoice in God my Saviour! I went through Cecil county, and part of Delaware state. A precious flame was kindled in many hearts, and many were brought to inquire what they should do to be saved. I visited Mr. Asbury at Judge White's, and found him very unwell. I had a sweet opportunity of preaching at his place of confinement. After some agreeable conversation with Mr. Asbury, I went on to Maryland, and had much liberty in preaching to our persecuted friends in Queen Ann.

"In this place they threatened to imprison me; but as they did not take me in the public congregation, I concluded they did not intend to lay hands on me: however, the next day, as I was going to Kent, John Brown, who was formerly a judge in that county, met me on the road. When I came near him, he made a full stop as if he wanted something; apprehending nothing, I stopped and inquired the distance to Newtown. His reply was, You must go to jail, and he instantly took hold of my horse's bridle. I desired him in the Lord's name, to take care what he was about to do; assuring him I was on the Lord's errand, and requesting him to show his authority for his proceedings. He immediately alighted from his horse, and taking a large stick that lay in the way, for some time beat me over the head and shoulders. Not being far from his quarter, he called aloud for help. I saw several persons, as I thought, with a rope, running to his assistance. Providentially, at this moment he let go my bridle: had not this been the case, it is probable they would have put an end to my life; for the beasts of the field seemed to be in the utmost rage. I thought the way was now open for my escape; and being on an excellent horse, I gave him the whip, and got a considerable distance before my enemy could mount; but he, knowing the way better than myself, took a nearer route, met me, and as he passed, struck at me with all his might; my horse immediately made a full stop, my saddle turned, and I fell with force upon the ground, with my face within an inch of a sharp log. The blows I had received, together with my fall and bruises, deprived me of my senses. Providentially, at this time, a woman passed by with a lancet. I was taken into a house not far distant, and bled; by which means I was restored to my senses, but it was not expected I had many minutes to live. My affliction was good for me; and I can confidently say, nothing induced me to wish to stay any longer in this world, but the thirst I had for the salvation of my fellow creatures. The heavens, in a very glorious manner, seemed to be open; and by faith I saw my Redeemer standing at the right hand of the Father, pleading my cause; and the Father smiling as if reconciled to my poor soul.

"I was so happy I could scarcely contain myself. My enemy was walking to and fro, in great agitation, wishing he had not molested me. I had a heart to pray for him, and desired him to sit down by me and to read such and such chapters. He did so; I told him if he did not experience that blessed work he would surely go to hell. I said, if the Lord should take me away, I had a witness within me that I should go to heaven; that I had suffered purely for the sake of our Lord's blessed gospel; and that I freely forgave him. I entreated him to seek the salvation of his soul, and never again to persecute the followers of our Lord. The poor unhappy man did not know which way to look. "I will take you in my carriage," said he, "wherever you want to go." Notwithstanding this, when he perceived I was likely to recover, he went to a magistrate who was nearly as bitter against us as himself, and brought him to me.

"They both appeared as if actuated by the devil. With a stern look the magistrate demanded my name: I told him; and he took out his pen and ink, and began to write a mittimus to commit me to jail. Pray sir, said I, are you a justice of the peace? He replied that he was: why then, said I, do you suffer men to behave in this manner? If such persons are not taken notice of, a stranger can with no degree of safety travel the road. 'You have,' said he, 'broken the law.' How do you know that? answered I; but suppose I have, is this the way to put the law in force against me? I am an inhabitant of this state, and have property in it; and if I mistake not, the law says for the first offence the fine is five pounds, and double for every offence after. The grand crime was preaching the gospel of the Lord Jesus Christ, in which I greatly rejoice. My enemy, said I, conducted himself more like a highwayman, than a person enforcing the law in a Christian country. Be well assured, this matter will be brought to light, said I, in an awful eternity. He dropped his pen, and made no farther attempt to send me to prison. By this time the woman who bled me came with a carriage; and I found myself able to rise from my bed and give an exhortation to the magistrate, my persecutor, and others who were present.

"I rode to the house of old brother Dudley, and preached with much delight, in the evening, to a few despised disciples, as I sat in the bed, from John xvi, 33. 'These things I have spoken unto you, that in me ye might have peace. In the world ye shall have tribulation, but be of good cheer: I have overcome the world.'

"I can truly say, what I suffered was for my good, and I think it was rendered a blessing to the people in the vicinity: for the work of the Lord was carried on in a blessed manner, and I met with very little persecution in that county afterwards. (Some time after I preached the funeral sermon of the wife of the above magistrate, and he was very much moved.) In the morning I awoke about four, and desired the friend of the house, if possible, to prepare a carriage for me by six; as I had a long way to go and to preach twice. But being disappointed in getting a conveyance, though scarcely able to turn in my bed, my body being so bruised, I looked to the Lord for help, which was granted with sweet consolation. I mounted my horse about seven o'clock and rode about fifteen miles, and preached at eleven o'clock. O! what a nearness I had to the Lord, while I held up a crucified Jesus to upwards of five hundred persons! My face bruised, scarred, and bedewed with tears! the people were for the most part much affected. I rode afterwards ten miles farther, and preached to hundreds with great freedom. O! how sweet my Saviour was to me! It seemed as if I could have died for him.

"After a few days respite I went to the place where I was beaten, and found that the persecuting spirit had in a measure subsided; and that my way was surprisingly opened. I had many hearers, and the word was much blessed to many souls. The language of the hearts of many was, Surely this must be the right way.

"The Lord was very kind to me in making a discovery, in a vision of the night, of the things I was to pass through; and they came to pass just as they were made known to me.

"From Queen Ann's, I again travelled through the Delaware state, and had many blessed opportunities of enforcing the truth on the attentive multitudes that flocked together from various quarters. In the neighbourhood of Mr. S. the people had been deprived of the privilege of hearing for some time, so that when I came among them I found them hungering for the word. I preached from 'Who is she that looketh forth as the morning, fair as the moon, clear as the sun, and terrible as an army with banners?' Solomon's Songs vi, 10. I was so wonderfully drawn out, and my spirit so taken up with divine things, that I almost thought myself in heaven; and many of the persecuted children of God seemed as if they would take wings and fly away. O! it was a great day of awakening power! The love feast was also remarkable for the sanctifying operations of the blessed Spirit. Many of our happy friends came from afar, and returned with their hearts all on fire for God. Many happy moments have I had among those loving followers of our blessed Lord.

"Sunday, July 19, I visited and preached to the people of Marshey Hope. I was sorely tempted of the devil all the morning before preaching; he strove to destroy or weaken my faith. I was afraid I should not be a means of doing any good. I wept and mourned in secret, and sensibly felt the power of darkness, tempting me to believe I never had a commission to preach the everlasting gospel. There was an unexpected congregation; and shortly after I stood up before the people, the devil and unbelief fled; and I gave out, 'How shall we escape, if we neglect so great salvation?' Heb. ii, 3. The word ran through all the congregation, and there was a great shaking among the people. Among the rest, a woman was struck under conviction, and she cried for mercy until she fell to the ground. Her husband was much offended, and I was informed that he threatened me, as he said, for killing his wife. After sermon I spent some time in praying for the distressed. In the afternoon, accompanied by many, I rode four miles, and preached from 'Cut it down, why cumbereth it the ground?' and I found myself greatly at liberty. In this place a few months ago, the people were fast asleep, but now many are awaking up, and several united to Jesus.

"After travelling and preaching with great freedom and success in the Delaware state, I was brought on my way in the heat of July to Talbot county, in Maryland, where I laboured for about two weeks night and day with tears. Many souls were refreshed, and I thought it good for me to be there. Sweet refreshing seasons had I among those dear *loving* people: I shall not soon forget those mothers in Israel, sister Parrot and sister Bruff, who are now lodged in Abraham's bosom. They, I trust, lived and died witnesses of perfect love.

"In August I left Talbot, and accompanied by several friends went to Kent Island. I preached frequently to a very gay, high minded people, with freedom. An admirable change for the better has since taken place in that island. From thence I attended the August quarterly meeting in Kent, and had none to assist me except a few local preachers; but the Lord was powerfully present, both in public worship and at the love feast.

"I cannot help thinking the circumstance I am going to relate very remarkable. One day after meeting, my brother John came up to me and shook hands; and looking me very wishfully in the face, without any explanation, said, 'I shall never see you again in this world.' It was even so; for by the time I got round as far as Cecil, he was taken very ill;- and a few hours before I got to his house, he was interred on the east side of the preaching house, at the place where he bade me his last farewell, not more than two weeks before. He was my second spiritual son; and there was an uncommon intimacy between us. His dissolution was revealed to him some time before he died. An eminent physician was with him the evening before his death; and when his wife, speaking low to the doctor, inquired how soon he supposed her husband would die, and was told that his life would not be prolonged until the morning; he overhearing them, said, 'Doctor, I shall not go till eight o'clock in the morning.' He had his senses perfectly in his last moments, and the exhortation which he gave was striking. After exhorting his wife and a brother who lived with him, to stand fast in the faith, and entreating the servant to love the Lord; in a very affecting manner, he said, 'Now there is but one thing which lies heavy on my mind, and that is, the case of two unconverted brothers. Tell them,' continued he, 'from me, I never expect to see them in heaven,' (they lived on the western shore) 'unless they repent, and turn to the Lord.' This he said to my brother Richard. Not long after they heard the message, they both sought and found the Lord. Thus were his prayers answered. At eight o'clock, as he had said, he resigned his spirit to his God, a witness of perfect love. He was beloved by all the people of God, and spent much of his time in the public and private exercises of religion.

"This is the brother, who so solemnly covenanted with God, on a sick bed, that if his life were prolonged, he would give himself to the service of his Maker. To show the mercy of the holy God, I must say, after his recovery, he was as careless as ever. I did not at that time enjoy the liberty of the gospel, yet at times I endeavoured to talk to my brother, and impress his mind with the solemn promises he had made, and how merciful his heavenly Father was in sparing him, &c, but he would not hear, was rather displeased, and gave me to understand that he did not wish me to revive that subject.

"Shortly after I was brought to an evidence of salvation by the forgiveness of sin, my brother John lay with great weight on my mind. I accordingly visited him, and while I was telling him my experience, I believe the blessed God touched his heart. With his consent I appointed a prayer meeting at his house; many attended, and among others he was powerfully awakened and cried for mercy. About three months after this, he received a clear evidence of his acceptance with God, and walked humbly before him. In the spring of 1775, he married a pious young lady in Cecil county, after which I saw very little of him for two years, as I was travelling in distant parts; but I have every reason to believe, that he maintained a heavenly walk with God.

"In May, 1778, I came to his house, and found him an humble follower of Jesus, and had sweet communion with him. He had the charge of three classes, in which there were about sixty members, walking in love and harmony, and they esteemed him as a father and guide.

"He gave the greater part of his time to meeting the classes, and visiting from house to house as long as he was able. In his last sickness he praised God wonderfully, testifying to all around that he had found the blessing he had been long seeking for, the perfect love of God. So my dear brother John lived, and so he died. I was about forty miles off—they sent for me, but a little before I arrived he was interred, so I did not, according to his word, see him again, neither shall I, till I see him in a better world.

"In September, 1778, I returned to Delaware state; and on the 5th, for the first time, preached at Mr. Williams's in Muskmelon, a kind man who had been a Quaker. I had for several days suffered deep exercises of mind, especially while on my way to this place. The enemy of my soul suggested that the Lord was a hard master. The whole sabbath morning I was sorely tempted in this way. This appointment was made for Mr. Asbury, which caused my trial to be greater. At the meeting there were between five hundred and a thousand people; many of whom came out of curiosity. I preached under a large spreading tree; but the wind being high, I concluded to preach the second sermon in the house; but the house could not contain half of the people. I gave out, 'One thing I know, whereas I was blind now I see.' Glory to God! Jesus makes use of clay, in this our day to open the eyes of the blind. While, I was in the first place describing the blindness of the human mind, the Lord displayed his almighty power. There was a great weeping and mourning among poor sinners : I likewise felt much happiness, while describing the Lord's method in bringing sinners to himself, and in showing the blessed privileges they enjoy. How many were then convinced, and how many converted, I will not undertake to say, but I believe the number of both was great. I shall take notice of one instance of the power of God displayed at this meeting. A man noted for wickedness, came cursing and swearing, as he has since told me, but under the first head of the discourse, his sins fell, as it were, with the weight of a mill stone on him. 'I would,' said he, 'have run out ; but I was afraid to put one foot before the other, lest I should drop into hell, for the pit was disclosed to my view; and I saw no way to escape it: I thought every minute I should fall; but I held myself up by the chair. O! said he, under the second head of your discourse, while you were holding up Christ, I saw a beauty in him; and without any dependance on myself, I cast my soul on Jesus; in a moment the burden fell, my soul was happy, and I went home rejoicing in my Saviour.' I knew him six years after, and had no cause to doubt the soundness of his conversion. Among the rest an officer was cut to the heart, who soon after gave up his commission, and became a pious follower of Christ. I do not think I ever saw a more powerful day in a new place. After meeting the people all around were begging to have preaching at their houses. Among other places, I appointed to speak at Mr. Lewis's whose heart the Lord had touched; he lived in Mother Kill, a place famed for wickedness. Previously to my entering this place, the Lord awakened a woman of distinction by an earthquake ; she found peace to her soul shortly after I came to the place, and about a year after, she died a witness of perfect love;

I preached at a variety of places in the country, and the work of the Lord went on prosperously.

"When first I preached at Mr. Lewis's only a few came to hear; but the numbers gradually increased; souls were awakened, and I joined many to the society. In the second sermon, among others, a youth by the name of Caleb Boyce was awakened, and after a time became a light in the church of God. I preached at his father's, and the work of the Lord prospering, a large society was raised in that neighbourhood, which did honour to the cause of God!

"I bless God for it, I had many hearts, hands, and houses, opened around me; and many inquired, 'What shall I do to be saved?' The people about Mother Kill were brought up Presbyterians, and their pastor strove by every means to keep them from the Methodists; but all in vain; they were convinced there was more in religion than a mere form. Multitudes gathered to hear the word, and many large societies were formed in different places.

"September 12th, 1778, was the first day of my entering the town of Dover, quite an irreligious place. I had desired for some time to attack this place, but had no opening, till an old gentleman came one day and heard me preach at Mr. Shaw's: his heart was touched, and he gave me an invitation to preach in the academy. Scarcely had I alighted from my horse before I was surrounded by hundreds; some cried one thing, some another; some said, he is a good man, others said nay, he deceiveth the people —and I was also accused of being a friend to King George. They cried, 'He is one of Clowe's men—hang him—hang him.' I know not what the event would have been, had not the Lord interposed. There were so many voices heard, that I had no possible chance to speak for myself; and to all human appearance, I was in a fair way to be torn in pieces every moment: I was, however, rescued by several gentlemen of the town, who hearing the uproar ran to my assistance.

"The chief of these were Mr. Pryor, a merchant, who was formerly awakened under Mr. Whitefield, Mr. Lockerman, and the alderman of the town. The little squire pressed through the crowd, Zaccheus like, and taking me by the hand, led me through the mob, desiring me to preach and he would stand by me. I mounted the stage at the door of the academy: the people flocked round, both within and without. After singing and prayer, I gave out, 'If it bear fruit well, and if not, then after that, thou shalt cut it down.' The Lord was with me in truth. It was not difficult for me to speak so as to be heard a quarter of a mile. Many who did not come to the place, heard me from their gardens and windows. We had much of the presence of the Lord with us. We rarely see such a weeping company in a new place. One woman, who sat in her window more than a quarter of a mile off, was powerfully wrought upon. She knew no rest day nor night, till she found a resting place in her heart for the God of Jacob. It was thought by some of my Christian friends, who accompanied me, that very few of the extensive congregation were left without a witness on their hearts of the truth of what was delivered: more than twenty got the word of truth so fastened, that they did not desire to lose it, and it terminated, I trust, in a sound conversion of the souls of many.

"The mob hung their heads; many of them were affected; their ringleader said, as I was informed, he would come and ask my pardon if he thought I would forgive him: I understood he betook himself from that day to reading the Bible; and never again, to my knowledge, persecuted the children of God.

"In the evening I lectured at Mr. Smether's, the old gentleman who had first given me an invitation to the town. Many of the chief people of the place came to hear, and we had a very solemn time. When I withdrew to my room, I was severely buffeted by Satan. I felt as miserable as Jonah under his withered gourd; it seemed as though

I had given all to the people, and had nothing left for myself. Ah! said the enemy, the Lord will make use of you for the good of others, and then cast you away, as a parent does a rod after correcting the child. I was in such deep exercise, that I could scarcely close my eyes throughout the night, but passed the greater part of it away in sighs and groans and silence before the Lord. I believe I was permitted to be thus tried in order to keep me at the feet of my Saviour, and hope I shall be always thankful for his kind dealings with me.

"Monday, September 13th, I preached a few miles out of town, accompanied by many, and the Lord was with us. In the afternoon I returned and found many mourning after Christ; but the devil and some of his adherents were striving to make them believe that what I had told them was a delusion; but they were not successful. I joined those who were deeply awakened into a society; and the Lord was with them, spreading his work and converting the souls of many: among the rest there was an old lady stripped of her own righteousness, who had been a communicant in the church for many years; also ten of her children with their husbands and wives were brought under concern for their souls. I preached at her house, when sixteen or eighteen of her children and children in law were present. The old lady was mourning; but several of them the Lord had set at liberty; and before many months he visited the old lady with his forgiving love, as well as the most of her children. Such a family as this I have seldom seen in any part of America.

"The fields appeared white for harvest; but the labourers were very few. I was engaged in strong cries to the Lord, to open the way and send out more; and blessed be his name, he raised up several young men, and sent others from the western shore. I wrote to Mr. Asbury, who was at Judge White's, informing him how matters were, that his way was open into any part of the state, and

I requested him to make a visit to Dover: he did so, and brought in many whom I could not reach. The Lord gave us great favour in the sight of Dr. Magaw, minister of the church, and he proved a great blessing to the cause of Methodism. The prejudices of the people began to fall astonishingly, and hundreds were enabled to rejoice in the kingdom of grace.

"The 19th of September, 1778, I attended the funeral of my brother, and a solemn season it was; my youngest brother was there from Baltimore, a wild youth, but the Lord laid his convincing hand upon him, and he returned a penitent mourner. In a few weeks he returned to see me, and continued with me till the Lord set his soul at liberty.

"Monday, September 20th, as I was meditating and walking through the fields, I heard the cries of one on the top of a tree: and lifting up my eyes, I saw a man about taking away his own life. A rope was tied to a limb with a noose in it, and the poor wretch bemoaning himself thus—'O what a wretch I am! once I had a day of grace, but now it is a gone case with me!—I may as well put an end to my wretched life!' He then made a motion to put the rope over his head, bidding the world farewell. I instantly called to him, and told him to stop a few minutes while I conversed with him. He did so; and after some time I persuaded him to refrain from his wicked intention, and come down from the tree. In the course of our conversation, I found the good Spirit had from time to time strove with him, but he had rejected the offers of mercy. At length the arch fiend persuaded him his day of grace was past, and that he had better know his doom as quickly as possible. My being an instrument (to human appearance) of saving the life of a human being, as well as, perhaps, an immortal soul, was no small comfort to me.

"Tuesday I rode as far as Queen Anne's, and found a very prosperous work going on. I was very comfortable in my own soul; and experienced it to be sweet to wait on

God in secret. I found many hungering for the word, and had liberty in preaching.

"Wednesday, September 22d, I awoke and arose early from my pillow, felt a great nearness to the Lord, and had a sweet time in secret. I visited poor John White, a brother of the Dr., and found him near death, and in his sins. In his health he was a great persecutor; but now a penitent, begging the prayers of those he once despised.—O! how did he exhort his old companions to flee from their sins, and to take warning from him. I was greatly affected with his situation, and did not find freedom to leave him in the arms of the devil. 'O!' cried he, 'I am sleeping over hell!' I prayed with him frequently, and still it was impressed on my mind not to leave him. I had a travail of soul for this young man; and retiring into a secret place, I wrestled with the Lord for him a long time; and I thought the Lord would surely grant him favour. When I returned to the house and called the family together again for prayer, several of them were happy in the Lord. In the time of prayer the Lord set his soul at liberty; and I do not entertain a doubt but that he went to rest.—O! what a blessed thing it is in such a case to have Christian friends!—He spoke freely of the love of God which he felt in his soul, and of his willingness to die. Numbers attended his funeral; and I preached a sermon with much liberty on 'I heard a voice from heaven, saying unto me, Write, Blessed are the dead which die in the Lord, from henceforth: yea, saith the Spirit, for they rest from their labours, and their works do follow them,' Rev. xiv, 13. The Lord was present, and I trust measurably accompanied his word.

"Individuals thought me an enthusiast, because I talked so much about feelings, and having impressions to go to particular places. I know the word of God is our infallible guide, and by it we are to try all our dreams and feelings. I also know, that both sleeping and waking, things of a divine nature have been revealed to me. One night the state of the people in Somerset and Sussex counties seemed to be shown me. In my dream I thought I had a large circuit formed ; and the people were gathering to the banner of our Lord. On Friday, October 22d, I set out to form a circuit in those counties. On Sunday 24th I arrived, and had an opportunity of preaching in a forest, both morning and afternoon, to hundreds who gathered to hear the new doctrine. I suppose many of them expected to be greatly diverted : for they were a people who had neither the form nor power of godliness. My text was, 'Behold the Lamb of God, which taketh away the sin of the world,' John i, 29. The first sermon was only preparatory to the second, which I preached after a few minutes intermission, from 'And I saw the dead, both small and great, stand before God, and the books were opened, and another book was opened, which was the book of life, and the dead were judged out of those things written in the books, according to their works,' Rev. xx, 12. I was convinced my impressions in respect to this place were not enthusiastic, for the power of God was very manifest in the congregation ; and there was weeping on every side. I suppose that more than thirty were powerfully wrought upon, all of whom not long after joined the society. I had invitations to preach from various quarters. The way was prepared in the same manner in which the Lord had revealed it to me ; and sinners flocked to Jesus. Some of the people among whom I went, appeared as familiar to me as if I had been there frequently before.

"Monday, September 25th, I preached a funeral sermon in the same neighbourhood ; and the devil sent out a woman with a pistol or two to shoot me. While I was preaching from ' Acquaint now thyself with him, and be at peace, thereby good shall come unto thee,' Job xxii, 21, she came in, and made so much noise that I stopped till they put her out and shut the door. O! how precious this season was to me! The divine power was sensibly felt among the people. After the sermon many hung around me in tears, begging of me to pray for them, and likewise to visit them, and not to let the disturbance prevent my coming among them again.

"The wife of Mr. Nellum, a merchant in Salisbury, was powerfully awakened, with many others who came from a distance. This part of the world was famous for gambling and dancing; but as the word spread these vices fell; until there was scarcely a frolic heard of in Broad Creek. About this place I joined many broken hearted sinners in society, many of whom, I trust, became acquainted with the power of religion.

"Saturday, Nov. 7th, on my way to Talbot quarterly meeting, I preached at Mr. Parrot's. Two very gay young women, who came on a visit to their relations, were wounded, and I left them crying for mercy.

"On Sunday, Nov. 8th, our quarterly meeting commenced.

"Monday 9th, love feast began in the morning, and it was a refreshing time. Many rejoiced in the Lord, and spoke freely and feelingly of what God had done for them. After the love feast I found great freedom to preach from 'The Lord knoweth how to deliver the godly out of temptation,' 2 Pet. ii, 9, and we had a time not soon to be forgotten.

"Tuesday, Nov. 10th, I called again at Mr. Parrot's, and found those young women dressed very plain, and under deep distress. In the evening I read and lectured on the 16th of John, and the Lord was with us of a truth. The power of the Lord was sensibly felt, and his presence filled the room, where about fifteen of us were met for prayer. Brother Hartley, my brother Richard, (who had come from some distance to see me,) and myself, continued in prayer, including the time we spent in singing and exhorting, from about eight o'clock, till nearly two; and in that time five souls were set at liberty: the two young women of whom I have spoken, Dr. White and his two sisters, who came from a distance to quarterly meeting. This was an extraordinary night to my poor heart, and to the souls of most present.

"Wednesday, Nov. 11th, greatly refreshed and strengthened, I set out again on my way to Somerset, and found my young disciples growing in grace, as well as increasing in number. In my way round, having an invitation from Mr. Nellum, I preached in Salisbury, where the Lord began a blessed work; but enemies were raised up against me, who sent the sheriff with a writ to take me to jail. After he served it on me, he told me I must be confined. I told him I was a servant of the Lord Jesus, and that if he laid a hand on me, it would be like touching the apple of his eye. He was afraid to injure me: and friends and enemies followed me to the next preaching place. Many assembled from all quarters, and I preached from 'Behold, ye despisers, and wonder and perish; for I work a work in your days, a work which ye shall in no wise believe, though a man declare it unto you,' Acts xiii, 41. It appeared to me as if the place was shaken by the power of the Lord; many of my enemies trembled like a leaf; I had faith to believe they had no power to stop me; and so it proved, for I went on my way rejoicing in God my Saviour. This day one soul was set at liberty.

"I preached at a place called Quantico, and a similar work broke out there. The Lord raised a society, and many souls were converted; among others, old sister Rider, who was formerly a hearer of Mr. Whitefield, was raised up as a pillar in our society; and she became a mother indeed to the preachers. This society was mostly composed of young people, who were as tender as lambs."

In a note Mr. Garrettson gives the following account of the manner in which he was first introduced to the above place:

"I will briefly narrate the method the Lord took to bring me first to Quantico. Old Mr. and Mrs. Rider, who were on a visit among their friends, heard me preach, and were much affected. After the congregation was dismissed, they advanced towards me in tears, and the old lady spoke as follows,—'Many years ago we heard Mr. Whitefield preach, and we were brought to taste the sweetness of religion. Till we heard you, we had not heard a gospel sermon for about twenty years. The first time I heard you preach, I knew it was the truth, but I only had a little spark left. Yesterday we heard you again, and the little spark was blown up to a coal; and glory to God, to day the coal is blown up to a flame. We cannot hide ourselves any longer from you; our house and hearts are open to receive you, and the blessed word you preach.' The dear old people seemed to see, feel, and think alike. I went to their house, and it appeared as if there were many in that vicinity just ripe for the gospel. O! there was a sweet gathering to the fold of Jesus.

"In April, 1779, I was led still farther into the wilderness, and though I met with a variety of trials, and was severely buffeted of Satan, yet my Lord was with me daily. Although in those new places I had none to converse with, at first, who knew the Lord, yet Jesus was blessed company to me in my retirement. Often the wilderness was my closet, where I had many sweet hours in communion with God. Whose heart can help rejoicing to think of the kind condescension of our blessed Lord to permit them to have such heavenly converse with *him!*

"Saturday, April 3d, I preached at a place called the Sound, for the first time, near the sea shore, to about two hundred people. They had been as sheep without a shepherd; but I preached not without hope. There were several who are under the appellation of Baptists in this place; and one of their preachers who spoke after me, cried down *baby sprinkling*, as he called it. I requested the people to attend the next day at an appointed place, and I would preach on the subject.

"Sunday, April 4th, a number of people assembled, and I preached from 'Go ye into all the world, and preach the gospel to every creature. He that believeth and is baptized shall be saved; but he that believeth not, shall be damned,' Mark xvi, 15, 16. Very great attention was paid; and as my hearers were principally Presbyterians and Churchmen, a vindication of infant baptism was very agreeable to them. If it was of no other service, it prepared their minds for what was to follow; for they knew not who or what I was. I told them that after a few minutes intermission I would preach again; which I did from these words, 'If the righteous scarcely be saved, where shall the ungodly and the sinner appear?' 1 Pet. iv, 18. This day will not soon be forgotten: the work of the Lord broke out. Though I continued more than three hours in the two sermons, the people, after I concluded, appeared as if nailed to their seats; for they did not seem as if they wished to move from the place; and weeping was on every side.

"Monday, April 5th, I preached still nearer to the sea; and the same convincing power ran through the audience: some of them thought but little of walking ten or twelve miles to hear the word. I appointed a day to read and explain the rules of our society; and many came together: I preached with great freedom: then explained the nature and design of our society; and desired such of the weeping flock as wished to join, to draw near and open their minds. I examined and admitted about thirty; but being weary, I declined taking any more at that time. Weeping and mourning were heard among the people.

"I went to a place some distance off, and preached to a gazing company: and while I was speaking, a man started from his seat, saying, 'Sir, it is a shame for you to go on as you do; why, do you think you can make us believe your doctrine is true?' I stopped immediately, and desired him to point out wherein it was false. I conversed with him before the people, until he asked my pardon, being sorry he had exposed his ignorance. As he was a man of some note, it proved a blessing to the people.

"I returned to the Sound, and preached two, three, and frequently four times in a day. They were so hungry for the word, that many would follow me to the house where I was to stay, inquiring, 'What they should do to be saved?' The devil in this, as well as other places, had his factors: one man of note set up a reading meeting in opposition to the society; but the power of God reached his heart, so that he gave it up and joined the society. Several hired a clergyman of the Church to come and preach against us. He came once, and appointed to come again; but before the time, I met him on the road, and told him I was the man against whom he preached in such a place. I asked him if he had ever heard a Methodist? He told me he never had. After explaining to him our doctrine, and conversing with him more than an hour, he promised that he would never do the like again, and confessed that he was led into it by a few individuals: and his people could never after persuade him to preach against us.

"In this neighbourhood I have preached to a thousand or fifteen hundred souls assembled together under the trees; and many were brought to experience justification by faith."*

* Respecting the people in this place, Mr. Garrettson makes the following observations in his notes to this part of his journal, that an admirable change soon took place for the better in this region of country. When he first went among them the people, their land and houses, with but few exceptions, were poor. What was worst of all, they were destitute of even the form of godliness. Many of them preferred fishing and hunting to cultivating the land. After the gospel came among them, religion spread rapidly, and the people became industrious and happy; left off gambling, tilled their land,

"My mind was amazingly exercised, and I believe the Lord permitted this affliction for the humiliation of my soul. I was frequently afraid, lest after preaching to others, I myself should be a cast away; and many hours I have spent in secret, weeping before the Lord. Sometimes I was tempted to think I did more harm than good, and that the people, after a while, would be worse than ever: or that they were hypocrites. At other times, the cross was so heavy a little before I had to preach, that I was constrained, like the prophet, to cry out, 'The burden of the Lord!' But at such particular times I was sure to have a happy meeting.

> O! to grace how great a debtor,
> Daily I'm constrain'd to be:
> Let that grace now like a fetter,
> Bind my wandering soul to thee.

"One day I was wandering through the wilderness in search of poor lost sheep, and called at several houses; but they did not want me. At length night came on; and I had been all day, at least from the morning, without any refreshment for myself or horse. I finally found myself lost in a thick wilderness, called the Cyprus Swamp. The night was dark and rainy; and after wandering about for a considerable time, I concluded to take up my lodging as well as I could; for this purpose I stopped my horse; but before I got down, I espied a light, by following which I was led to a house, where I was most kindly entertained. I sat down, and found my soul very happy and thankful. The man of the house fixed his eyes upon me, and at last built houses, and attended to their spiritual interests, so that, says he, "after a few years, in retracing my footsteps in this country, I found that my younger brethren in the ministry who had succeeded me, had been blessed in their labours, and every thing appeared to wear a different aspect. Experience had taught many that there is nothing like the gospel in its purity to meliorate both the temporal and spiritual condition of man: and my prayer is that it may find its way throughout the whole world, to the destruction of idolatry and infidelity."

said, 'What are you, or who are you? for I am sure' I never saw such a man as you appear to be.' I told him I was a follower of our blessed Saviour; and asked him if he would join me in prayer; I then read the 7th chapter of Matthew, and lectured from it; and found great sweetness in prayer. After I withdrew to bed, the wife said to the husband, 'That is a man of God; one whom the Lord hath sent to reform the world.' When I arose in the morning, he asked me to what place I was bound, and offered his service and company. I perceived that the Lord had reached his heart; and I now saw for what purpose the crook was in my lot the day before. I asked the woman if she had a love for the Lord? She said, 'Yes.' I asked if she ever prayed? She replied, 'I pray always.' I asked if she knew her sins forgiven? She said, 'she did not; but she knew that she should go to heaven when she died. And,' said she, 'I know that you are a servant of God; but you cannot teach me, for I understand all the Scriptures, and I know what kind of death I am to die.' After breakfast we went on our way, and as we rode the man asked me what I thought of his wife. I told him she was a mystery to me. 'Why,' said he, 'some time ago she was taken in a kind of melancholy way, and no one knew what was the matter; for thirteen days she would neither eat nor drink, and frequently she would embrace the pitcher and kiss it, but would not take a drop, till at length she became so weak, that she betook herself to her bed; and the thirteenth day of her fasting, a number of people waited around, expecting to see the last of her; but all on a sudden she raised up, and said, "You thought that mine was a bodily disorder; but it was not. Now," said she, "I know that my Maker loves me." They gave her food and she eat as heartily as ever: and she has been in that serious way ever since.' She appeared to be a very solemn woman, and I had a hope that the Lord had taken her into his favour.

"On my return I called on him again, and conversed more fully with the woman, who continued to believe that man could not teach her. I suppose the people in this part of the country had scarcely ever heard any kind of preaching, and knew no more about the new birth than the Indians. I met a man one day, and asked him if he was acquainted with Jesus Christ. 'Sir,' said he, 'I know not where the man lives.' Lest he should have misunderstood me, I repeated my question; and he answered, 'I know not the man.'

"Glory to God! I preached in a variety of places through this wilderness: and many were convinced and brought to the knowledge of the truth. They built a church, and the Lord raised up several able speakers among them. There was an amazing change both in the disposition and manners of the people. The wilderness and solitary places began to bud and blossom as the rose; and many hearts did leap for joy. Hundreds who were asleep in the arms of the wicked one awoke, and were inquiring the way to Zion with their faces thitherward.

"As my brethren in rotation began to travel largely through this part of the work, I had an opportunity to visit the friends in various parts of Maryland; and found it good for me to be among old established Christians.

"On the 1st of June I returned back to the Sussex circuit in Delaware; and June 6th I preached with great freedom at Thomas L.'s in the Fork, from 'Friend, how comest thou in hither, not having on a wedding garment,' Matt. xxii, 12. I rode six miles and met brother M. We held a watch night, and I had much satisfaction in hearing several of the exhorters, and gave them notes of permission to speak.

"Sunday, June 7th, I spent the morning in retirement, sorely tempted by the devil; and after I went to my appointed place, my mind was so bewildered, I thought there was not a text in the Bible that I could speak from.

I felt myself less than the least. At eleven o'clock there was such a number collected, that I was obliged to preach under the trees. I had been before the people but a few minutes, till the Lord blessed me with great light, and the Bible seemed all plain to me."

In reference to silent meetings, Mr. Garrettson has the following very pertinent observations among his manuscript notes.

"It is said, in favour of silent meetings, that Job's friends waited in silence seven days, and then they began to speak. Why was this silence? Before Job's affliction he was thought to be a very good man. His friends were in council to make up an opinion respecting his case. It was a received opinion with many in that country and age, that the Almighty would not lay so heavy an affliction upon a good man. From such an opinion, their decision must be, that Job was a bad man, or that his Maker dealt unjustly by him: but the judgment of the counsellors was, that the Almighty was perfect in wisdom and goodness; and that Job was a bad man, and having made up their minds on the occasion, they began to load Job with accusations of base hypocrisy, and to preach to him repentance, or banishment from the presence of God. Had they known how to reconcile those deep afflictions with the mercy and goodness of God, they might have begun their discourse when they first approached Job, and not have accepted a false vision.

"I grant, in several instances, the prophets waited in silence; but who cannot see the difference between foretelling future events, and declaring those sacred truths of the gospel which have been revealed to every regenerated child of God, and especially to his ministers? Before a person professes to be an ambassador of Jesus Christ, he must know that he has a commission from him, and the pious man with the commission, receives a holy unction, and if he is faithful, he will be taught every necessary truth, and certainly he will be taught to be instant in season and out of season. I know that the nearer we live to the fountain head, the more plentifully will the water flow. A Christian minister should always have the holy spark with him, and certainly he should have the faculties of his soul so well regulated, as to know when to speak, and when to be silent. I myself one day heard three men speak, after brooding over it for nearly an hour, and I verily believe I have heard a pious sister in a love feast speak more to the purpose in fifteen minutes. What would you think of E. H., who by some is cried up to be a great man, after professing to have waited a considerable time for the Spirit, rising up and declaring that there is no more merit in the blood of Jesus Christ, than in the blood of any common animal, and inveighing against almost all the duties enjoined by the Christian religion. I speak thus, because I think it a pity that any respectable society of professing Christians should be imposed on by such men, and such doctrine.

"Whenever the Lord begins his work in any place, the devil and his children are sure to rise up against it. After preaching, I set out for my afternoon's appointment, accompanied by about thirty, whose hearts the Lord had touched. I was pursued by a party of men who way laid me, and the head of the company, with a gun presented, commanded me to stop. Several of the women who were with us surprised me; they were in an instant off their horses, and seizing hold of his gun, held it until I passed by. That same man was a penitent some time after, and became a member of the society. I went on and preached at old Mr. T—'s to a large attentive company, and united a prosperous society.

"It appeared as if hundreds in the congregation were more or less wrought upon, and many appeared to be broken hearted. We could never get a society in this place till now. I know the day when the Lord began his work in the Fork: I preached from these words, 'And in hell he lifted up his eyes, being in torment;' and intended, if I saw no fruit, to leave them: but blessed be God, he visited the place in mercy, and the devil's kingdom is like to receive a wonderful shock."

About this time Mr. Garrettson laboured under peculiar and heavy temptations, often repelling them by earnest prayer to God, wrestling in holy violence for the victory. He continued, however, steadfast in his Master's work, preaching successfully to large congregations. Under a feeling sense of his inward conflicts, he says, "What is the devil afraid of? Why does he chase me in this manner? I do not know that I have given way to sin, either inwardly or outwardly; and yet he tells me frequently, 'my commission is run out, and that my labours never will be blessed again.' I have had great strugglings in my mind to know my standing; not that I doubt my adoption into the family of heaven; but respecting my salvation from all inward sin. From this quarter have arisen my greatest fears, for more than twelve months past. I know that my Lord has given me power to serve him, and that I love him supremely; but these are comprehensive words, 'to love the Lord with all the heart.' My prayers have been frequent, being desirous of a stronger assurance of this perfect love which casteth out fear. I have thought sometimes that I should doubt no more; but fearfulness has again assaulted me.

"This day I felt strangely: I was so burdened, not with guilt, blessed be God! that I could scarcely bear my own weight. None know what I mean, but such as have received a commission to deliver a message for the Lord. The prophet knew when he cried out, 'The burden of the Lord;' Jonah knew something of it when he was called to go to Nineveh, and Jeremiah was well acquainted with exercises of this kind. It is a sweet thing to preach the gospel, but the cross is to be borne.

"I crossed the river and went to my appointment, which

was at J. More's on Broad creek. The people assembled from all quarters; and many came out, some from afar, who were enemies to the way. I had scarcely opened my mouth when my burden dropped off, and in an uncommon manner the Holy Scriptures were opened to me, and the flame ran from heart to heart. I felt as though I had almost faith enough to remove mountains. One thing was noticed, not only by my friends, but likewise by those who were enemies,—there had been a great drought, so that the vegetable creation hung in mourning; and it was thought by many they would lose their crops if it continued much longer. In a particular manner I was led to pray for rain; and a few minutes after the congregation was dismissed, the face of the sky was covered with blackness, and we had a plentiful shower. This greatly surprised and convinced the people. I was now happy enough to see the prosperity of the young converts. While the Lord was plentifully watering the earth, I collected the family for prayer; and we had a great time of refreshing from the presence of the Lord. My soul was so happy while the Lord was uttering his voice in thunder, that it seemed as if I saw, by an eye of faith, the blessed Jesus; and the glorified company around him, in exalted strains, singing and shouting his praise. And this joy continued with me till some time in the night; I then sweetly rested in the arms of my Lord.

"Thursday, June 11th, I preached to a poor people. Some who came from a distance thought I pointed my discourse at them. Thursday was a very solemn day of fasting. I have noticed that the evil one is more spiteful on my fast days than at other times. But I feel there is a necessity of keeping my body under, lest after preaching to others I should be a cast away. My public labours this day, as I was among a curious people, were to reconcile some seeming contradictions in Scripture. After I had done, I was warmly opposed by an enemy to the cross of

Christ. I visited one of the spiritual children of Mr. Whitefield, on her death bed; and I trust her soul was happy in the Lord.

"In the evening I met and examined a large society, and we had a comfortable time. I had a sweet night's rest, and awoke at my usual hour with a happy mind, and prayed earnestly to the Lord, to grant that every moment of my life might be given to him.

"I rode to Quantico to visit the young lambs. I expected that the Lord intended to do something for them, for the devil pursued me all the way even till I got to the place. An unexpected congregation assembled in the afternoon, and the Lord was with us of a truth. Several were set at liberty; and the cries of the distressed were heard—O Jesus, thou art lovely to my soul!—Thou hast overcome me with thy loving kindness. I found great freedom in meeting the society, and in the morning I met them again, and a precious time we had.

"Sunday, June 14th, I felt this morning as if the Lord intended to do great things for the people. I spent the morning in wrestling with the Lord for a blessing on my labours. I preached at old brother Rider's at eleven o'clock: the old judge who came as a hearer gave great attention, and we had a melting time. I rode ten miles to Salisbury; when I came in, the man of the house took me into a room, and told me I had better leave the town immediately; for a mob was waiting and intended to send me to jail. 'They came to my house last night,' said he, 'expecting to find you here; but when they found you not, they laid hold on me, and dragging me down the chamber stairs, hauled me along the street till my arms were as black as ink from my wrists to my shoulders; and I know not what would have been the consequence, if I had not been rescued by a magistrate.' This mob was made up of what they call the first people in the county. I told my informer that I had come to preach my Master's gospel, and that I was not afraid to trust him with body and soul. Many came out to hear me; I understood the mob sent one of their company to give information of the most convenient time to take me. While I was declaring 'The Lord knoweth how to deliver the godly out of temptation, and reserve the unjust unto the day of judgment to be punished,' the heart of the spy, who sat close by me, was touched, and tears plentifully ran down his face. After service he returned to his company, and told them I had preached the truth, and if they laid a hand on me he would put the law in force against them. They withdrew to their homes, without making the slightest attempt upon me. O, who would not confide in so good a God! After our blessed meeting was over, I rode three miles and had a pleasant time with a few of my friends. Glory be to God! he is carrying on a gracious work about this place. All this week I spent in preaching and visiting the young societies.

"Sunday, June 21, I was to preach at the Sound. In the morning I intended meeting the society at eight o'clock; but such a crowd gathered that I declined it; and preached a sermon. At twelve about fifteen hundred were assembled under the spreading trees, and the Lord made bare his arm. After a short intermission, I preached another sermon; and it seemed as if the whole country would turn to the Lord. While preaching I was so wonderfully drawn out, that it appeared to me as though I saw our blessed Saviour working prosperously through the assembly. Weeping was on every side. I spent a week in the neighbourhood, preaching several times a day, besides visiting and conversing with the distressed. I believe this work was greatly hindered by the Baptists, who came among the people, drew off a few, and set others to disputing about the decrees, and their method of baptizing.

"Sunday, June 28th, when I came to brother Williams's in Muskmelon, I found that a Nicolite preacher had been sowing his seed in the young society, and endeavouring to destroy the new-born children. He told them, 'It was a sin to wear any kind of clothing that was coloured; and that they ought never to pray but when they had an immediate impulse, and that it was wrong to sing.' Many people came together, but I perceived a considerable alteration; for some would not sing at all, and others sat both in time of singing and prayer. Some had taken off the borders of their caps, and condemned those who would not do as they had done: in short, some of my own spiritual children would scarcely hear me, because I wore a black coat. I gave out my text, 'The kingdom of God is not meat and drink, but righteousness, and peace, and joy in the Holy Ghost,' Rom. xiv, 17. The Lord made bare his arm and humbled me among them; and there was a shaking, convincing power. After sermon was ended, I met the society and excluded the leader and one or two more; those that remained seemed to grow in grace more than ever. I spent the week in Mother Kill, and several other places, and was greatly comforted among the growing societies.

"Sunday, July 5th, I preached in Dover a little after sunrise, then rode four miles and preached at brother B.'s at nine, to hundreds who stood and sat under the trees for want of room in the house, from 'Behold a sower went forth to sow,' Matt. xiii, 3. I was in my element, and we had a great display of the power of the Lord. Many about this place are inquiring, 'What shall I do to be saved?' I rode on six miles and preached at one o'clock to a listening multitude, under the trees in Mother Kill. O how good the Lord was to my soul! It was little trouble for me to preach, for the Scripture seemed all open. I rode five miles and preached again in Muskmelon at brother W.'s, and had I think more freedom than at either of the other places. At the last sermon there was a Quaker preacher present, and after meeting was ended he told a person that I 'spake by the Spirit, if ever man did.' The person said it was my fourth sermon that day; he then altered his mind, and replied, 'If that was the case, I was a deceiver, for it was nothing but will worship.' This day I stood upwards of six hours in the four sermons, and concluded about sunset. My spirit was so united to my Jesus, and so transported, that I scarcely felt the fatigues of the day; and the only sustenance I had taken was a little milk and water. I have seldom seen a greater day than this: I do not know but I may say thousands are flocking to Jesus. There is a childlike fondness in these people, and I feel unwilling to leave them; but the will of the Lord be done.

"Monday, July 6th, having it on my mind, I set out to make an inroad through the Delaware state, where I had never been: I had appointed a friend, who had given me an invitation to Lewis Town, to meet me at such a time, and conduct me through the country: so that numbers had knowledge of my intention to pass that way. All along the road many were standing at their doors and windows gazing, and I could hear some of them say, as I passed, 'There he is;' 'O,' said another, 'he is like another man.' I rode about thirty miles and got to my appointment about three; about four o'clock I began, and shortly after I gave out the text, J. Wolf, brother to the man at whose house I was to preach, came to the door with a gun and a drum, and several other utensils, and after beating his old drum a while, he took the gun, and was dodging about as though he was taking aim to shoot me: this greatly terrified the women, so that there was nothing but confusion. I then stopped and withdrew to a private room. Soon after, the town squire and several other magistrates came, and among the rest the Presbyterian minister. The town squire commanded him to depart immediately to his own house, or behave himself, otherwise he would send him to jail. We now had peace, and I found great freedom to finish my sermon. I have no doubt but the Lord began this work. The minister told some of the people afterwards that I held out nineteen errors. The town squire told me the court house was at my service, and I should be welcome to his house.

"Wednesday, July 8th, my old enemy W——f by nature and name, set on by a few others, came into the court house while I was preaching, not with a gun and drum, but with fire which he put in the chimney, and then began to heap on wood, though the day was exceedingly warm: finding that this did not disturb me, he brought in a bell, and rung it loudly through the house. I stopped and inquired if any would open a large private room. Many were offered, and I withdrew and finished my sermon at the house of a kind widow woman. In spite of all the opposition, the word found the way to the hearts of the hearers; and though severely tempted of the devil, and persecuted by many of his servants, my heart was with the Lord; and many were the sweet moments I had in secret.

"Sunday, July 12th, my appointments were at nine in the morning, and three in the afternoon, that I might not interfere with the hours of the Church. The court house was crowded at nine, and a most pleasant time I had. In the morning it rained, so that Mr. —— did not make his appearance, and as the people were waiting, the squire said I had better begin my second sermon. Just as I began he arrived, and waited till I was nearly done; and then the bell rung over my head for church, but the people would not move until I concluded, after which we all went into church; but his pulpit and that of Mr. W. rang against me, and all such runabout fellows. His having the bell rung over my head much offended, not only those who were my friends, but many of his also. The more they preached and spoke against me, the more earnestly did the people search their Bibles to know whether these things were so.

"I had an appointment a few miles from the town by the side of a river; and some declared that if I went there they would drown me. I went and found a large concourse of people, and preached with much freedom, but no man assaulted me. I had five miles to my afternoon's appointment; and when I had got two miles on my way I looked behind and saw a man dressed like a soldier, riding full speed, with a great club or stick in his hand. I now found it necessary to exercise my faith. When he came up to me he reached out his hand, saying, 'Mr. Garrettson, how do you do? I heard you preach at such a time, and believe your doctrine to be true; I heard you was to be abused at the river to day, and I equipped myself as you see me, and have rode twenty miles in your defence, and will go with you if it is a thousand miles, and see who dare lay a hand upon you.' Friend, said I, the Scripture tells us that vengeance belongs to God, and not to man. 'Very true, sir,' said he, 'but I think I should be justifiable in so glorious a cause.' I travelled and preached all through the forest, and the Lord enlarged my heart, and gave me many precious souls; for numbers were brought to inquire after religion.

"Saturday, July 18th, I went to the Fork, accompanied by my dear old friends brother and sister White. July 19th, I preached again in the open air to many hundreds; and found that the work of the Lord was still going on. In the afternoon I preached to almost as many at old Mr. Turpin's. His daughter Rebecca is a very happy young woman. A few months since she was in the height of the fashion, but now sees the evil and folly of these things.

"Monday, July 20th, I went to preach at a house by the river, on the edge of Dorset county; here the Lord had greatly weakened Satan's kingdom. I preached at the door to abundantly more than could get into the house. I was so surprisingly drawn out, and the people so engaged, that I could not conclude under two or three hours. From the looks of the people, I should not have thought that I had an enemy in the congregation. After sermon, being much spent I withdrew. Shortly after a person came to me and said, 'two men wanted to see me.' I told him to desire them to walk up, thinking they were persons in distress, and wanted instruction; but when I saw them I discovered wickedness in their very looks. One of them was a magistrate, and he was a Churchman; the other was a Presbyterian, and he was a disputant. The magistrate brought him out in order to confute me in points of religion: and then his intention was to send me to prison. I desired them to sit down, and the disputant began; he said but a few words until I asked him if his soul was converted to God? I charge you, said I, in the presence of him before whom we shall shortly stand, tell me, is your soul converted to God? Do you know that your peace is made with God? He was struck, and knew not what to say; but at last he said, 'I do not know that I am.' Then, replied I, you are in the way to hell: and I began to exhort him to repent, and turn to the Lord. I think I never before saw a man so confused. He made attempts to quote Scripture, but could get hold of none. The magistrate seeing in what a condition his disputant was, in a rage said, 'Sir, do you know the laws of this state? You have not taken the oath, and you have broken the law by preaching; you must go to jail.' I bless God, said I, that I am not afraid of a jail. They withdrew, and after I had eaten dinner I mounted my horse and set out to attend my afternoon's appointment; but a sheriff met me a few rods from the house, and commanded me to stop. Many of my friends gathered around me, and offered to be security for my appearance at court; but I told them I would give no security. I had faith to believe that he had not power, or at least would not be permitted to stop me. I looked him in the face, and said, I am going on the Lord's errand, and if you have power, here I am, take me; but remember that the God against whom you are fighting, who made yonder sun, is just now looking down upon you; and I know not but that he will crush you to the earth, if you persist in fighting so furiously against him. ' I am now on my way to Philadelphia, to preach the glorious gospel of my Redeemer; and the consequence of your stopping me in this manner will be rueful. After conversing with him a few minutes, I perceived his countenance fall, and he said, 'It is a pity to stop you;' and so turned his back upon me. I went rejoicing on my way, accompanied by many of my kind friends, some of whom were weary and heavy laden; and had an opportunity in the afternoon to inculcate precious truths on as many people as could crowd into a large house standing by the river side.

"After attending several quarterly meetings, where we had a very large number of people, and great displays of the power of convincing and converting grace, I pursued my journey to Philadelphia, accompanied by several of my friends from that city. In my way I preached at Mr. Sadler's in Queen Anne's: and after preaching, to get clear of a mob which they expected would surround the house, (for there were many violent opposers in this part of the county) I rode, accompanied by a tender friend, the best part of the night, and got into another county. The next day my friends met me: we then went on together and arrived safely in Philadelphia."

CHAPTER VI.

Leaves the Peninsula, and at the request of Mr. Asbury goes to Philadelphia—Society there in a depressed state—British army had just left the city—Citizens returned to their employments—Success in New Jersey—Conversion of an old man—Remarkable account of a young woman.

MR. GARRETTSON had laboured in the Peninsula in the manner related in the preceding chapter about fifteen months. During this time several new circuits had been formed, and the work of God had prospered in his hands; so much so that the number returned in the societies in

Delaware and Kent county, was 1288 in the year 1779. When the many difficulties they had to contend with, in consequence of the war which was now raging with increased violence, are considered, we can but admire the good hand of God that was with them in the awakening and conversion of so many souls. Notwithstanding these obstacles, Mr. Garrettson was enabled to prosecute his labours in the gospel with increased vigour and perseverance, and with great success; so that at the time we are now speaking of, there were no less than forty nine preachers and 8577 members in the societies. Mr. Asbury was still confined, principally at Judge White's, so that the chief management of the affairs fell upon Mr. Garrettson, so far as active labour was concerned. It is true he corresponded with Mr. Asbury, and acted according to his advice and under his direction. It is not to be wondered at that "all manner of evil" should be said of a man who was thus instrumental in the hand of God in giving such a shock to Satan's kingdom.

Having given such evident proofs of his designation to the work of the Christian ministry by the supreme Head of the church, and of his skilfulness in conducting the spiritual interests of the societies, Mr. Asbury requested him to leave his present field of labour, and pay a visit to the city of Philadelphia, the society in this place being in a very depressed state.

The British army had been for a considerable time quartered in this city, and at this time had just taken their departure. The confusion occasioned by this state of things, tended very much to obstruct the work of God. Previously to the entrance of the British into the city, many of the inhabitants had fled into the country, and it was some time even after they had departed, before the citizens returned and arranged their affairs, so as to feel themselves in a settled state. "I stayed," says Mr. Garrettson, "about two months in Philadelphia, and though I did not see much fruit of my labour, I found many of my dear friends near and precious to me."

Being relieved in the city by Mr. Cox, he took a tour into several parts of Pennsylvania and New Jersey, "preaching," he says, "from ten to twelve sermons a week. I bless God for the prosperous journey he gave me through the state of New Jersey: several were awakened, and some brought to know the Lord Jesus.

"One day after preaching, an old man came to me and said, all in tears, 'This day I am a hundred and one years old, and this is my spiritual birth day.' The dear man's soul was so exceedingly happy, that he appeared to be ready to take his flight to heaven.

"I preached at a new place, where the congregation consisted mostly of young people, from 'The Son of man is come to seek and to save that which was lost,' Luke xix, 10. We had a wonderful display of the power of the Lord. After I had finished my discourse, the young people hung around each other crying for mercy. Many, no doubt, will praise the Lord eternally for that day. A remarkable circumstance happened respecting a young woman who was brought up in the Quaker persuasion. It pleased the Lord to awaken her when very young. She experienced the pardoning love of God, and continued to enjoy it for some time. By degrees, however, she got off her watch, having none to strengthen but many to draw her away. She at length fell from God, and became as wild and trifling as ever. Soon after this she was entirely deprived of her speech; the enemy of her soul persuaded her to believe that it was a sin for her to do any kind of work, or even to dress herself; and if they gave her a book to read she thought it sinful to turn over a leaf, and would read no more unless some one would perform this office for her. It was impressed on her mind that there was a people in a particular place who served the Lord; and if she could get among them, they would be a means of restoring her to her speech. She had never heard of a Methodist; and the place which was revealed to her was nearly twenty miles from her residence, where there was a young, loving society. Though she knew nothing of the way, she sat off to find that place and people. Her family missing her, pursued and brought her back. Not long after she made a more successful attempt, and found the society. The Lord revealed her case to them. There was a preacher present, Mr. Daniel Raff, who consented to call a meeting, and they cried to the Lord in her behalf that day and the next. She then went into a private room, kneeled down to prayer, and continued therein till the Lord blessed her soul. At the same time her tongue was loosened, and she could speak forth the praises of Israel's God. She had been dumb about two years. Some time after I came into this neighbourhood and sent word to her mother that I would preach such a day at her house. When the day arrived, I took the young woman home, accompanied by many friends, and we were received like angels: some thought the Methodists could work miracles. Many of the friends and neighbours came, and could not but observe how angelic this young woman appeared. She was now able to speak and work as well as usual. I bless the Lord who gave me great freedom in preaching on this remarkable occasion. The people seemed to believe every word which was delivered. The old lady was ready to take us in her arms, being so happy, and so well satisfied with respect to her daughter.

CHAPTER VII.

Returns to the Peninsula—Introduction of Methodism into Dorset county—Peculiar exercises, and happy deliverance—Escapes an attempt to take his life—Taken by a mob—Imprisonment of J. Hartley—Maltreated and imprisoned—Happy in his own soul—Is set at liberty—Strange visions of the night.

Having completed his mission in this part of the country, in the autumn of the same year he made his second visit to the Peninsula, the place where the Lord of the harvest had given him so many souls. Here he travelled extensively through the winter, preaching with his usual diligence and success.

The following account of the commencement and progress of the work of God in Dorset county, where the citizens were principally members of the Church of England, is taken from his printed journal and his manuscript notes. It began by means of a young lady who was niece to Judge E., of Dorset county, and sister to the wife of the honourable Mr. Basset. Being on a visit, she fell in company with the Methodists, by whose means she was awakened to a sense of her lost and guilty state, and finally converted to God, and so became a pious follower of the blessed Jesus. When she returned to her uncle's in Dorset, they thought she was beside herself. She, however, persevering in her Christian course, became instrumental in the conversion of her sister Mary, and a few others. Her sister became as zealous for God as herself; and soon after another sister, Mrs. Basset, became a most blessed woman. "I have no doubt," says Mr. Garrettson, "but that she lived and died a bright witness of sanctification."

The honourable Mr. Basset was an eminent lawyer in the state of Delaware. After he embraced religion, he became a member of congress, was afterwards appointed one of the United States' Judges; and finally, a governor of the state of Delaware. The substance of what follows Mr. Garrettson says he had from Mr. Basset's own mouth. At the time of the conversion of his lady and her sisters, who all three were eminently pious, Mr. Basset being a man of the world, and moving in the higher circles of fashionable society, became greatly distressed in mind on account of the Methodists, so that he had but little rest day or night. A court being soon to be held in Lewiston, in which he had a cause to manage as counsel, he concluded that when that should be completed, he would sell his property, and move to some distant part of the country, so as to rid himself of the "noisy Methodists." One night during the session of the court, he went to his bed chamber to rest. After falling into a profound sleep, he dreamed that he saw two devils in black standing by his bed side, who, he thought, had come to take him away. He trembled, and began to pray. The devils thereupon soon vanished; and were succeeded by two beautiful angels dressed in white, standing near his bed. These, thought he, are messengers for good. Casting his eye towards the farthest corner of the room, he saw an aged, and very grave looking man, sitting in a large arm chair, frowning upon him, the angels still standing by his bed. He looked, and beheld a beautiful child advance to the aged man, and smiling pleasantly, began to fondle around him; but the aged man continued to frown. On this his sins were brought to his recollection, and it appeared to him that God the Father, represented by the aged man, was frowning on him, while Jesus Christ, represented by the little child, was interceding for him. The angels might justly represent the Holy Spirit directing the ministers of Christ, or his holy sisters presenting his case in prayer to a throne of grace.

He awoke in a sort of rapture, and immediately dedicated himself to the God who made him, and became a happy Christian. "From what I understood," says Mr.

Garrettson, "Mrs. Basset had been praying for her husband's conversion, and that very night she dreamed that God had converted his soul."

On returning home from court he met his family, and especially his pious lady joyfully. When he related to her what the Lord had done for him; "I know it," said she, "the blessed God told me so." So far from indulging in a desire to move away from the Methodists, they now became the people of his choice. "I knew him," says Mr. Garrettson, "many years after this, and he lived I believe like a Christian, and I doubt not died like one and is gone to glory. Mrs. Basset lived but a short time after she embraced religion. I was often at the house, and was with her in her last sickness, when she seemed filled with the perfect love of God. I felt as if the room was filled with ministering spirits; and she left the world praising God."

Equally remarkable was the conversion of Henry Arey, Esq., who was a relation to Mary, the young lady above-mentioned. "As he was a man of fashion, and an entire stranger to inward religion, he was much afraid she would drive his wife out of her senses. He undertook to show his *visiter* that the Methodists were not in the right way; and for this purpose he chose an old book written by a Puritan divine, a hundred and fifty years ago: but he had not read many minutes before conviction seized him, and the tears flowed from his eyes. He withdrew and read till he thought he must go among the Methodists with his book, and compare it with theirs. He did so, and found the Methodist publications to agree in substance with that. On this occasion I first met with him at Mr. White's. After he had laboured some time under distress of soul the Lord gave him rest—he felt the burden of guilt removed—and now expressed an anxious desire that I should come to the county where he resided, being determined to stand by the cause as long as he lived.

"Thursday, Feb. 10th, 1780, I arose very early in the

morning, and addressed the throne of grace. The Lord wonderfully refreshed my soul, and I felt a willingness to suffer whatever he might permit to come upon me for the sake of his cause. I opened my mind to Mr. Asbury who was at Mr. W.'s, and he seemed very desirous I should accept the invitation. He then commended me to the Lord in prayer, and I set out in good spirits with a strong hope that good would be done. The first day I got half way, and had a comfortable night. February 11th was a day of deep exercise. Are others distressed in the way that I have been? I travelled on seemingly with the weight of a mill stone. I wept bitterly as I passed along, and several times stopped my horse intending to turn back, but was still induced to pursue my way. I got to my dear friend Mr. Arey's some time before night; and the burden which I felt all the way left me at his door. The dismission of it was perceptible, for my spirit did rejoice in God my Saviour. I was conducted into a private room, where the Lord let me know that I was in the very place in which he would have me.

"In the evening the family were gathered together for prayer: I shall never forget the time: I suppose about twelve white and black were present. The power of the Lord came among us: Mrs. Arey was so filled with the new wine of Christ's kingdom, that she sunk to the floor, blessing and praising the Lord. And many of the blacks were much wrought upon. This night was a time of great refreshment to me."

The three following days Mr. Garrettson preached in the neighbourhood to numerous and attentive congregations, most of whom were greatly affected under the word, and a gracious work commenced among the people. Proceeding to another part of the country, he observes, "One man was deeply affected only by seeing us. I preached at Colonel Vicery's, a clever man, who afterwards became a great friend to us, and to himself too. The fields are white for harvest, but the wicked rage, and invent lies and mischief. The county court was sitting, and some of the heads of it were determined by some means to clear the place of such a troublesome fellow. For a pretence they charged me with toryism; and I was informed, gave a very wicked man liberty, and promised to protect him in taking my life. For this purpose he was to lie in wait for me the next day. It providentially reached my ears that night before I went to bed, and as the wicked seemed thus inclined, I thought it expedient to withdraw to Mr. Arey's, where I remained two days; but being pressed in spirit, I could stay no longer, so I went to another part of the county. Many came out to hear, and the word was still attended with power to some hearts.

"Saturday 25th, my spirit was solemn and I could not but expect that something uncommon would transpire. I withdrew to the woods, and spent much time before the Lord. I preached with freedom to a weeping flock, my friend Arey, who was a magistrate, and a man of note in the county, accompanying me to the place. In the evening we were repairing to his house, being about to preach there the next day; when a company of men, who had embodied themselves, way laid me, with an intention to take me to jail. About sun set they surrounded us, and called me their prisoner. They beat my horse, cursed and swore, but did not strike me. Some time after night they took me to a magistrate who was as much my enemy as any of them. When I was judged, and condemned for preaching the gospel, the keeper of the peace who sat in his great chair, immediately wrote a mittimus and ordered me to jail. I asked him if he had never heard of an affair in Talbot county. Brother I. Hartley* was committed to jail

* Mr. Garrettson adds the following particulars in a note:—
"Brother Hartley, a dear good man, and an excellent preacher, was so pressed in spirit, he could no longer contain, and the rulers laid hands on him, and confined him in Talbot jail; but he preached

for the same crime, that of preaching the gospel; soon after the magistrate was taken sick unto death, and sent for this same preacher out of confinement to pray for him. He then made this confession, 'When I sent you to jail,' said he, ' I was fighting against God, and now I am about to leave the world, pray for me.' His family were called in, and he said to his wife, ' This is a servant of God; and when I die, I request he may preach at my funeral. You need not think I have not my senses; this is the true faith.' He then gave brother Hartley charge of his family, and desired them to embrace that profession. Now, said I, I beseech you to think seriously of what you have done, and prepare to meet God. Be you assured, I am not ashamed of the cross of Christ, for I consider it an honour to be imprisoned for the gospel of my Lord. My horse was brought, and about twelve of the company were to attend me to jail. They surrounded me, and two, one on each side, held my horse's bridle. The night was very dark; and before we got a mile from the house, on a sudden there was a very uncommon flash of lightning, and in less than a minute all my foes were dispersed: my friend Arey was a little before the company, so that I was left alone. I was reminded of that place of Scripture, where our Lord's enemies fell to the ground, and then this portion of Scripture came to me, ' Stand still and see the salvation of God.' It was a very dark cloudy night, and had rained a little. I sat on my horse alone, and though I called several times there was no answer. I went on, but had not got far before I met my friend Mr. Arey returning to look for me. He had accompanied me throughout the whole of this

powerfully through the window. The blessed God owned his word, and he was instrumental in raising a large society. He was confined a long time, till finally they thought he might as well preach without as within jail. Shortly after he was set at liberty, he married a pious young lady, and located. He did not live many years, but while he did live, he was very useful, and adorned his Christian and ministerial character. He died in the Lord, and went to glory."

affair. We rode on talking of the goodness of God till we came to a little cottage by the road side, where we found two of my guards almost frightened out of their wits. I told them if I was to go to jail that night, we ought to be on our way, for it was getting late. 'O! no,' said one of them, 'let us stay until the morning.' My friend and I rode on, and it was not long ere we had a beautiful clear night. We had not rode far before the company collected again, from whence I know not. However they appeared to be amazingly intimidated, and the leader of the company rode by the side of me, and said, 'Sir, do you think the affair happened on our account?' I told him that I would have him to judge for himself; reminding him of the awfulness of the day of judgment, and the necessity there was of preparing to meet the Judge of the whole earth. One of the company swore an oath, and another immediately reproved him, saying, 'How can you swear at such a time as this?' At length the company stopped, and one said, 'We had better give him up for the present;' so they turned their horses and went back. My friend and I pursued our way. True it is, 'The wicked are like the troubled sea, whose water casts up mire and dirt.' We had not gone far before they pursued us again, and said, 'We cannot give him up.' They accompanied us a few minutes, again left us, and we saw no more of them that night. A little before midnight we arrived safe to my friend's house. Blessed be God, the dear waiting family were looking out, and received us with joy: and we had a precious sweet family meeting. I retired to my room as humble as a little child, praising my great deliverer.

"During the remainder of the night, though asleep, I was transported with the visions which passed through my mind. I had a confidence in the morning that my beloved Lord would support me. I saw in the visions of the night 'many sharp and terrible weapons formed against me; but none could penetrate or hurt me; for as soon as they came near me they were turned into feathers, and brushed by me as soft as down.

"Sunday 27th, at eleven o'clock many came out to hear the word, and it was expected my enemies would be upon me. I was informed that not a few brought short clubs under their coats to defend me in case of an attack, for many had just about religion enough to fight for it. As I was giving out the hymn, standing between the hall and room doors, about twenty of my persecutors came up in a body. I was amazed to see one of them who was an old man and his head as white as a sheet. The ringleader rushed forward, presented a pistol, and laid hold of me. Blessed be God! my confidence was so strong in him, that I feared none of these things. Some of the audience, who stood next to me, gave me a sudden jerk; I was presently in the room, and the door shut. As soon as I could I opened it, and beckoning to my friends, desired that they would not injure my enemies; that I did not want to keep from them, but was willing to go to jail. If I had not spoken in this manner, I believe much blood would have been shed. I began to exhort, and almost the whole congregation were in tears. The women in a particular manner were amazingly agitated. I desired my horse to be got, and I was accompanied to Cambridge, where I was kept in a tavern from twelve o'clock till near sun set, surrounded by the wicked; and it was a great mercy of God that my life was preserved.

"I told my enemies not to give themselves any uneasiness, for I thought it an honour to suffer in the cause of Christ. After my horse and baggage were ready, and I was equipped for the expedition, we started, two and two. My friend and I rode together, and half the company before, and half behind. This was on the Lord's day. When we came to the hotel, my friend and I were permitted to occupy a room adjoining the large public room. The inhabitants of the place seemed to be coming and going the whole of the day, and kept the room filled the whole of the time, drinking and rejoicing over their prey. My friend was a young soldier, and the trial was too great for him. One of the company, a stout man, was about to break in to abuse, (for their hatred against him was almost as great as it was against me,) and actually did strike at him with all his force with a large loaded whip, and in all probability would have killed him, had not the whip struck the top of the door. My friend was young and active, and he instantly sprung, and as quick as a flash, sent his fist into the fellow's temple, who like a Goliah under David's sling, fell flat to the floor, and there was a roar of laughter through the house, and a declaration, 'the Methodists will fight.' At a convenient time I got my friend round the neck, and wept and told him he had grieved my spirit. He said he was sorry on account of grieving me; but that it was almost as sudden as thought: that it appeared to him that his arm was nerved for the purpose, and that he did not feel as if he had done wrong. And I must say I think they behaved rather better afterwards.

"A little before night I was thrust into prison, and my enemies took away the key that none might administer to my necessities. I had a dirty floor for my bed, my saddle bags for my pillow, and two large windows open with a cold east wind blowing upon me: but I had great consolation in my Lord, and could say, 'Thy will be done.' During my confinement here, I was much drawn out in prayer, reading, writing, and meditation. I believe I had the prayers of my good friend Mr. Asbury; and the book which he sent me, Mr. Rutherford's Letters during his confinement, together with the soul comforting and strengthening letters which I received from my pious friends, were rendered a great blessing to me. The Lord was remarkably good to me, so that I experienced a prison to be like a paradise; and I had a heart to pray for my worst enemies. My soul was so exceedingly happy, I scarcely knew how my days and nights passed away. The Bible was never sweeter to me. I never had a greater love to God's dear children. I never saw myself more unworthy. I never saw a greater beauty in the cross of Christ; for I thought I could, if required, go cheerfully to the stake in so good a cause. I was not at all surprised with the cheerfulness of the ancient martyrs, who were able in the flames to clap their glad hands. Sweet moments I had with my dear friends who came to the prison window.

> Happy the man who finds the grace,
> The blessing of God's chosen race,
> The wisdom coming from above,
> The faith which sweetly works by love.

"Many, both acquaintances and strangers, came to visit me from far and near, and I really believe I never was the means of doing more good for the time: for the county seemed to be much alarmed, and the Methodists among whom I had laboured, to whom I had written many epistles, were much stirred up to pray for me. I shall never forget the kindness I received from dear brother and sister Arey. They suffered much for the cause of God in Dorset county, for which, if faithful, they will be amply compensated in a better world.

"Mr. and Mrs. Arey were remarkably kind, and sent me every thing which was necessary. My brother Thomas, who lived about a hundred miles off, heard of my imprisonment, and came to see me, and brought a letter from Judge White to Mr. Harrison, a gentleman of note, who was the greatest enemy I had in town. After reading the letter, he not only invited my brother to put up at his house, but went and got the prison key, let my brother come in, and next morning he came to the jail and invited him out to breakfast, and told me he would do any thing he could for me. Before this he was as bitter as gall. One day when an old Quaker friend came to see me, he came and abused him, and strove to drive him away: the Quaker made him ashamed of his conduct. My enemies sent a spy, who feigned himself a penitent, and as I was coming down stairs to converse with him through the window, it came powerfully to my mind, he is an enemy sent if possible to draw something out of you concerning the war. He cried, and said he was a miserable sinner, that he was afraid he would go to hell, and wanted to know what he should do to be saved. I told him to leave off swearing and drunkenness, and return, and I would give him farther directions. I afterwards found he was the very character I had supposed.

"My crime of preaching the gospel was so great, that no common court would try my cause. There appeared to be a probability of my staying in jail till a general court, which would not convene in nearly twelve months. My good friend Mr. Asbury went to the governor of Maryland, and he befriended me: had I been his brother, he could not have done more for me. The manner in which he proceeded to relieve me was this:—I was an inhabitant of Maryland by birth and property: I could likewise claim a right in the Delaware state, which state was more favourable to such *pestilent fellows*. I was carried before the governor of Delaware. This gentleman was a friend to our society. He met me at the door, and welcomed me in, assuring me he would do any thing he could to help me. A recommendatory letter was immediately despatched to the governor of Maryland; and I was entirely at liberty. O! how wonderfully did the people of Dorset rage: but the word of the Lord spread all through that county, and hundreds both white and black have experienced the love of Jesus. Since that time I have preached to more than three thousand people in one congregation, not far from the place where I was imprisoned; and many of my worst enemies have bowed to the sceptre of our sovereign Lord. The labours of Caleb Peddicord and Chew were much blessed in this place, in the first reviving and spreading of the work.

"After I left my confinement, I was more than ever determined to be for God and none else. I travelled extensively. The Lord was with me daily, and my spirit rejoiced in God my Saviour. In visiting the young societies, after I left jail, we had blessed hours: for many came to hear, sinners cried for mercy, and God's dear people rejoiced.

"Friday 24th, was a solemn fast, being good Friday, the day on which the great Redeemer gave up his precious life. Three days after, being in a blessed family, I had great sweetness both in public and private; and before I laid down to rest, I was very desirous of being lost and swallowed up in the love of the Redeemer, and of feeling the witness of perfect love. After I laid down to rest, I was in a kind of visionary way for several hours. About one I awoke very happy, arose from my bed, and addressed the throne of grace. I then lighted a candle and spent nearly two hours in writing the exercises of the night. I saw myself travelling through a dismal place, encompassed with many dangers; I saw the devil, who appeared very furious; he came near to me and declared with bitterness that he would cause my death; for he seemed to suggest, you have done my kingdom much harm: thus saying, he began pelting me with stones, and bedaubing me with dirt, till I felt wounded almost to death, and began to fear I should fall by the hand of my enemy. But in the height of my distress, my adored Saviour appeared to me, whom I thought the most beautiful person that ever my eyes beheld. 'I am your friend,' said he, 'and will support you in your journey; fear not, for your enemy is chained.' I seemed to receive much strength, and the power of my enemy was so broken that he could not move one foot after me; all he could do was to threaten, which he did loudly till I got out of his hearing. Being safe from these difficulties, I looked forward and saw a very high hill which I was to ascend, but feared that I never should be able to reach the top: I entered on my journey, and got about half way up, so fatigued that I thought every moment I must sink to the earth. I then laid down to rest myself a little, and seemed to fall into a kind of doze; but I had not lain long before the person who met me in the valley passed by, and smote me on the side, saying, 'Rise up, and be going, there is no rest for you there.' With that I received strength, and arrived at the top of the hill. I then looked back and saw my enemy at a great distance. I was greatly surprised when I saw the place through which I had passed; for on every hand there appeared to be pits, holes, and quagmires in abundance. I was much wounded, and all bespattered with dirt. I looked around to see if I could find any house: and at a distance I espied a little cottage, and made up to it: when I got near the door, two angels met me and said, "Come in, come in, thou blessed of the Lord, here is entertainment for weary travellers.' The interior of the cottage appeared to be the most beautiful place I had ever seen. After I went in I thought it was heaven filled with blessed saints and angels. One and another broke out 'Glory, glory,' &c, &c, till the place was filled with praises. One spake to me and said, 'This is not heaven, as you suppose, neither are we angels, but sanctified Christians: and this is the second rest. And it is your privilege, and the privilege of all the children of God.' With that I thought I had faith to believe, and in a moment my spotted garments were gone, a white robe was given me, and I had the language and appearance of one of this blessed society : I then awoke.

"Before this, I had an ardent desire truly to know my state, and to sink deep into God. When I awoke I seemed all taken up with divine things. I spent part of the remainder of the night in writing, prayer, and praises: and had a strong witness of union with my blessed Lord. My brother T. from the western shore came to see me, travelled several weeks with me, with whom I had blessed times; for I believe it was on this visit he felt a witness of pardoning love to his soul.

"Upon a certain occasion, I was wonderfully led to think of the place called hell, and was severely buffetted by the devil. 'Hell,' he suggested, 'is not as bad a place as you represent: how can God be a merciful being, as you set him forth, if he sends people to such a dismal place to be tormented for ever for a few sins?' I was earnestly desirous to know what kind of place it was; and the Lord condescended to satisfy me in the dead season of the night. After I fell into a deep sleep, I seemed to enter through a narrow gate into eternity, and was met by a person who conducted me to the place called hell; but I had a very imperfect view of it. I requested to be taken where I could see it better, if that could be done. I was then conveyed to a spot where I had a full view of it. It appeared as large as the sea, and I saw myriads of damned souls in every posture that miserable beings could get into. This sight exceeded any thing of the kind that ever had entered into my mind. But it was not for me to know any of them. Were I to attempt to describe the place as it was represented to me, I could not do it. Had I the pen of a ready writer, and angelic wisdom, I should fall short. I cried out to my guide, it is enough. With that he brought me to the place where he first met me. I then desired a discovery of heaven: my guide said, 'Not now, return: you have seen sufficient for once; and be more faithful in warning sinners, and have no more doubts about the reality of hell.' Then I instantly awoke."

CHAPTER VIII.

Disputes respecting the ordinances—Mistakes corrected—Breach healed, and harmony restored—Mr. Asbury's account of this affair —Goes to Baltimore—Thence to the Peninsula—Singular dream.

The Methodists in this country, as well as in Europe, were considered at this time only as a society. The preachers were not ordained, and therefore did not claim the right of administering the ordinances of baptism and the Lord's supper, nor of performing the rites of marriage and burial of the dead. These circumstances became the source of considerable uneasiness in the societies. Not having fellowship with many of the parochial clergy of the Church of England on account of the irregularity of their lives, and the want of evangelical doctrine in their sermons, the Methodists were unwilling to receive the ordinances of Christ at their hands.

In addition to this, many places, particularly at the south, were entirely destitute of a settled ministry of any denomination. To remedy the inconveniences arising from this state of things, some of the preachers, no doubt from the best of motives, for they appear to have been a company of holy men, seconded the views of the people in respect to having the ordinances among themselves. Mr. Asbury, however, and most of the northern preachers resisted these measures, and endeavoured to persuade them to remain as they were until they could advise with Mr. Wesley and receive his directions.

In the opinion of Mr. Garrettson, who was present when the question respecting administering the ordinances was discussed, those brethren in Virginia who advocated the measure have been misrepresented, as though they were at the head of a schism. In his manuscript notes, Mr. Garrettson says, "Since the death of Mr. Asbury, I am the oldest preacher in the American connexion, and therefore I think it my duty to explain this business." He then goes on to state, that at the Deer-creek conference, which was held May 20th, 1777, Mr. Rankin in the chair, it was asked, "Shall the preachers in America administer the ordinances?" The answer was, "We will suspend them until the next conference."

May 19th, 1778, the regular conference was held in Leesburg, Virginia. Mr. Rankin and his British brethren, except Mr. Asbury who was not present at this conference, were gone home. Mr. William Watters, being the oldest American preacher, was called to the chair. The same question was proposed again, "Shall we administer the ordinances?" "I was present," says Mr. Garrettson, "and the answer was '*lay it over until the next conference*,' which was appointed to be held in Fluvanna county, Va., May 18th, 1779, at what was called the broken back church." In consequence of the troubles arising from the state of the war, which then raged with increased violence, the northern brethren did not attend the Fluvanna conference; but for their "convenience," says Mr. Garrettson, "called a little conference in Kent county, in the province of Delaware, April 28th, 1779, at Judge White's, where Mr. Asbury had been confined to avoid the rage of his enemies. At this conference Mr. Asbury was present and presided."

At the time appointed, the southern brethren met in the regular conference, and the same question respecting administering the ordinances was discussed, and was finally decided in the affirmative. They accordingly set apart several of the oldest preachers to travel extensively, and to administer the sacraments of baptism and the Lord's supper, and to perform the marriage ceremony; and at the conclusion, appointed their next conference to be held in May, 1780, at Manicantown, Virginia. "We at the north," says Mr. Garrettson, "were opposed to this innovation, and it was our pleasure to meet in Baltimore, April

24th, 1780, and brother Asbury, William Watters and myself were appointed a committee to meet those brethren at their conference, and endeavour to effect a reconciliation. After much prayer and consultation, they unanimously agreed to a suspension of the ordinances for one year, and to call a general conference in Baltimore the next spring; in the meantime to consult Mr. Wesley, by whose judgment they would abide."

Now although these brethren erred in their judgment, they undoubtedly manifested much of the meekness of Christianity, in agreeing, for the sake of peace and harmony, to relinquish their project, and wait for farther advice from their venerable founder. No doubt, also, they were prompted to this step, not from a restless ambition, but from a love to the souls of the people who had been converted to God by their ministry, and who were anxious to receive the ordinances of Christ at their hands.

In preventing a division in the societies at this time, which must have been attended with very deleterious effects on the work of God, Mr. Garrettson took a very active and efficient agency, in conjunction with Messrs. Asbury, Watters and Drumgole. Mr. Asbury says, "When we could not come to a conclusion with them, we withdrew and left them to deliberate on the conditions I offered, which were to suspend the measures they had taken for one year." To this they refused to submit, until the next day, when, says Mr. Asbury, "they were brought to an agreement while I had been praying, as with a broken heart, in the house we went to lodge at, and brothers Watters and Garrettson had been praying up stairs where the conference sat. We heard what they had to say, and surely the hand of God may be seen in all this. There might have been twenty promising preachers, and three thousand people seriously affected by this separation; but the Lord would not suffer this." Thus, by the mutual endeavours of these holy men of God, this breach, which seemed to threaten the dissolution of the body, was healed, and peace and harmony restored. Mr. Garrettson says, "having accomplished our business, we set our faces to the north with gladness of heart, praising the Lord for his great goodness." Returning to Baltimore, where he was appointed to labour, he set apart a day for fasting and prayer, and the Lord abundantly blessed him. Such, however, was the ardour of his soul in behalf of lost sinners, that he did not long confine himself to the city; for we soon find him in the country, where he makes the following reflections: "With delight I viewed the rising morn; the fields are clad with a beautiful green; the creation is smiling, and the birds tuning their notes. Surely an immortal spirit ought to praise the Creator of the universe." After labouring for several weeks in Baltimore and the adjoining county with great success, he crossed the Chesapeake again to the Peninsula. "Having," says he, "a good horse, and being seldom sick enough to desist from travelling, or weary enough to complain, I could travel from twenty to fifty miles a day, and preach from one to four sermons. During the five or six weeks I remained here, I visited most of the circuits; the congregations were larger than usual, and never for the time had I brighter prospects. Many evil reports were raised against me; but my manner was to go straight forward in the line of my duty. When I returned many gathered at the Fork chapel from all quarters; and among the crowd, I espied my old uncle T. who had heard and believed the reports; and was determined, as I understood, to detect me in the midst of the people. Never shall I forget the day; for the Lord manifested his power: the heart of my dear old uncle was softened, and tears flowed down his face. After he left the chapel, he said to some of his acquaintances, 'Surely my cousin is belied.' He came and begged me to go home with him, which I did. The next day he followed me five miles; and the tears flowed plentifully.

When we were about to part, he asked me what compensation he should make me, for the benefit which he had received. 'Will you,' said he, 'receive a suit of clothes?' I thanked him kindly, telling him that I had as much clothing as was necessary. He then put his hand in his pocket, and pulled out eighty continental dollars, which at that time were worth about twenty hard dollars: at first I refused; but he would not be denied. So I took them, and some time after gave them to brother S., a man who needed them. When we parted he told me that he expected to see me no more: it was even so, for some time after the Lord called him away.

"I continued in this circuit till the following spring, and enjoyed precious moments. Many were brought into gospel liberty, and added to the society; and some received the second blessing. I trust I grew in grace and knowledge during my stay; and felt myself an unprofitable servant: very unworthy of the many favours which I received from the precious, loving followers of Christ in this circuit."

Just before Mr. Garrettson visited the Peninsula, he gives the following account: "I went to bed very happy, but my night visions were uncommonly strange: I thought I was taken dangerously ill, and expected shortly to be in eternity. I doubt not but I felt just as dying persons do. I appeared to be surrounded with thousands of devils, who were all striving to take from me my confidence; and for a time it seemed almost gone. I began an examination from my first awakenings—then my conversion—my call to preach—the motives which induced me to enter this great work—my intention, and life from the beginning. In the time of this examination, every fear was dismissed, —every fiend vanished; and a band of holy angels succeeded with the most melodious music that I ever heard. I then began to ascend, accompanied by this heavenly host; and thought every moment the body would drop off, and my spirit take its flight. After ascending a vast height, I was overshadowed with a cloud as white as a sheet; and in that cloud I saw a person the most beautiful that my eyes ever beheld. I wanted to be dislodged from this tabernacle, and take my everlasting flight. That glorious person, more bright than the sun in its meridian brilliancy, spoke to me as follows, 'If you continue faithful to the end, this shall be your place; but you cannot come now, return and be faithful; there is more work for you to do.' Immediately I awoke, and my spirit was so elevated with a sense of eternal things, that I thought I should sleep no more that night. Great and glorious discoveries have been made to me both sleeping and waking; but all the promises of heaven and eternal glory have been conditional. In Scripture we have a little, but significant word, *if*—If you are faithful until death, you shall have a crown of life. I would advise all the children of God to be very careful and watchful, and continue in well doing until death. Some suppose that we ought not to put any dependance in dreams and visions. We should lay the same stress on them in this our day, as wise and good men have done in all ages. Very great discoveries were made to Peter, Paul, and others in their night visions. But is there not a danger of laying too much stress on them? We are indeed in danger from a variety of sources; and the only safe way to escape from the illusions of error is to try every thing by the written standard: if enlightened by the Holy Spirit, by taking heed to that word which is *a lamp to our path*, we shall not be suffered to go astray."

CHAPTER IX.

Goes to Little York—Curious account of the conversion of a man and his wife—Effects thereof on the people—Goes to Colchester—Curious account of a deluded woman—Persecution rages—Visits a distressed man—Opposed by some soldiers who were quartered in the town—Powerful effects of the word preached—Attends conference in Baltimore where unanimity prevails—Great distress in Virginia—Rev. Mr. Jarret friendly to the Methodists.

On the 24th day of January, 1781, Mr. Garrettson set off to visit Little York in Pennsylvania. Stopping at a tavern for the night, he lectured on the 7th chapter of St. Matthew, and in time of family prayer the Lord powerfully awakened a gentleman who lodged there also.

"Tuesday 25th, I went into the town, and in the afternoon the bell rang, and I preached in the Dutch church. The gentleman's lady (who was awakened the evening before) got her heart touched. When he came home in the evening, he spoke to this effect, 'My dear, I heard such a man last night as I never saw or heard before, and if what he said be true, we are all in the way to hell.' 'I suspect,' said she, 'he is the same man whom I heard this afternoon in Wagoner's church. I believe his doctrine is true, and that we are all in the way to ruin.' 'Well,' said he, 'let us set about our salvation.' 'I am willing,' said she.

"Having an appointment, I preached at Mr. G.'s, the Lutheran minister: and after meeting we had an agreeable conversation. His mother and sister, whose hearts the Lord had touched, accompanied me to Berlin, where I preached to a large congregation with great freedom. I again had an opportunity in the evening to hold up a loving Saviour to the listening multitude.

"By this time a persecution had arisen among the people in Little York and its vicinity: the enemy of souls had taken an advantage of my two friends who were awakened:

Being under deep distress, and sorely tempted by the devil, not knowing what to do, at length they prepared water, and washed themselves; then put on clean clothes, and concluded that it was the new birth. After they came from their room, they kissed their two children, a son and daughter well nigh grown, and told them they were new born. Being in a great measure bereft of their senses, and the enemy ready to take every advantage, 'Come,' said they, 'old things must be done away, and all things must become new.' They then began to throw their old clothing and blankets on the fire; and among other things they threw on a large bundle of paper money. 'This,' said he, 'is an old thing, and must be done away.' The neighbours being alarmed, ran in and saved many things; but I suppose they did not sustain less than fifteen pounds loss. A minister was sent for, and he desired a doctor to be called; for they knew not what was the matter. A Quaker woman came to see them, who said, 'she did not know of any one that could be of service to them, unless it was the man that was the occasion of it.' The cry was, such a man ought not to go through the country; and that some desired me to be apprehended and put into jail. I was about twenty miles off, but as soon as I heard of it, mounted my horse and got to them as quickly as possible. When the neighbours saw me, several gathered into the room. When I entered the house, I perceived that the woman looked strange, and the man was in bed under the hands of the doctor, with several blister plasters on him. I sat down by his bed side (she sat on the foot of the bed) and asked him what he wanted—'To be new born,' said he. Taking out my little Bible, I read and lectured on a chapter; and sensibly felt that the Lord was present to heal. It brought to my mind the time when St. Peter visited Cornelius. I believe in the time of the exhortation and prayer the Lord not only opened the way of salvation to those two distressed ones, but to several others who came in; and we had a precious sweet time. I desired them to take his blister plasters off. Glory to God! he restored them, not only to their natural but spiritual senses. A good and gracious God has his own way of working among the children of men. Though at first this circumstance caused me great distress of mind, in the end it was for good; many were astonished and brought to a serious consideration. Although the church door was shut against me, a large school room was opened, in which I preached a sermon on the occasion, to about three hundred souls: the Lord touched the hearts of many; and my two mad people (as they had been called) were able to rejoice in the Lord. Soon after this a loving society was formed in the neighbourhood.

"Wednesday 22d, I had a tedious journey to Colchester; but found the parents of one family, who were awakened when I was there before, mourning for Jesus; and I had freedom to preach to the people. In the morning I sat out again for Berlin, and missed my way. I am burdened—surely it is a burden which the Lord hath laid upon me, and it is for the best. I called at a house to inquire for the road; I heard a dismal groaning and lamenting within. I alighted from my horse and went in; and found the woman of the house wringing her hands and mourning bitterly. Good woman, said I, what is the matter with you? 'Sir,' said she, 'have you never heard what has happened? I have sold my three little children to the devil, and on such a day he is to come for them.' I can prove to you, said I, that it is out of your power to sell your children to the devil, for they belong to God. I read and explained to her parts of several chapters; but it seemed all in vain. Her husband came in, and I desired him to get a horse and take her to preaching that afternoon. After he had got the horse, I desired her to make ready, and go to preaching with her husband. 'O,' said she, 'I cannot think of leaving my dear little children in the arms of the devil.' After some time she was prevailed on to go. Her husband told me, that she had carried a razor in her bosom for three weeks, with an intention, first to take the lives of her children (before the day came that she thought the devil was to come for them) and then to take her own life. I preached a sermon suited to her condition, and it pleased the Lord to visit her soul in mercy; so that after preaching she came to me in a rapture of joy, blessing and praising God that she ever saw my face. She became a blessed pious woman. I then knew the cause of my being lost. O God, thou art good, and I will praise thee! thou art kind, and I will give glory to thy holy name!

"Friday, February 24th, I returned to town, and the persecution raged so furiously, that I thought it most expedient to preach at Mr. W.'s, a mile out of town. Many gathered, and we had a moving time. The next day we had a powerful season; and the hearts of some of my enemies were reached.

"Sunday, February 26th, I never saw so many out in this place before, and even some who had thought it a sin to hear me were present, and I never witnessed a more general moving in any place where preaching had been so short a time. In this county there were, I think, sixteen different denominations, and some of all seemed zealous in their way. In the afternoon I again returned and preached at D. W.'s, where one woman was struck under conviction, and cried aloud for mercy. There was a shaking through the whole assembly; I felt the power of faith, and was greatly enlightened in the Holy Scriptures."

Returning to town again, he found more peace than formerly.

"Tuesday, March 1st, being desired the day before to visit a distressed man, one who was troubled with an evil spirit, between day break and sunrise I called his minister out of bed, and desired him to go with me. We went, and I desired all to leave the room, except the distressed man, his wife, the minister, and myself. I then desired him to open to me his case. He said that 'for a long time the devil had followed him, and that he had frequently seen him with his bodily eyes.' The dear man was under conviction, but knew not what was the matter with him. I told him my experience, and gave him as good directions as I was capable of. I prayed for him, and so likewise did his minister in Dutch. I understood afterwards that he was troubled no more in the same way, and he became one of my quiet hearers.

"I visited the country and experienced great displays of the awakening power of God; for many precious people, both Dutch and English, were inquiring the way to heaven. I again returned to town, and preached to about three hundred people by candle light; but some were offended. I appointed to preach the next evening. In town there were many soldiers billetted, and the officers declared that if I attempted to preach again, they would take me to jail: so I understood by my friends, who desired me to decline. I was not afraid of their threats, but in the evening attended the appointment. Shortly after I had taken my text, 'Quench not the Spirit,' 1 Thess. v, 19, several officers with a company of soldiers came to the place, but the house was so crowded that none could get in but the officers, who fixed themselves by my right hand, one of whom stood on a bench with his staff in his hand, lifted up several times either to strike or frighten me; but had a bat, or an owl lighted on the wall, I should have been as much afraid. The devil cannot lead his factors farther than the length of his chain. After sermon was ended, all withdrew, and no harm was done. I was surprised to see the same officers come peaceably to hear the word the next night. The next day I had an invitation to preach to the soldiers; but as I was under a necessity of leaving town, I could not."

Notwithstanding the opposition of some, Mr. Garrettson continued to travel through the country, and to preach with his usual zeal and success. While one cried out, "Sir, can you tell me what I shall do to be saved, for I am the wickedest man in the whole county," others said, "This is the right religion;" and so great was the influence of truth, that although he observed that he was never in a place where there was such a variety of sects, it seemed to him as if sects and names would be lost, and the name of Christ be all in all. During his labours in this part of his Lord's vineyard, which was a little over two months, he says that he "preached in more than twenty different places, and thought that more than three hundred people were under powerful awakenings, besides a number who had already found the pearl of great price. About one hundred had joined the societies."

On the 22d he left the circuit for conference in the city of Baltimore, where he arrived, after a ride of sixty miles, about sunset, and heard a sermon in the evening.

At this conference they had great peace, as all the preachers agreed to abide by the decision of Mr. Wesley respecting the ordinances.

This year, 1781, in Virginia, where Mr. Garrettson was appointed to travel, was a time of great distress, on account of the war. Lord Cornwallis was then harrassing the people with his army, and the Americans were exerting themselves to oppose his progress; so that by the marching and countermarching of armies, and frequent skirmishes, the minds of the people were constantly excited with fear and perplexity; a state of mind very unfavourable to the progress of religion.

Another circumstance tended not a little to arrest the progress of truth and righteousness. Though the disputes respecting the ordinances were amicably terminated among the preachers who composed the conference, yet in Virginia and North Carolina, there were some local preachers, and many of the private members who were not so easily pacified. One object in sending Mr. Garrettson into those parts appears to have been, being a son of peace, and possessing considerable influence among preachers and people, that he might be instrumental in restoring union and confidence among the brethren. This, after considerable labour, accompanied with much prayer, he in a great measure accomplished before the end of the year.

Amidst the troubles arising from these sources, Mr. Garrettson found his mind much refreshed, and his hands strengthened by the good countenance and spiritual conversation of the Rev. Mr. Jarrat, a pious clergyman of the Church of England. Mr. Jarrat received the Methodists with open arms, invited Mr. Garrettson into his pulpit, and as the Methodists had not the ordinances of God's house among themselves, Mr. Jarrat supplied this lack of service by inviting them to the table of the Lord in his church, and occasionally administering baptism and the Lord's supper to them in other places. Of this pious and zealous clergyman, Mr. Garrettson makes honourable mention.

"I have had," says he, "some happy seasons in his congregation, particularly on sacramental occasions. At one time about three hundred of his parishioners communed, and the place seemed awful on account of the power and presence of God. Mr. Jarrat told me that when a lad, while studying under President Davies, he was brought under a travail of soul, and that when the burden was removed, and he received regenerating grace, he was as sensible of it as he would have been, (to use his own expression,) if a ton weight had been rolled from his body."

He arrived on his circuit, Essex, in Virginia, June 4th, 1781, and going to an appointment at Ellis's chapel, he says, "As I entered the door I saw a man in the pulpit dressed in black, engaged in prayer. I soon perceived he was a man bereft of his reason. I went into the pulpit and desired him to desist. After he ended, I gave out his text, and began to preach. But I had no other way to stop him, than to desire the people to withdraw. His testimony was, that he was a prophet sent of God to teach the people; and that it was revealed to him a person was to interrupt him in his discourse. After a few minutes the people returned, and all was still. I then gave out, 'Feed my sheep,' John xxi, 17. I had liberty in showing, 1. The character mentioned in the text—sheep; 2, why the followers of our Lord might be called sheep; and 3, how the sheep are to be fed. 1. The Shepherd; 2, the food; and 3, the manner of feeding the flock. The prophet returned home, and that night he told his family, at such an hour he would go into a trance; and that they must not bury him till after such a time, should he not survive. Accordingly, to appearance he was in a trance. The next day I was sent for to visit him. Many were weeping around the bed, in which he lay like a corpse, for I could not perceive that he breathed. He was once happy in God, and a sensible useful man. About the time of which he spoke, he came to himself. Satan was partly disappointed; for in some measure he was restored to his reason, and I took him part of the way round the circuit with me. What was the cause of this? Satan prompted him to think more highly of himself than he ought to think; and so he fell into the condemnation of the devil. I had a hope before we parted, that his fallen soul was restored. Some time after this he began again to preach Christ; and I trust was more humble than ever. I continued on this circuit about three months, had many happy hours, and some distressing ones. Two things were a great distress to my mind: 1. The spirit of fighting; and 2, that of slavery, which ran among the people. I was resolved to be found in my duty, and keep back no part of the counsel of God. Day and night I could hear the roaring of the cannon, for I was not far from York town during the siege and the surrender of Cornwallis. Many of our pious friends were absolutely against fighting, and some of them suffered much on that account, for they were compelled, or taken by force into the field; though they would sooner have lost their own lives than take the life of any human creature. I saw it my duty to cry down this kind of proceeding, declaring that it could not be justified in the oracles of God. I was, in a particular manner, led to preach against the practice of slave holding. Several were convinced of the impiety of the practice, and liberated their slaves: others who did not liberate them, were convinced that they ought to use them better than they had done. Had it not been for these two evils, I might have been more popular among the people. I preached at a quarterly meeting at Mabery's chapel, where there were about two thousand present, of all ranks; and being pressed in spirit, I cried, 'Do justice, love mercy, and walk humbly with thy God.' There were more than a thousand people who could not get into the chapel, and some of those without called out for an officer to take me. After meeting was ended, I walked through the midst of them, but no one laid hands on me."

After preaching in several places, in all of which he found the power and presence of God to be with him, it seems he went to form a new circuit; for he says, "I am now in my element, forming a new circuit, and I have pleasing prospects. I preached in one place, and there was a great shaking among the people. I preached again the next day, and the power of the Lord in a most wonderful manner came down. I was somewhat surprised—the rich are brought to mourn for Christ. Several fell under the word. A major was so powerfully wrought on, that I suppose he would have fallen from his seat had not the colonel held him up. A large society was united in this place, mostly of the rich. About this time I received a letter from Mr. Asbury, in which I was informed that he could not visit the south, and that it was his desire I should see to stationing the preachers."

It seems that at the request of Mr. Asbury, who was the general assistant under Mr. Wesley, Mr. Garrettson travelled through several circuits, attended the quarterly meetings, held love feasts, and exercised a sort of general superintendency over preachers and people, in the absence of Mr. Asbury. Hence at his request he visited the circuits on the north side of James' river, where he found them in some confusion respecting administering the ordinances, and not a little disturbed on the question of slavery. Some, however, had liberated their slaves, and those who yet plead for the ordinances were tolerably pacified through his mediation. In this tour he had the satisfaction of meeting his brother Richard, a travelling preacher, with whom he was much refreshed, and whose labours had been greatly blessed among the people. Coming from thence to Baltimore, and finding the small pox raging, he was inoculated. He concludes his account of his labours on this tour, with the following reflections: "I think my Lord made me instrumental in uniting to us many brethren, both preachers and people, who had disagreed with us about the ordinances. I can say it was a year of humiliation, and believe I grew in knowledge as well as in grace."

CHAPTER X.

Travels extensively through Virginia and North Carolina—Political difficulties—Goes to Little York—Preaches in the fields—Preaches on the doctrine of perfection—Remarkable dream—Remarks on infant baptism—Greatly encouraged to persevere—Visits and rejoices with his old friends—Mourns over the stupidity of the people—Attends conference in Baltimore—Account of a blind man—Interesting account of a young female—Attends to the people of colour—Conversion of a great opposer—Meets Dr. Coke—Reflections on Mr. Wesley's plan for the organization of a church—Goes to call a conference of the preachers at Baltimore.

THERE is a chasm here in his printed journal of about three years, from 1781 to 1784. This, however, is supplied in the manuscript journal which he has left behind, and which has been carefully transcribed by his surviving and only daughter, Miss Mary R. Garrettson, whose pious and affectionate duty to her father was a solace to him in the decline of his life, and especially in his dying moments. During the year 1781, Mr. Garrettson says, "I travelled about five thousand miles, preached about five hundred sermons, visited most of the circuits in Virginia and North Carolina, and opened one new circuit, in which the Lord began a blessed work, so that many, both rich and poor, joined the society." It was a year of great distress, in consequence of the sanguinary conflicts between the British and American armies. And as Mr. Garrettson was averse to war from principle, as well as to slave holding, a practice so prevalent in the country in which he then laboured, he met with no little difficulty: but he says, "Though some threats were uttered against me, I passed on unhurt, looking continually to Jesus; for I can say I did not think my life dear to me, if I could only win souls to Christ, and get safely to heaven myself."

From the conference in Baltimore, he took his journey to Little York, where he was joyfully received by his friends. From the almost daily notices in his journal, in which we behold the same constant breathing after God, the same thirst for the salvation of sinners, it appears that he continued from place to place, preaching a free and a full salvation, with a diligence and success rarely to be met with. On Friday, April 18th, he paid a visit to a place called Devil's Island, where he says he had "glorious times" in preaching to the people. A faithful class on this island bid him welcome, and added much to his comfort, and gave a pledge of future good. Passing thence to the continent, he frequently met such crowds of people at his appointments, as no house would contain; and therefore was obliged to preach to them after the example of the venerable Wesley, in the open fields, or in the groves.

After noticing that, on one occasion, he had preached to some hundreds under the trees, he says he had "seldom seen a more solemn time."

"Monday 28, the stewards, leaders, exhorters, and local preachers, met at seven o'clock. Our love feast began at nine, and public preaching at twelve. I had promised the day before to preach a sermon on perfection; but knowing that many gainsayers of this doctrine would be at the meeting, I felt that the cross was very heavy, and I arose with fear and trembling; but glory be to God! no sooner had I opened my mouth, than I felt sensibly the presence of my Saviour; and although the house was crowded, and many who could not get in were standing without, and a company of soldiers who came to seek for a deserter, were there, yet I know not that I ever preached to a more solemn audience: most of them were in tears, and many who had been opposed to the doctrine of holiness were convinced of its truth. My own soul was wrapped in love. O that I could always be in such a frame as this! Blessed be God, I hope many of the friends are on stretch for more of the mind of Jesus. O for that love that casts out fear!"

It would seem that the subject of these memoirs, notwithstanding his entire devotedness to the service of his God, was often reduced to great trials of mind, and sometimes to a depression of spirits. On some of these occasions it appears that the Lord instructed and encouraged him in dreams and visions of the night; and though implicit confidence may not be placed in dreams, because "we have a more sure word of prophecy," yet who that reads his Bible but what knows that "in a dream, in a vision of the night, when deep sleep falleth upon man, in slumbering upon the bed, then he openeth the ears of men, and sealeth their instruction." We have in some of the preceding chapters noticed the thoughts which often occupied this holy man upon his bed. The following is no less remarkable than any of the preceding.

"Monday 5th, I think I shall never be satisfied until I have a deeper work of grace in my soul.

'I drink, and yet am ever dry.'

In my way to Devil's Island I called in at a friend's house, where I laid down on a bed in a private room, and fell into a sound sleep. I began to dream, and thought some wicked people came to the place where I was, and spoke evil of the ways of God: the man of the house asked me to go to prayer; but it seemed as if I could neither sing nor pray with them: after a while they began to sing— Satan was striving against me, and I was struggling with all my might. I wanted to call for help, but could not. It appeared to me that in a great measure I got the victory: in a short time I seemed to be dying. I began to search for my witness of God's favour, and I sensibly felt that I might have been more faithful. I wished to live longer that I might be instrumental in bringing souls to Jesus. Instead, however, of dying, I imagined that I fell into a trance, and was taken into the other world, where I had a view of hell. At first I had an imperfect view of it, and it was thought expedient for me to enter its mouth. O what an awful scene was presented to my mind. What feelings I had for precious souls! all my pain was for them, as I thought the fire had no power to hurt me; but I trembled to think of their agonies: on looking forward I could see no end to that sea of fire, whose high surges, one after another, with the interval of a few minutes, continually rolled along. I looked at them as they came, and saw the damned beat about by them in all the tortures of agony—toiling and striving to stem the waves, which, like molten metal, drove them back, while the place resounded with their bitter groans. O, it was indescribably awful! sometimes the sea would sink into a black calm, and a dismal noisome smoke would ascend. I stood and trembled while I saw the damned rising out of the embers, and then other waves of the liquid fire would arise and beat them back. As I stood looking, it was said, 'Will you after this be faithful in warning sinners?' I thought I would be more faithful than ever, and that my whole life should be spent in warning them. I then requested to be carried to heaven; but the answer was, 'You have seen enough; return and be faithful.' On awaking I sat up in the bed in wonder; then kneeling down, I found that the Lord Jesus was precious to my soul. At four o'clock I preached on the island. Thanks be to my Saviour for these precious happy souls. Jesus was near to me! O Lord, make me more faithful than ever."

Whatever may be thought of the above dream, it is certain that there is a place of endless torment for the wicked in a future state, "where the worm dieth not, and the fire is not quenched." And as "eye hath not seen, nor ear heard," the things that God hath prepared for those that love him, so hath it not entered into the heart of man to conceive the things, the terribleness of that "blackness of darkness" which those must inherit who die unreconciled to God. Mr. Garrettson observes,

"Thursday 15th, in my sermon at —— I endeavoured to discover the propriety of infant baptism. 1. If any of you can prove that infant initiation was ever thrown out of the church, then it will be time for me to prove that it was again received. St. Paul tells us that the 'unbelieving husband is sanctified by the wife, and the unbelieving wife by the husband; else were your children unclean, but now are they holy,' 1 Cor. vii, 14. It is obvious the apostle was speaking to those Gentile converts who were for leaving their heathen wives and husbands. He here recommends them to live together: tells them their children are holy. They possessed a covenant holiness: though but one believed, their children had a right to baptism. 2. The reason why we have so large an account of adults being baptized, was because the gospel dispensation had just commenced; and all believers were to be made partakers of the ordinance, as well as their children; for, 'the promise is to you and to your children,' Acts ii, 36. Whole households were baptized. I proved infant justification by Scripture, Rom. v, 18, 19, &c.

"On the evening of the 25th, I preached Prudence Hudson's funeral sermon to about five hundred people. It was three years last winter that I first came into this place, when she, though moral, was with others going on in the way to ruin. When she heard of salvation by faith she was convinced of her undone condition. She followed the preaching night and day. Go where I would, if within eight or ten miles, she was there, and she generally walked to the meetings. For some months she groaned under a spirit of bondage; but God in his own good time delivered her soul from the guilt and power of sin. She received the spirit of adoption, whereby she was enabled to cry, Abba Father. I frequently met her in class, where she always seemed to be desirous of loving God supremely. I believe from the time she became religious, she never did any thing to grieve her brethren, or wound the cause of God. She afterwards married a pious young man, and after the birth of her first child, she was impressed with an idea that God would take her out of the world. She expressed a fear that she was not cleansed from all sin, and desired her husband to pray for her. Shortly after, as she was lifting her heart to God, he in great mercy poured his love into her soul in a manner which caused her to cry out, 'Come, Lord Jesus, come quickly, and take my raptured soul away.' To her weeping friends she repeated the goodness of God—whose grace, she said, had sanctified her wholly, and made her meet for glory. She bid them dry their tears, for she was going to heaven. She embraced her parents and thanked them for their kindness, and exhorted her class mates to faithfulness. Many a time, said she to them, have we walked together to our meetings; and now I am going to receive my reward. She warned her husband against keeping slaves. Her soul seemed to be so enraptured with the love of God, that she would frequently cry out, 'O death, where is thy sting! O grave, where is thy victory!' Thus she continued some days exhorting all around her, and so fell asleep in the arms of Jesus. O that Christians would bestir themselves to greater faithfulness."

After passing through various places, and preaching to crowded audiences, he observes under date of Nov. 12, 1782, "I rode down in the Neck, and preached near Delaware bay. Four years ago I preached in this house, when the whole Neck seemed to be in Egyptian darkness. I never visited them again until now: and though I then laboured (as I thought) to little purpose, I now find among them two scores professing the knowledge of Jesus, many of whom date their conversion from that day: this encourages me to draw the bow at a venture, and leave the event to God. Lord, increase my faith, and give me greater deadness to the world."

How consoling and encouraging is it to a faithful minister, to witness the salutary effects of his ministry in the holy lives and triumphant deaths of his spiritual children! These are the living and dying witnesses of the power and truth of that gospel he preaches, and will be his "crown of rejoicing in that day." This solace was imparted, in a high degree, in numerous instances, to Mr. Garrettson. The following instance he relates, under date of Dec. 29: "I met G. M., we rejoiced together in considering the good which God has done in this part of his vineyard. On the 28th, preached a funeral sermon over our dear departed brother Smith, who lived for many years a life of piety. He was a man of affliction, but he bore it with Christian patience and fortitude. He, in a measure, lost his speech for some months before his death. I visited him several times in his sickness, and though he could not speak so that I could understand him, my soul was refreshed, and by the signs he made, and the tears which so plentifully flowed from his eyes, I had not a doubt or fear but his soul was transported with joy. Happy he lived, happy he died, leaving a family happy in God; and glory to God! I have no doubt but his soul is happy at God's right hand. O that all my dear friends and children may make as happy an end! I rode to Mr. Barcel's chapel, and spent two or three hours in watching for the coming of Christ; and blessed be God, we found him in our hearts.

"Sunday 29th, preached again in Barcel's chapel. This week I spent in preaching and visiting the friends: my soul is sweetly drawn out to serve God; and if I had a thousand tongues, I would employ them all in praising my dear Master."

None but those who have had an experience of it can fully realize the happiness resulting from the visits of ministers after a long absence, among those who had been converted under their ministry, and still finding them "steadfast in the faith." "I have no greater joy than to find my children walking in the truth," said St. John. The following circumstances related by Mr. Garrettson will illustrate the truth of this remark:—

"Jan. 5, 1783, I am once more among my Dover friends. Surely God is among these people. The last sabbath I preached here, the Lord in mercy laid his hand upon one of the greatest persecutors in the town; finding no rest, he cried mightily to God, and he converted both himself, his wife, and his brother's wife: they are now happy in religion, going on hand in hand with the brethren; and he is resolutely determined on building a brick chapel. Shall we not give the glory to God, who can change the hearts of lion-like men and women in so short a time? I have great freedom both in preaching, exhorting, prayer, and visiting the friends. God has done and is doing great things for the people in this town. I visited sister Basset, who has been a long time under the afflicting hand of divine Providence. I think her one of the happiest women I have met with. I believe her to be a living witness of sanctification; her soul seems to be continually wrapped in a flame of love. Several of this family are happy in the love of God; four of whom enjoy that degree of it which casts out fear. Surely God has a church in this house.

"On the 30th I sat out to visit the societies in Kent and Newcastle: I generally preach once and twice every day, besides meeting the classes; and I bless God for the sweet consolation I have. Many are happily going on to perfection. I think if I know myself, I have set out in this new year, (1783,) to live a life of devotion to God."

The following item in his journal may be considered as descriptive of a heart deeply penetrated with the worth of immortal souls, as well as of the exercises peculiar in some sense to a true minister of Jesus Christ. Such often cry out, "The burden of the Lord! the burden of the Lord are these." Those who "prophesy for hire, and preach for gain," may think lightly of such exercises; but the true "minister of the sanctuary" often "weeps between the porch and the altar, saying, Spare thy people, good Lord, and give not thine heritage to the heathen."

"Thursday 6th, I began this morning to read Nicodemus on the fear of man, and in the afternoon preached to a crowded audience, many more than could get in the house. I thought during the sermon, surely these people must be convinced; they were in a flood of tears: how is it? I fear they weep, and repent, and sin again. When I was in this neighbourhood several years ago, they were in the same condition; nearly thirty in society, and but two believers! O God, thou must do the work: stretch forth thy powerful hand. My soul is distressed for the people: many who, I fear, live in sin, appeared to be as glad to see me as if I had been their father. I always endeavour to preach as plain truths to them as I possibly can. This has been a day of temptation: Satan would persuade me that my life was a life of misery; but I am sure one soul is of more value than ten thousand worlds! Lord give me a more earnest desire for all the mind that was in Jesus. O that I may give an account before my Master for the improvement of this comfortable room: though an unprofitable servant, God gives me great favour in the sight of the people."

It seems that Mr. Garrettson was now travelling over ground which he had been the means of ploughing and sowing some years since. He found that in most places the good seed of the kingdom had taken deep root, and was now springing up and bearing fruit; while in other places there was reason to believe the seed had fallen "by the way side, or upon stony ground." In this visit among his old friends and spiritual children in Kent and Dorset counties, his spirit was much refreshed and strengthened, while he preached in crowded houses, and sometimes in the fields, to from one thousand to one thousand five hundred people. On the 27th of May, 1783, he attended the conference in Baltimore, at which there were, he says, about sixty preachers, all of whom appeared to be in the spirit of the gospel.

From this conference he went to Talbot circuit. While he rejoiced over some who had remained steadfast, and amidst the persecution they endured, loved and supported each other, he had to mourn over others who had departed from the faith, particularly some who had been guilty of a practice plainly repugnant to the economy of the gospel. Mr. Garrettson gives the following interesting account of a blind man: "The man of the house is entirely blind, but glory to God! I believe he has spiritual eye sight, and can view the Redeemer by faith. I was very much surprised the next day to find him, as he rode with me to preaching, directing the boy who was to have been our guide, but whose horse took the wrong road, he having fallen asleep; the blind man soon detected his mistake, roused him from his sleep, and set him right. In passing the fields of corn or wheat, he would make very judicious remarks on the state of the crops. When he came near a house, he would point to it, and tell me the owner's name; and when we came nearly opposite the paths, &c, which intersected the road, he would direct the boy which way to turn; or when he came to a gate, would say, 'Boy, open that gate.' He could walk about his plantation; go to what room of his house he pleased, or to any desk or chest he pleased. He said he could count money by the feeling. He is of a family who generally lose their eye sight when they arrive at the age of twenty or twenty-two. I think he is a precious happy soul, and can praise and bless God for spiritual eye sight. His wife is as blind spiritually as he is literally."

The following narrative is no less edifying and interesting: "I preached in Hopkins's Neck to many precious souls and was much quickened among them. After preaching, I visited a beautiful damsel, about the age of fourteen, the only child of her tender father. She appeared to be in a deep decay, and there was little expectation of her staying in this world much longer. Her mother, a few months ago, went out of the world triumphing in the faith, and is now, no doubt, praising God in heaven. God refreshed my soul abundantly while praying for this damsel. After prayer, I asked her if she saw her way clear to the heavenly world? 'Blessed be God!' said she, 'I do.' I asked her if she was willing to die. 'I do not,' said she, 'wish to remain here any longer.' I asked her if she was prepared to die: she replied, 'God loves me, and I love him: I know,' said she, 'that he loves me.' I said, do you know your sins forgiven? 'I have not,' said she, 'the witness; but I believe God will give it me before he takes me hence.' Said I, were you willing to die when you were first taken ill?' She replied, 'No.' 'I asked her why? 'Because I was a sinner. I knew God was angry with me. I was under distress of soul, but the Lord has turned his anger away.' How did you feel, said I, in time of prayer? 'My soul,' said she, 'was happy!' I had the witness that she was a favourite of heaven. Child, said I, believe that God loves you; look to him now for a witness of his favour. 'I am looking,' said she, 'for a bright witness; and I believe God will give it to me.' I left her: my heart was full of love, hoping one day to meet her in glory. Her father accompanied me nearly a mile. I asked him if she had been under serious impressions any time before she was taken sick. He said from the time that preaching was first established in the neighbourhood, she had had a great love for the way, and wanted to join the society; but the preachers thought she was rather young: but, said he, since her sickness she has gone through deep distress."

Among other blessed effects of the Methodist ministry, was the conversion of many of the coloured people in that part of the country, both among the slaves, and those that were free. These people, who seem destined by an all-wise, but inscrutable Providence, to suffer many privations in this world, in consequence of the forced and cruel manner in which they had been removed from their own country, as well as the manner in which most of them were treated here, had been hitherto destitute of spiritual instruction, and generally treated as if they had no souls either to save or lose. To them particular attention was paid by the Methodist preachers.

Such, however, was their situation, that they could not assemble at the usual hours for preaching. To meet their case, therefore, appointments were made especially for their benefit. This, in many instances, made double work for the preachers. Frequently after preaching to the white people, they had to meet the coloured population.

This Mr. Garrettson often did. On one of these occasions he says, "This night my soul was transported with joy when meeting the black class, a company of humble, happy souls. And a little below he says, "for these last five days I have been employed in preaching every day, and in meeting several coloured classes, and was much comforted among them."* Such, indeed, is the state of many of those ill fated people.

What can more strongly attest the truth, and may we not say the *divinity* of the gospel, than the conversion of some of its warmest opposers? Hence the conversion of St. Paul has been ever considered an irrefragable argument in favour of the power and truth of the gospel of Christ. Many similar instances are recorded in the history of the church,

* It may not be amiss to observe here, that from the beginning of the Methodist ministry in this country, particular attention has been paid to these ill-fated people. And who knows but that the entrance of the gospel among them in this way may not be a prelude to the entire conversion of the African race, not only those who inhabit this country, but even those who remain in their native land! Though some who are either wilfully blind, or inexcusably inattentive to the history of events, seem to think, and even to affirm that these people have been entirely overlooked by the Christian community until quite recently, it is well known to others, that ever since Methodism was planted in this country, they have been the special objects of its ministry; and that the Methodists have had, since the year 1787, when the late Dr. Coke first landed in the Island of Antigua, flourishing missions in nearly all the West India Islands; and that at this time they number nearly 30,000; and that in these United States there are about 60,000 of the coloured population members of our church, besides a number, no doubt truly pious, who have separated from us, and set up for themselves.

The Wesleyan Methodists have also established several missions in Africa. These, together with the infant colony now rising into notice under the fostering care of the American Colonization Society, give a fair promise of the future reformation of the vast continent of Africa to the principles of Christianity. May not these things be reckoned among the "signs of the times," which indicate the near approach of that day, "when the knowledge of the Lord shall cover the earth, as the waters do the sea?"—ED.

and not a few in the journal of Mr. Garrettson. At the time we are now speaking of, he says, "I was rejoiced to converse with one who, a few weeks since, was a great enemy to religion, but has now a broken heart."

Mr. Garrettson continued his labours in these parts of the country among his old friends with various success, and oftentimes exposed to much fatigue and suffering, until September 3, when he was preparing to take his departure for Charleston, S. C., but was arrested in his progress by the arrival of Dr. Coke, who was empowered by Mr. Wesley to organize the Methodist societies in this country into a separate and independent church. On this event he makes the following reflections: "In the evening news came to my room that Dr. Coke had arrived. I felt a spirit of rejoicing, and hastened down stairs to receive him. I was somewhat surprised when Mr. Wesley's plan of ordination was opened to me, and determined to sit in silence. I thought it expedient to return with him to a quarterly meeting held in Kent county, where I expected to meet Mr. Asbury, and a number of the preachers. About fifteen met in conference, and it was thought expedient to call a general conference at Baltimore; and that I should decline my expedition to Charleston. I was accordingly appointed to go and call a conference. I sat out for Virginia and Carolina, and a tedious journey I had. My dear Master enabled me to ride about twelve hundred miles in about six weeks; and preach going and coming constantly. The conference began on Christmas day."

Dr. Coke in his journal alluding to the same event, says, " Here I met with an excellent young man, *Freeborn Garrettson*. He seems to be all meekness and love, and yet all activity. He makes me quite ashamed, for he invariably rises at four in the morning, and not only he, but several others of the preachers. Him we sent off, like an arrow, from north to south, directing him to send messengers to the right and left, and to gather all the preachers together at Baltimore on Christmas eve."

CHAPTER XI.

State of the societies at the conclusion of the war—Destitute of the ordinances—Mr. Wesley solicited to supply this deficiency—Finally consents—Ordains Dr. Coke, who arrives in America, in company with Richard Whatcoat and Thomas Vasey—Christmas Conference—Mr. Asbury ordained a superintendent, and Mr. Garrettson and others, elders—He volunteers for Nova Scotia—Pastoral letters—Embarks for Halifax—Stormy passage—Kindly received at Halifax, preaches and forms a society—Makes a tour into the country, and preaches with success—Account of the Allenites—Letter to Mr. Wesley—Mr. Wesley's answer—Visits Liverpool—Society doubled by his labours—Commencement of Methodism in Liverpool—Visits Shelburne—Kindly treated by the rector of the parish—Society increases amidst opposition—Returns to Liverpool—Thence to Halifax—Correspondence with Mr. Wesley, Dr. Coke, and Bishop Asbury—Anecdotes and reflections—Leaves Nova Scotia for Boston—Origin of Methodism in Boston—Mr. Garrettson preaches there—Passes thence to Providence—Newport—New-York—Philadelphia—to Baltimore, where he attends conference.

WE come now to a very important era in the history of Methodism, as well as in the history of our country. After a long and severe struggle, the revolutionary war ended in the independence of these United States. With the annihilation of the political power of Great Britain over this country, ceased all its ecclesiastical jurisdiction. While, however, the contest lasted between the two countries, the Methodist societies had continued to increase under the faithful labours of the preachers, Mr. Garrettson and others; but these preachers not being ordained, the societies had remained destitute of the ordinances, only so far as they received them from the hands of other ministers.

This deficiency in the ministrations of the Methodist ministry, as has already been observed, had occasioned much uneasiness in the societies. From time to time, Mr. Wesley had been solicited to grant them relief; but being unwilling to disturb the order of the church to which he belonged, until the independence of this country had been achieved, and acknowledged by the English government, Mr. Wesley remained deaf to their solicitations. This event, however, so auspicious in its consequences to this country, to the church, and perhaps I might add to the world at large, tended to remove all scruples from his mind respecting the expediency of the measure. He saw a large field opened for the future usefulness of a well organized ministry; a ministry constituted according to the Scripture model. To this work, with a view to supply the spiritual wants of so many thousands who were looking to him for direction in this important affair, Mr. Wesley believed himself providentially called. He, therefore, with all the despatch the nature of the business would allow, concerted measures for the organization of the Methodist societies in America into a church, according to what he considered to be the primitive model.

With a view to accomplish this object, Mr. Wesley first directed his attention to the most suitable men and means. Thomas Coke, LL. D., and a presbyter in the church of England, had been led by a train of providential circumstances to connect himself with the body of Methodist preachers in England, and had, for a number of years, been one of Mr. Wesley's most active and efficient assistants. Mr. Wesley had received unequivocal proofs of his entire devotedness to the cause of his divine Master, of his hearty concurrence in the general plans of usefulness to the souls of men; and of his firm attachment to the doctrines and discipline of the Methodist societies. To him, therefore, Mr. Wesley directed his attention as the most suitable person to organize the societies in this country into a church, and to be the instrument of furnishing it with the ordinances of the gospel. Accordingly, being assisted by other presbyters of the Church of England, on the 2d day of September, 1784, Mr. Wesley set apart Dr. Coke as a superintendent of the Methodist societies in

America, and gave him letters of ordination. At the same time Mr. Wesley, with the assistance of Dr. Coke and Mr. Creighton, another presbyter of the Church of England, ordained Messrs. Richard Whatcoat and Thomas Vasey, who had volunteered their services for America, as presbyters, and recommended them to the brethren in this country. They accordingly accompanied Dr. Coke, who left England in the month of September, 1784, and arrived in this country, at New-York, on the third of November following.

It is not my intention to enter into a detailed account of the transactions of this period. Those who wish for such an account, and for the arguments in vindication of the conduct of Mr. Wesley, Dr. Coke, and Mr. Asbury, in these important matters, may consult Moore's Life of the Messrs. Wesleys, Drew's Life of Dr. Coke, Lee's History of the Methodists, Vindication of Methodist Episcopacy, and the Defence of our Fathers.

We have already seen the manner in which Mr. Garrettson was employed in calling the preachers together, and the opinion expressed by Dr. Coke of his diligence and activity, his meekness and love. The preachers, about sixty in number, assembled in Baltimore, December 25th, 1784, and held what has been designated the "Christmas conference." The plan recommended by Mr. Wesley was unanimously approved of by the preachers present; and on the 27th of the same month, Mr. Francis Asbury, according to the appointment of Mr. Wesley and the unanimous vote of the conference was consecrated by Dr. Coke, assisted by Mr. Otterbine, a German minister, of undoubted piety, and for whom Mr. Asbury entertained an affectionate and high regard, and other elders, to the office of a superintendent of the Methodist Episcopal Church. According to Mr. Lee's History of the Methodists, there were thirteen elected to the office of elders, eleven of whom only were ordained at the conference.

Among those consecrated to this office was the subject of this memoir.

At the conclusion of the revolutionary war, a number of persons who still retained their attachment to the British government, removed to the province of Nova Scotia. Among these emigrants there were some who had been members of the Methodist society in this country; others had emigrated from Europe. These were as sheep without a shepherd. They therefore expressed a strong desire to have Methodist missionaries sent among them. As their circumstances and wishes became known to Dr. Coke, he deeply interested himself in their behalf, and contemplated making them a visit, but was providentially disappointed by a violent storm, which finally compelled the captain, with whom the Dr. sailed, to seek a shelter in one of the West India islands. At this conference, therefore, through his solicitations, Mr. Garrettson volunteered his services for Nova Scotia. While preparing for this enterprise, he wrote the following letters, one of which appears to be addressed to members of some former charge, and the other to a respected friend:

"*My dearly beloved friends and brethren,*

"Peace and consolation attend you for ever, through Jesus Christ, Amen! I had great expectation of paying you a visit before I took my departure to some other quarter of my Master's vineyard; but had not had an opportunity, being confined to other places. I send this epistle, hoping it will, in some sense, supply my lack of service. Through the mercy of our God I enjoy health of body; and blessed be his dear name, I think my love and zeal for his glory are as great as ever; desiring to spend, and be spent in the best of causes, not counting my life dear, so I can win souls, and at last stand blameless before the throne of my God, not having on my own righteousness, but a righteousness through the faith of the Son of God.

"My dearly beloved friends, you very well know what you were before the great Shepherd and Bishop of your souls gave me entrance among you: this I can say, my trials were great and manifold; yet our great Master stood by me. You know very well I was among you with tears and fasting; labouring both night and day, and glory be to God, I hope not altogether in vain. 'Ye were once darkness, but now are ye light in the Lord; walk as children of the light.' When I shall be among you again, I know not, being straitened between two, whether to go out into the wilderness, or to tarry with the children of the kingdom. It is the most pleasing to nature to tarry, but having a great sense of the deplorable condition thousands of souls are in, I feel a willingness to tread unbeaten paths in the wilderness, and call home hundreds and thousands of the lost sheep of the house of Israel, who now (as you once did) sit in darkness, that we all may be of one fold, feeding in one pasture, under one great Shepherd. I long to see the happy time, when the knowledge of God shall cover the earth. Who among you will join, *faithfully join,* to pull down the kingdom of the devil? Shall I be so happy as to meet you *all* in glory?

"I shall speak my mind freely, though at a distance: when I was with you last, I was afraid that some of you were waxing cold, and that others were too much glued to the world. O! my friends, better you had never heard the glad sound of the gospel—better you had never been born, than in the midst of such privileges to be lost! O what a cutting sight, should I see any of you at the left hand, with whom I have taken sweet counsel. May Jehovah for his mercy's sake forbid it! I now come to speak of great matters:—' As you have received Christ Jesus the Lord, so walk you in him.' How was Christ received? not in neglect of prayer, not in trifling, not in associating with the wicked, not in worldly mindedness, nor in neglect of any of the means of grace; but in an earnest, fervent, humble, holy looking to God by faith. This is the way you are to walk in him; to be as much engaged for perfect love, as ever you were for justifying faith. What is the reason we are not more holy? Why do we not walk more closely with God, and live more in heaven? Why are we not more dead to the world? Because we are enthusiasts, looking for the end, without using the means. O! that you may stir up the gift of God, by earnestly groaning, both day and night, for full redemption in the blood of Jesus: look for the blessing *now;* this moment look up by faith. You must *feel* the need of it; then, and not till then, will you seek it with all your powers. O that you may receive it now, while these lines are read to you. By and by, our sabbath opportunities, praying opportunities, preaching opportunities, hearing opportunities, and class meeting opportunities will all be passed away: the harvest shortly will be ripe, Christ will appear, his labourers will be called home, and each of us will have to give an account of his stewardship. O what a dismal day it will be to the impenitent; to swearers, drunkards, liars, defrauders, the worldly minded, to all those that have been covered with a web of their own weaving, and particularly to hypocrites and backsliders. The backslider may then say, 'Once I went in and out with the people of God, tasted his goodness, and felt his power; but wretched me, I departed from his holy commands, pierced the Saviour afresh, yea, I wounded his cause, by stabbing him in the house of his friends; and now an eternal storm must for ever beat upon my guilty soul.' O my God! who can bear the thought. While I am writing, the worth of your souls lies near my heart, and blessed be God, I feel a sense of his dying, forgiving love to my own soul.

"I shall now close with an address to you in the several stations you occupy in the church of God. Some of you God has set apart to speak in his name: O that you may do it faithfully. To the leaders I would say, keep the life and power of God in your souls, that your prayers and admonitions may have the happy effect of kindling all around you the flames of holy, pure love: then will you long for your class day to come. The private members I would enjoin to love each other, and to bear each other's burdens: be watchful, sober; train up your children in the fear of God, and be as burning lights to all around you: then will you force the heathen world to say, 'See how these Christians love one another.' You that are young men and women, be sober minded, and be not unequally yoked together with unbelievers. Considering that light has no communion with darkness, or Christ with Belial, I earnestly exhort you all to receive with kindness, and esteem highly, those who labour among you in word and doctrine; they watch for your souls, as they that must give an account, that they may do it with joy. God has already in his wisdom seen fit to remove some from among you into eternity, I hope, to surround his glorious throne.

"I now commend you to the fatherly goodness of Jehovah, praying and beseeching him to keep you all by the power of his Spirit, that if I never enjoy your company here, I may eternally enjoy it in heaven.

"I desire the prayers of all my dear friends and children, that I may stand fast in the faith, and finish my course with comfort: may we all meet to be crowned with an eternal crown. Friends meet and part here, but there we shall meet never to part more. Our sorrows will be wiped away; the wicked will cease from troubling, and our weary souls will for ever be at rest; to which happy place may God in his infinite mercy grant to bring us all, for the sake of his dear Son. Amen.

"I remain your sincere, though unworthy servant, in the bonds of the peaceful gospel of Christ,

"F. GARRETTSON.

"An epistle to all the brethren on the sea side. Care of brother John Coe—to be read."

"*Dear Brother,*

"God in his wisdom has altered my station from the south to the north, and I am now on my way as far as Mount Holly. There seems to be a loud call for the gospel in Halifax, Shelburn, and many other places in Nova Scotia. I am willing, and want to go in the power of the blessed Spirit. I hope I shall have an interest in the prayers of all my dear friends. I shall never forget you for the acts of kindness you have showed. Lord, grant you may ever continue an humble, zealous follower of the Lamb, that I may one day meet you in glory everlasting.

"Blessed be God, my mind is sweetly drawn out in the work of the ministry, and I hope I shall ever be little and mean in my own eyes, and that I may ever be rising higher and higher in the divine image. Brother Kent informs me that the work seems still to prosper, which rejoices my heart. O that Jesus may still go on in the power of his Spirit. Give my kind love to sister Hopper, and to all inquiring friends. I hope you will write to me often: direct to Halifax. I am more and more convinced that our new plan is of God. I hope and trust the Lord is about to raise up a glorious church.

"I commend you to Jesus, trusting you will be faithful unto death. In great love believe me

"Your friend,
"F. GARRETTSON."

About the middle of February, in company with Mr. James O. Cromwell, Mr. Garrettson embarked for Halifax in Nova Scotia. They had a very tedious voyage, suffering much from cold and wet, having in a small vessel, deeply loaded, encountered a severe storm. "I never," says he, "saw so dismal a time before; but through the amazing goodness of God, we were brought safely to Halifax, and were very kindly received by a Mr. Marchington, a true friend to the gospel." Through the exertions of this pious gentleman, a convenient place was fitted up for preaching, and in a short time Mr. Garrettson united a few serious persons together in a class.

Shortly after his arrival, he wrote the following letter to Dr. Coke:—

"*Halifax*, 1785.

"*Rev. and dear sir,*—After a stormy and dangerous passage of thirteen days, we arrived safely at Halifax, where we met with a kind reception from Mr. Marchington, and a few other poor sheep in the wilderness. As yet I do not know as much of the country, or the state of affairs, as I shortly shall, God being my helper.

"A few days ago brother Cromwell set sail for Shelburn. Brother Marchington has hired a house at ten dollars a month, that will contain about three hundred souls. I have preached five sermons. The number has increased so that we now have our little apartment filled. I cannot speak of any visible good, more than that they seem to hear with attention and solemnity, and I have joined a society of seven or eight members. Shortly after I came to town, I waited on the old rector. 'Sir,' said he, 'you are on a blessed errand; I will do what I can in assisting you. I desire to see the gospel spread.'

"The next day I waited on his excellency, the governor, accompanied by Mr. Marchington. I found him very accessible. After telling him my business, from whence I was, and by whom I was sent: 'Mr. Wesley,' said he, 'is a good man—a very good man. How long do you purpose to stay?' I told him twelve months, or two years. 'I am glad you called upon me: you have my approbation, and whenever you call for my assistance, if I can help you I will.' I could but humbly thank him.

"God willing, on Monday next I purpose to take a tour through the country, to collect, if possible, the sheep so widely scattered. I believe there are many precious souls who desire to hear us. I am well assured we shall have hard work this year; but who would not labour, and suffer in so good a cause. I bless God for health, and as great a desire as ever to do his blessed will, and spend and be spent in the best of causes. We shall, as the people are poor, do little in the sale of books. Indeed I expect we shall be under a necessity of giving some of the small tracts away. The travelling here is extremely expensive. The packet has no less than four or five dollars for carrying a person from Halifax to Shelburn, and as much to Annapolis or St. John's Town: besides long journeys by land to the different towns and settlements. I am fully persuaded that our voyage to this part of the world is of God; the very time when preachers of our order ought to have come. But if possible we must be assisted, for our preachers are left without horses, and but four pounds a piece. Next year I trust the people will be able to support the gospel. When I am more acquainted with the country, I shall send on another letter to conference. By the grace of God I shall do all that lies in my power to promote the Redeemer's kingdom.

"Dear sir, I remain your affectionate friend and brother,
"F. GARRETTSON.
"To the Rev. Dr. Coke."

In another letter he says, "The secretary sent for me, to know whether it would not be expedient for me to take the oath of allegiance to his majesty; but on my objecting to it, and stating my reasons for so doing, he told me there was not the least necessity: he also told me if there should happen any disorders in our meeting, to apply to a magistrate, and I should find favour. So far is well, is it not? My congrogation has been increasing ever since I came; so that on the sabbath evenings many return home for want of room in the house. The last week night I preached, the house was nearly full. For two nights we had a little disturbance. On one night the stones flew, and one stone of nearly a pound weight was levelled at me, but missed its aim, and struck out two panes of glass near my head. This is but trifling, if I can win souls to Jesus."

After continuing a short time in Halifax, during which he preached almost every night in the week, and three times on the Lord's day, in the latter part of March he set out on a tour through the country. "I have," says he, "travelled, though the snow was deep, about three hundred miles in two weeks, and preached twenty sermons to many attentive hearers." Among others, he found some old members of society, who had emigrated from Europe, and who rejoiced much to hear from his lips the same truths they formerly had heard in their own country. Indeed, some time prior to this, Mr. William Black, a native of Yorkshire, who had been converted to God, had gone to that province, and had been instrumental in diffusing gospel light and truth among the people in New Brunswick, and some other places. On the arrival of Mr. Garrettson, Mr. Black and those who were associated with him were much encouraged.

In this country Mr. Garrettson preached the word with a success similar to what had attended his evangelical labours in the United States. Among others who had begun to "taste of the good word of God," he found a society of coloured people, with whom he was much comforted, whom he endeavoured to bring into gospel order, by forming sixty of them into a class, administering baptism to nineteen, and the Lord's supper to about forty, most of whom he trusted loved God and one another.

It is not one of the least perplexing difficulties connected with ministerial duty, to be under the necessity of either disentangling the sophistries of error, or of suffering vain and deluded mortals to remain under the influence of their fatal delusion. It is more especially so, when this error is nourished and strengthened by pride and self conceit,—vices not uncommonly united,—and adhered to with all the tenacity which ignorance and bigotry inspire. To remain silent under such circumstances, betrays a want of zeal in the cause of truth, and an indifference to the salvation of souls. To undertake to unravel the knotty threads of error is often a task no less difficult and irksome to ourselves, than it is offensive to those whom we labour " to convert from the error of their ways."

These remarks were suggested by the following account which Mr. Garrettson has recorded respecting a people he found in Nova Scotia, who seem to have adopted all the offensive peculiarities of Calvinism, called *Allenites*, one Mr. Allen being their principal leader. Though he might have been a good man, it is certain that some parts of his doctrine must have had a very pernicious influence. "Some of them seem to have the fear of God; but in general they are as deluded a people as I ever saw. Almost all of them preach in public. I was conversing with one who seems to be a principal person among them. She said she believed death would slay more sins for her than were ever destroyed before. 'As for sin,' said she, 'it cannot hurt me: not even adultery, murder, swearing, drunkenness, nor any other sin, can break the union between me and Christ.' They have passed judgment upon us, that we are neither Christians, nor called to preach.

"Thursday I preached at Mr. Woodworth's, to a crowded audience. A little before preaching time, two old Calvinists came into my room to have a conversation with me before preaching. 'I understand,' said one of them, 'that you hold with falling from grace: I heard it, but did not know how to believe it, and should be glad to know whether you do deny the perseverance of the saints?' I answered, I do not, for my desire is that they should persevere: I do not hold with man's persevering in wickedness, neither do I believe that a man can have grace while he lives in sin. Let us take the Bible, and see what is said there: I read part of the 15th of John, and parts of several chapters in Hebrews, Romans, and Peter. Now, said I, this is the language of many other passages. We have no promise for any but such as do persevere to the end, and we have had many unhappy instances of men running well for a time, and then turning back: read the 18th chapter of Ezekiel. Now what harm can there be in enforcing our Lord's, the prophets', and the apostles' exhortation? 'Very good,' said he. Why should we do it if there was no danger? and what harm can there be in the doctrine; suppose you are a Christian, and your neighbour is one also: you believe in the unconditional perseverance of saints; he in the conditional: who, sir, is the safest? If you are right, surely he cannot fall. 'I never,' said he, 'saw so much in it before.' They stayed to hear the sermon, and afterwards one said, 'I never heard these men before, but they are better than I thought.'

"Friday morning I sat out for Granville. I had not got far, before a man came running out. 'Sir,' said he, 'I like part of your doctrine well, but part I do not like.' What part don't you like? 'You say, sir, that a saint may fall. Will you answer me one question?' said I. Do you know that you were ever converted? 'I do,' said he. Pray tell me how matters are at present between God and your soul? 'Why,' said he, 'it is a winter state.' But, said I, are you not now living in open sin against God? He paused awhile. I ask, said I, in the fear of God, and desire an answer in truth. 'I confess,' said he, 'I am living in sin.' And yet you do not believe in falling from grace! I believe it because you have fallen. This is what you call a winter state! I call it lying in the arms of the wicked one, and you may talk as you will about your past experience; but I would not give a straw for your chance of heaven, if you die in this state. You are reconciling Christ and Belial together. 'O,' said he, 'I shall be raised up at the last day.' You will, said I; but, unless you repent, it will be to be cast into the lake of fire. He seemed much affected and left me.

"January 19th, I preached opposite Granville to a number of serious hearers, and was invited home to dinner by an old gentleman, who, soon after we were seated at table, said, 'I understand you preach perfection.' I do, said I, and have done so for a number of years; and shall do so as long as I find the doctrine in the Bible. 'Why, sir,' said he, 'Paul was not perfect, he complains of a thorn in the side.' The *heart* is the place for sin, said I, and not the side. He then mentioned several other passages of Scripture which he thought were opposed to holiness of heart, which I explained to him. Pray, said I, let us come to the point at once. Do you believe that an unholy creature can enter into heaven? 'No.' Pray when is sin to be destroyed? 'At death.' You must then hold with death as being part of a Saviour, or with a purgatory after death, or you must come to perfection on this side the grave. He sat amazed, and seemed to give up the argument. We rose from the table: I went to prayer, then went on my journey, and preached at six o'clock in the court house. When I left the old man, he desired me to make his house my home. I left Fletcher's Checks with him. Shortly after I received a few lines from him to this effect:—'I believe you to be a servant of God. I hope the Lord will bless you, and those that sent you here. I want to see you at my house at every opportunity. I thank you for the book.'"

Mr. Garrettson, in another place, gives the following summary of their leading absurdities:—"1. They think they can tell whether a person is a Christian at first sight. 2. They say that we are leading people blindfolded to hell. 3. They are, they say, as sure of heaven, as if they were already there, for sin cannot hurt them." "I never met with such a people in my life. There are about fifty of them in Liverpool."

From the date of the following letter found among his papers, it must have been written about this time. It seems to contain a short account of his experience and labours up to that time.

AN UNFINISHED LETTER TO MR. WESLEY.

"*Halifax, April* 20, 1785.

"*Rev. and dear Sir*,—Known to me, yet unknown, I have many things to write, but am afraid of burdening you, or of taking up your precious time, which I believe you are redeeming moment by moment. I bless God that I ever heard of your name, or read your numerous works. Close doctrine and discipline I dearly love. This spring is fourteen years since I was powerfully convinced without the use of human means. The doctrine of the first Methodist preacher I ever heard was as precious ointment to my poor wounded soul. I was sure he was a servant of the living God. I have been travelling in your connexion nine years, during which time (I desire to write it with humility) God has granted me health, so that I have seldom missed preaching the whole of that time. My lot has mostly been cast in new places, to form circuits, which much exposed me to persecution. Once I was imprisoned; twice beaten; left on the high way speechless and senseless; (I must have gone into a world of spirits, had not God in mercy sent a good Samaritan that bled, and took me to a friend's house;) once shot at; guns and pistols presented at my breast; once delivered from an armed mob, in the dead time of night, on the high way, by a surprising flash of lightning; surrounded frequently by mobs; stoned frequently; I have had to escape for my life at dead time of night. O! shall I ever forget the Divine hand which has supported me. O that I could love my God more, and serve him with a more perfect heart. It was three years from my conviction, before I was brought through the pangs of the new birth. Eight months elapsed after I was called to preach, before I was willing to leave my all and go out. I wanted to live in retirement, and had almost got my own consent to sell what I had in the world, and retire to a cell. God withdrew himself from me. I was very near desperation, for I was travelling, as it were, alone. I betook myself to my room, except when I was wandering through the woods and fields, till I was worn away to a skeleton; and all this time I was kept from unbosoming myself to the lovers of Jesus. Strong impressions I had to go forth in Jehovah's name to preach the gospel. When I thought of it, I was pained to the very heart: it seemed like death, so great was the sense I had of my weakness and ignorance. By day I was drawn out in the study of the Holy Scriptures, and in the night season, when fast asleep, preaching aloud, till I have been as wet with sweat, as if dipped in a river. O! what a precious time I had when I gave up my own, to the will of God. I saw there was no other way for me to be saved. I was determined, if required, to go to the ends of the earth; yea, I promised the Lord if he would stand by me, and required it, I would go to the very mouth of hell. Blessed be God, he has been very kind and good to me ever since.

"The second year I travelled, I was powerfully convinced of the necessity of holiness. For a considerable time I waded through deep, but sweet distress. I had a discovery of the purity of the law, and the impurity of my own heart: being conscious it was my privilege to become pure in heart, I determined not to stop short of it. Sensible I was it came by faith. I was under deep exercises to preach no more, till I received that blessing. There was a time when I had a greater nearness to God, but I did not receive the witness till a twelve-month afterwards.
"F. GARRETTSON."

Soon after writing the above, it seems he received the following from Mr. Wesley, which will show in what high estimation he was held by that eminently useful man of God:—

"*Dublin, June* 16, 1785.

"*My dear brother*,—Dr. Coke gives some account of you in his journal, so that although I have not seen you, I am not a stranger to your character. By all means send me, when you have opportunity, a more particular account of your experience and travels. It is no way improbable that God may find out a way for you to visit England, and it may be the means of your receiving more strength, as well as more light. It is a very desirable thing that the children of God should communicate their experience to each other; and it is generally most profitable when they can do it face to face. Till Providence opens a way for you to see Europe, do all you can for a good Master in America.

"I am glad brother Cromwell and you have undertaken that labour of love, the visiting Nova Scotia, and doubt not but you act in full concert with the little handful who were almost alone till you came. It will be the wisest way to make all those who desire to join together, thoroughly acquainted with the whole Methodist plan, and to accustom them, from the very beginning, to the accurate observance of all our rules. Let none of them rest in being half Christians. Whatever they do, let them do it with their might, and it will be well, as soon as any of them find peace with God, to exhort them to go on to perfection. The more explicitly and strongly you press all believers to aspire after full sanctification as attainable now by simple faith, the more the whole work of God will prosper.

"I do not expect any great matters from the bishop. I doubt his eye is not single, and if it be not, he will do little good to you, or any one else. It may be a comfort to you that you have no need of him: you want nothing which he can give.

"It is a noble proposal of brother Marchington; but I doubt it will not take place. You do not know the state of the English Methodists. They do not roll in money like many of the American Methodists. It is with the utmost difficulty that we can raise five or six hundred pounds a year to supply our contingent expenses, so that it is entirely impracticable to raise five hundred pounds among them to build houses in America. It is true they might do much; but it is a sad observation, they that have most money have usually least grace. The peace of God be with all your spirits.

"I am your affectionate friend and brother,
"J. Wesley."

After visiting Digby, and forming a small society, on Tuesday, July 26th, he set sail for Liverpool; but in consequence of head winds, he did not reach his place of destination until Friday morning. Here he preached on the same evening in the Congregational meeting house, and again on Saturday, with much freedom to a people manifesting great willingness to hear the word. He continued in Liverpool about four weeks, constantly preaching and visiting from house to house, and many hearts were powerfully touched under the word, so that when he took his leave, the society had doubled its number, increasing from twenty to forty members, several of whom were savingly converted to God.

In the month of August, Mr. Garrettson left Liverpool for Shelburn; and after a passage of forty-eight hours, he arrived safely, and found a society of sixteen members. Though at the commencement of his preaching in Shelburn, he had only about fifty hearers, his congregation soon increased, so that their little chapel would not contain them all. Seeing the eagerness of the people to hear, one of the rectors of the parish, a Mr. W——, gave him the use of his pulpit, which he occupied until some of the vestry, excited to opposition by witnessing the manifest displays of awakening power under the preaching of Mr. Garrettson, interposed their authority, and he silently withdrew from the church, and immediately adopted means for enlarging their own house of worship: in the mean time he thanked the rector for his kindness, who very reluctantly acceded to the wishes of his vestry in their opposition to Mr. Garrettson.

Mr. Garrettson gives the following account of the commencement of Methodism in Liverpool. "Captain D., since gone to heaven, some time before any of us came to the place, met with Mr. Wesley's tract called *The Character of a Methodist*, and having a great desire excited to hear one of the Methodist preachers, he sent to Shelburn, and requested brother John Mann to visit them. Shortly after, Mr. Mann paid them a visit, and many of the people heard him gladly, though much opposed by the Allenites before mentioned. As he went one Lord's day to the meeting house to preach, a party of these zealous disciples were determined, if possible, to prevent it. Colonel P——, a very mild man, and a friend to all religious people, endeavoured calmly to reason with them, but to little purpose, until another magistrate spoke more authoritatively, which induced them to relinquish their design, and to permit Mr. Mann peaceably to proceed. From open opposition they resorted to secret insinuations, with a view to prejudice the people against us."

Though it had been only eight years since they began building the town of Shelburn, there were, on the arrival of Mr. Garrettson, about ten thousand inhabitants, mostly refugees—so rapidly had the town increased.

He remained about six weeks in this place, occasionally visiting some adjacent villages, during which time he received one hundred and fifty members into the society. It was not all fair weather, however, while he was here. He says he was stoned, had rotten eggs thrown at him, and when he embarked for Liverpool, the captain of a man of war cried out, "Hail for the Methodist preacher!" and soon a gun was fired, which obliged them to lower sail, and he had to submit to have his trunk examined, but was dismissed with no other annoyance than the sound of some blasphemous oaths from the sailors. "Blessed be God," says he, "they had not power to hurt me." After a stormy passage he arrived at Liverpool. Here he remained two weeks, preaching the word with much assurance and comfort. From thence he embarked for Halifax, and found the society he had left in peace. He remained in this place until the first day of February, during which time he had the happiness of receiving into society, as a broken-hearted penitent, a person who before had been famous for pouring contempt upon religion. He also visited the towns of Horton and Cornwallis, and preached with great freedom, evenings, as well as in the day time. To be idle, while he beheld so many precious souls "in the gall of bitterness and bonds of iniquity," he could not. We therefore find him braving the storms and tempests, from one place to another, travelling on foot through snow and mud, where the roads were too bad to admit his travelling on horseback, that he might, as widely as possible, extend the empire of his divine Lord and Master.

Mr. Garrettson, in his semi-centennial sermon preached and published at the request of the New-York conference, speaking of his travels in Nova Scotia, says, "I traversed the mountains and valleys, frequently on foot, with my knapsack on my back, guided by Indian paths in the wilderness, when it was not expedient to take a horse; and I had often to wade through morasses half leg deep in mud and water, frequently satisfying my hunger with a piece of bread and pork from my knapsack, quenching my thirst from a brook, and resting my weary limbs on the leaves of the trees. Thanks be to God! he compensated me for all my toil, for many precious souls were awakened and converted to God."

To these privations, labours, and sufferings, he voluntarily submitted. For however truly it may be said of some, that their circumstances in life might have compelled them to equal, or even greater hardships in another calling, that they might secure a scanty maintenance, this cannot be said of Mr. Garrettson. His patrimonial estate was amply sufficient to yield him a comfortable maintenance, simply by his exercising over it a prudential superintendence. But being called out from a sense of duty to his God and his fellow men, he willingly renounced the world "with all its pomps and vanities," and without pecuniary fee or reward, submitted to all this drudgery of labour, this "reproach of Christ," having respect solely unto the eternal "recompense of reward," and the salvation of sinners.

The following letters will more fully unfold the state and prospects of the work in which Mr. Garrettson was engaged in Nova Scotia, as well as the difficulties with which he had to contend. Those sent to him by Mr. Wesley are also inserted, because every thing coming from a man so eminently useful is very interesting: they serve moreover to explain some allusions in the letters of Mr. Garrettson, as well as to exhibit the deep interest which Mr. Wesley took in every part of the work of God, however remote from the immediate scene of his own labours.

"*Shelburn, April* 25, 1786.

"*Rev. and dear Sir,*—Some weeks ago I left Halifax, and went to Liverpool, where the Lord is carrying on a blessed work: many precious souls of late have been set at liberty to praise a sin-pardoning God. There is a lively society. Allen's small party oppose us warmly. The greater part of the town attend our ministry, and the first people have joined our society.

"A few days ago I came to this town, where I met dear afflicted brother Cromwell, and was glad to find him able to set out for Liverpool and Halifax. A negro man by the name of Morant, lately from England, who says he was sent by lady Huntingdon, has done much hurt in society among the blacks at Burch town. I believe that Satan sent him. Before he came there was a glorious work going on among these poor creatures, now (brother Cromwell not being able to attend) there is much confusion. The devil's darts are sometimes turned upon his own miserable head.

"Our chapel in Shelburn is not able to contain the congregation, and at present our friends are not able to build a larger. If I thought it right, I could wish, yea, beg for fifty or sixty pounds from England to promote the building one. Blessed be God, there are some precious souls here; but I expect many will be obliged to move to other places for want of business. The people in Halifax have had very little preaching of late, at which they are much tried. It is impossible for us to supply half the places where they want us. I have written to Mr. Asbury for help, but with no certainty of obtaining it, as the work seems to be spreading among them.

"I am an unprofitable servant, but blessed be God, the desire of my soul is to be instrumental in spreading the glorious gospel. I find a willingness to spend my all for God. I meet with many difficulties, but a moment's contemplation of the eternal world weighs down all. A man who labours for God in this country, needs a greater degree of grace, fortitude, and wisdom, than I possess. Dear sir, if you are disposed to send books to be given to the poor, or for sale, the sooner the better: let me know the conditions, and I will do the best in my power. The Saint's Rest and hymn books are wanted; the small select hymn book would sell; some pieces displaying the nature, manner, and doctrine of the Methodists; your journals and sermons; Mr. Walsh's Life; dear Mr. Fletcher's works have been a blessing in Cornwallis and Horton. I would to God they could be spread all through the country. I wrote in a former letter for some of the new prayer books adapted to the kingdom.

"We have bought two horses, which will do for the present. In some places the people will be able to support the gospel. In general they are poor; but in my opinion this country wants nothing but pure religion and industry to make it desirable. I have seldom seen a better spring in Pennsylvania or Maryland. The winter has been very moderate, except a few weeks. Much of the land is very good, and I am informed they get from twenty to forty bushels of grain from an acre; and hay and vegetables in great abundance.

"I want to die to the world, and live wholly to God. This is the constant prayer and desire of your unworthy servant,
"F. GARRETTSON."

"TO THE REV. FREEBORN GARRETTSON.

"*London, Sept.* 30, 1786.

"*My dear brother,*—I trust before this comes to hand, you and Dr. Coke will have met and refreshed each other's bowels in the Lord. I can exceedingly ill spare him from England, as I have no clergyman capable of supplying his lack of service; but I was convinced he was more wanted in America than in Europe For it is impossible but offences will come, and of yourselves will men arise speaking perverse things, and striving to draw away disciples after them. It is a wonderful blessing they are restrained so long, till the poor people are a little grounded in the faith. You have need to watch over them with your might. Let those that have set their hands to the plough, continually pray to the Lord of the harvest that he would send forth more labourers into his harvest.

"It is far better to send your journals as they are, than not to send them at all. I am afraid it is too late in the season to send books this year, but I hope Dr. Coke has brought some with him to serve you for the present. I was far off from London when he set sail. Most of those in England who have riches love money, even the Methodists, at least those who are called so. The poor are the Christians. I am quite out of conceit with almost all those who have this world's goods. Let us take care to lay up our treasure in heaven. Peace be with your spirit.

"I am your affectionate friend and brother,
"J. WESLEY."

"TO THE REV. FREEBORN GARRETTSON.
"—— —— Nov. 30, 1786.

"*My dear brother*,—You have great reason to be thankful to God, that he lets you see the fruit of your labours. Whenever any are awakened, you do well to join them together immediately. But I do not advise you to go on too fast. It is not expedient to break up more ground than you can keep; to preach at any more places than you or your brethren can constantly attend. To preach once in a place, and no more, very seldom does any good; it only alarms the devil and his children, and makes them more upon their guard against a first assault.

"Wherever there is any church service, I do not approve of any appointment the same hour; because I love the Church of England, and would assist, not oppose it, all I can. How do the inhabitants of Shelburn, Halifax, and other parts of the province, go on as to temporal things? Have they trade? Have they sufficiency of food, and the other necessaries of life? And do they increase or decrease in numbers? It seems there is a scarcity of some things, of good ink, for yours is so pale that many of your words are not legible.

"As I take it for granted you have had several conversations with Dr. Coke, I doubt not you proposed all your difficulties to him, and received full satisfaction concerning them. Commending you to him, who is able to guide and strengthen you in all things,

"I am your affectionate friend and brother,
"J. WESLEY."

"P. S. Probably we shall send a little help for your building, if we live till conference. Observe the rules for building laid down in the minutes.

"I see nothing of your journal yet. I am afraid of another American revolution. I know not how to get the enclosed safe to Dr. Coke, probably you know: on second thoughts I think it best not to write to him at present."

"A LETTER FROM MR. GARRETTSON TO MR. WESLEY.

"*Halifax, March* 10, 1787.

"*Rev. and dear Sir,*—I received yours dated London, September 30. As I have not had an opportunity of writing for a long time, I shall be the more particular in this. By a storm Dr. Coke was driven to Antigua, and it is not certain when he will be here. We are much disappointed, but hope it will all work together for good.

"My time this winter has been spent mostly in Horton, Windsor, and Cornwallis. In the former there has been a divine display; many convinced and converted to God. A few months ago the place was famous for the works of the devil—now for singing, praying, and hearing the word. If the work continue much longer as it has done, the greater part of the people will be brought in. I have had a blessed winter among them. The work greatly revives to the west. James Mann (a young man God has lately given us, whose praise is in the churches) writes, 'God is carrying on his work in a glorious manner in Barrington; the people flock from every quarter to hear the word: many have been convinced, and about fourteen have been set at liberty, some of whom were famous for all manner of wickedness. The fields here seem white for harvest.'

"Brother Cromwell has had his station in Shelburn, but is very poorly: he writes, 'There seem to be very dull times in this town: hundreds have the small pox, &c. The Lord enabled me to go on as far as Cape Negro. I could only stay to preach a few sermons, &c. It would do you good to see the dear people, some rejoicing, and others mourning. In this way they continued good part of the night: depend upon it there is a blessed revival here. I returned to Shelburn very poorly, and expect, if God spares my life, to go home early in the spring.'

"Brother John Mann at Liverpool writes, 'I am greatly comforted under an expectation of an ingathering here: the society is very lively; several added, and several lately converted,' &c. Dear sir, it would cause your heart to rejoice to know what a deadly wound Antinomianism has received in the town of Horton. My dear Master has given me one of the first lawyers in Cornwallis, and his lady.

"Brother Black is very steady and zealous in our cause, and has gone for a few weeks to the country. I can say this for Halifax, they are very kind in supporting brother Black's family: I think they give a guinea a week, and they have got a famous chapel nearly ready to preach in; it will contain a thousand people. Religion, I fear, is not very deep as yet.

"William Grandine, a young preacher, whom I mentioned in a former letter, has returned to his friends. I am under a necessity of going to the west to relieve brother Cromwell. I know not what will become of the young work in Horton: God can raise up or send us a preacher. Poor Cumberland is still mourning for want of one.

"I have received no books since I came to the province. We thought it expedient to have about fifty pounds' worth printed, as the printer was at leisure this winter. He printed several tracts very reasonably. Shall I ever see your face? Lord grant that I may be found worthy to meet you in heaven. So far I have been kept by the power of the Spirit, and I hope I shall never bring a reproach on the good cause. I want to be more given up to the work, with a greater nearness to God.

"I remain, as ever, your affectionate son,

"F. GARRETTSON."

"P. S. Since I wrote this letter I received one from brother Mann at Liverpool, saying, 'The Lord has broken in, in a wonderful manner, among the people, especially among the young. Within a few days twenty have been set at liberty: nine were converted one night.' Surely the Lord will do great things for us.

"A LETTER FROM MR. GARRETTSON TO MR. WESLEY.

"*Shelburn, Sept.* 25, 1786.

"*Rev. and dear Sir*,—Lest my other letter did not reach your hand I send this. My time this summer has been spent principally between this and Barrington, which has occasioned me many fatiguing journeys through the woods, many times half leg deep in mud and water. Blessed be God, he has supported me under all my difficulties.

"When I first made my entrance among the people at Barrington, Satan strove in every possible way to hinder. 1. The people were dissenters almost to a man. 2. There was a party of those they call New Lights, who stood in opposition, and a preacher of that denomination warned the people against me, telling them I was legal and destitute of faith. 3. A letter was sent by a Calvinist preacher who had ministered among them, warning them against an American. For a few days I was under great exercise about leaving the town, despairing of ever being the means of planting the gospel under these and other disadvantages.

"The second sabbath I preached among them many came out to hear, and a recommendatory letter was written on many hearts. Before, I had scarcely a place to lay my head; since, I have not wanted friends. I visited a small harbour a few miles off, where there were about ten families. We had a divine display of the goodness of God: very few were left behind. Of these families I have joined sixteen in society, ten of whom know the pardoning love of God to their souls. About thirty young and old have been baptized. One man cried out bitterly against his wife; went out to hear; was cut to the heart, and now both are rejoicing in the Lord. At the head of the harbour we had a gracious display; very few families escaped conviction more or less. I visited almost every family, as also on the two islands, and most of them were willing to submit to our American plan, as it is called. At the head the meeting house stands where I have joined a prosperous society, as also at another harbour. Blessed be God, there have been many as clear and as powerful conversions in this township, as I have seen in any part of the States. At different times this summer I have spent about eight weeks in the township, and have formed a small circuit, able, and willing, to support a preacher. There are about fifty members, twenty of whom I favourably hope have experienced the love of God, and many who are not in society are earnestly seeking. I appointed four leaders and two stewards. I am so far on my journey to Liverpool, and I expect to meet the Dr. in Halifax, in which place we are to hold a conference the middle of next month.

"My hope revives for Shelburn; there has been an addition, and the society has become more lively. I have given them my consent to take one hundred pounds on interest towards building a church. Most of the coloured people whom Morant drew off have returned. I shall not be satisfied till we get a preaching house in this place. I must beg some from Europe and some from the States.

"Some months ago I received a letter from Mr. Asbury, in which he intimated the desire they had of my being ordained to superintend the work in the north. I answered the letter. A few days ago I received one from *the Dr.* on the same subject. Three considerations caused doubts to arise in my mind in relation to this important question. 1. The great desire I have of seeing England sooner or later. 2. My unfitness for so great a work. 3. There are many in your connexion so much more fit for the place. I love the connexion, and want to do every thing in my power to promote it. Perhaps when I shall receive a letter from you, and meet with the Dr., more light will be cast on the subject. Don't think hard of my not sending my journal.

"I have not heard from brother Cromwell for some time. Brother Black informs there is a moving in Halifax. I desire your prayers and counsel God is love, and I wish to be more humble.

"I still remain your affectionate, though unworthy son,
"F. Garrettson."

"FROM MR. WESLEY TO MR. GARRETTSON.

"*Macclesfield, July* 16, 1787.

"*My dear brother,*—I have your letter of March 15, and that of May 20. In the former you give me a pleasing account of the work of God in Halifax and other towns in Nova Scotia; and indeed every where except poor Shelburn, from which I had an excellent account a few years ago. Shall the first be last? What could have occasioned the decrease of the work there? St. Paul's advice is certainly good for all Methodist preachers,—that it is good for a man not to touch a woman; and ' if thou mayst be free, use it rather:' and yet I dare not exclude those who marry out of our connexion, or forbid to marry; but happy are those who having no necessity laid upon them, stand fast in the glorious liberty. I commend you for laying as little burden upon the poor people as possible.

"Before I had printing presses of my own I used to pay two and thirty shillings for printing two and twenty pages duodecimo. The paper was from twelve to sixteen shillings a ream. I do not blame you for printing those tracts.

"But you do not send me your journal yet: surely you have had time enough to write it over. Dr. Coke seems to think you are irresolute, yet not willing to take advice.

I hope better things of you, and your heart says to God and man, what I know not, teach thou me.

"I am your affectionate friend and brother,

"J. WESLEY."

The following letter to Mr. Asbury, though dated before some of the preceding, is inserted here, that the whole correspondence with Mr. Wesley might appear together.

"A LETTER FROM MR. GARRETTSON TO MR. ASBURY.

"———— ———— 1786.

"*My very dear brother,*—I had the pleasure of receiving yours dated Charlestown, January 15, 1786, and considered the contents. I had strange feelings on reading the account of poor G———g, but was happy to hear of my dear old friend, brother Cole. I fear there is a wide door open for the last b———p to do us much hurt. O that our dear Lord and Master may lay to his hand, and let the blind world know that there is a God in Israel.

"I have seen neither brother Cromwell, Black, or Mann, since last fall, though I have frequently conversed with them by letter. My time this winter has been in Halifax, and in the different towns between that and Annapolis. In Cornwallis the last time I was there I put a chapel on foot; there were nearly five hundred dollars subscribed: how they will manage I know not. On my return I put one on foot in Windsor. In this town God has given us a loving society. A few friends are willing to build one at Annapolis, though they have had very little preaching for six months. This day they began to draw stone for building a church in this town also. It is to be the same size of that of Mr. White, except a pitch higher. I have preached several sermons in Dartmouth, a new town, six miles from this. They seem very desirous, and made an offer of erecting a small house of worship, if we would pay attention to them.

"God willing, what time I have to stay in this town I expect to spend as follows, viz. Sunday eight o'clock preach in our little chapel, which will hold about four hundred persons; ten o'clock preach in the poor house, where there are about a hundred people;—I gave them books which attached them to me; I hope great good will be done among them;—at twelve o'clock in the preaching house; four o'clock in a private house by the dock yard; and by candle light in the chapel. I preach every night in the week: Friday visit the prisoners. After all I feel myself a poor needy creature. You desired me to send our minutes. I wanted to have a little conference in this place the first of April, and to have sent a full account to your conference: but this cannot be, and as I know brother Cromwell's mind, I shall give you as full an account as I can. Halifax, where there are forty members, will employ one preacher; Horton circuit will employ another, where I left sixty members; Annapolis circuit will employ another, where I left nearly one hundred members last fall; but how they are now I know not. In these three districts I expect brother Cromwell, brother Black, and brother Grandine, will be stationed. This brother Grandine is a young man we have taken on trial: I think he will be a preacher. Brother Mann must take his station at Liverpool, where there are about forty members.

"There is Cumberland, where there is nothing but sin and the devil to hinder our gospel. This place would employ two preachers: however, one at present would do. There are about fifty members. In and around Shelburn there are between two and three hundred members, white and black. Much hurt has been done by a black man sent by lady Huntingdon, as brother Cromwell was not able to attend them constantly. Then there is the city of St. John's, and the country all around: I suppose there are twenty thousand souls. A few of our friends are scattered in that part; but in all that space there is only one clergyman, an old church parson. I was informed by a respectable man from the east, that there are hundreds of souls entirely destitute of the gospel. I have heard very little from Newfoundland: Mr. Wesley has sent brother Megary there, as I am informed by Dr. Coke. So you may see we are in want of three preachers. I made bold to open matters to Mr. Wesley, and begged of him to send one preacher from England, as a number of people would prefer an Englishman to an American. Many have refused hearing me on this account. However, this prejudice would soon wear away. The Lord knows I am willing to do every thing in my power for the furtherance of the gospel: but as to confining myself to Nova Scotia, or any part of the world, I could not; a good God does not require it of me.

"There are several thousand coloured people in this province, and the greater part of them are willing to be instructed. What do you think of sending Harry here this spring? I think he would be very useful. I have no doubt but the people will support their preachers in this country. It would be very well if the preachers who come would bring money to pay their passage; for we have but little money in hand, having been under the necessity of buying two horses.

"Next week I purpose to go to Shelburn, where I expect to meet brother Cromwell: if we think it expedient, and have an opportunity, one of us will attend conference, where we can state matters fairly. I send this letter lest I should have no other opportunity. A preacher will not do here unless he is able to take a circuit. Let him be in orders.

"Yours in love,
"F. GARRETTSON.

"P. S. In Horton the Lord has given us a kind friend, though not converted, Mr. Crane. He and his brother-in-law have offered two hundred dollars towards building a church in that town. There are many places I should be glad to visit, if there were preachers to supply the places already mentioned. Dr. Coke wrote to me to visit Newfoundland last fall, but it was not practicable."

The preceding letters contain so full and explicit an account of the state of things in Nova Scotia, as well as the manner in which Mr. Garrettson filled up every moment of time in his Master's work, that the necessity of copious extracts from his journal is superseded. As his travels in this province form a very important era in the history of his life, I thought it necessary to be as particular as the limits of this work will allow in the details of his sufferings and labours in that country. Certainly his diligence and zeal, his self-denial, his prayerfulness and watchfulness, as well as the privations endured in this cold region of country, while they speak in the language of rebuke to "the slothful servant," may be exhibited as an example of encouragement to those zealous preachers who are emulous to excel in "every good work" connected with their high and responsible calling.

The following anecdotes and reflections are from the pen of his amiable and pious daughter, to whose diligence in selecting from her venerable father's papers, and transcribing them, these memoirs are greatly indebted.

"Thus has my dear and honoured father ended his notes to his printed journal. When they were commenced and when ended I cannot precisely say, but I think it is one of the last testimonies which he has left, probably written very near the close of his devoted life. His memory was stored with a rich fund of anecdote, and I regret exceedingly that of many passages of his life he has left no record. His journals while in Nova Scotia, except those in print, are I believe lost. I have been able to find only short notices of his labours while there, and among my earliest and most pleasant recollections are the details which my dear father used to give me of his residence in that region of frost and snow. I well remember the delight with which I used to climb his knee, and the importunity with which I used to beg for a story about *Nova Scotia;*—and in riper years—but those halcyon days are for ever flown: tears will not recall them. At one time in order to attend his appointment, he rode through an unfrequented country, the hail driving in his face until nearly benumbed, he was obliged to lay the reins on the neck of his horse, and leave the animal by his own instinct to keep the road. There was no visible track, and turning out of the road in that country exposed the traveller to the greatest fatigue, as his horse sunk in the mass of unbeaten snow. At length he arrived at the only house he had seen; his horse stopped at the door, and he had only life enough left to walk in and throw himself on the bed. None but children were within, who covered him with plenty of bed clothes, while he lay almost insensible for nine hours, and had nearly forfeited his valuable life by too great eagerness in his Master's cause.

"He had often to cross the St. John's, whose tide recedes, leaving its bed nearly empty, and again comes roaring up with great velocity and force, sweeping every thing before it, and elevating on its waves the vessels and ships which it had left dry. During its recession its bed is fordable; but in winter the crossing is dangerous on account of the large masses of ice it leaves behind. On one occasion his guide, instead of leading him up the river, went down, and they were not apprized of their danger until they saw the tide fast roaring towards them. The guide shrieked out, 'Put spurs to your horse and make for the nearest land!' He did so, although uncertain whether it would be accessible when attained, for the shores thereabout were very bold and rugged. His horse was fleet; the shore was accessible; he outrode the wave, which swept over the back of his horse just as he had set foot upon the land. I have often heard my father say that if he had only been half the length of his horse's body behind, he should have been swept off like a feather on the tide."

It appears that Mr. Garrettson continued to travel and preach in this province until April 10, 1787, when he embarked for Boston, Mass., leaving as a testimony of his fidelity and success in his Lord's vineyard, about six hundred members in society. After a perilous passage of three days he arrived in Boston, where he was kindly received by a few pious friends.

About seventeen years before the visit of Mr. Garrettson, Mr. Boardman, one of the European Methodist preachers, had preached in Boston, and formed a small society; but not being succeeded by any minister of the same order, the society gradually diminished, so that at the time of which we are now speaking, there were only three left. Not being admitted to any of the pulpits in this city, Mr. Garrettson preached a few sermons in some private houses, and on Monday, April 17, he passed on to Providence in Rhode Island, where he says he found several who loved the Lord Jesus. Here he was invited by the Presbyterian minister, the Rev. Mr. Snow, who he says was a worthy and pious man, to preach in his church, which he did twice to a numerous and attentive audience. Passing from thence to Newport, he preached by invitation in the meeting house morning and evening to a numerous assembly, among whom he rejoiced to find some, as he believed, eminently pious. He then sailed for New-York, where, after a passage of forty-eight hours, he arrived in safety, and was much refreshed in meeting his old friends, and participating with their joy in a revival of religion with which they had been favoured. After preaching on the Lord's day with much satisfaction, and spending a few days in visiting some of his Christian friends, he went forward to Philadelphia, where he preached a few times, "took sweet counsel" with his brethren, and departed for Baltimore, where he arrived on Tuesday, and "my heart," says he, "was made glad while I sat in Conference with many of my old friends, the servants of Jesus."

It was now eleven years since Mr. Garrettson commenced his itinerating labours. When he entered this arduous field, there were three thousand one hundred and forty-eight members in the societies, and nineteen preachers; they were now increased to twenty thousand six hundred and eighty-one members, and one hundred and seventeen preachers; making an increase of seventeen thousand four hundred and thirty-three members, and ninety-eight preachers. Although others contributed their portion towards this extension of the work of God, it must be evident to all who impartially consult the preceding pages, that Mr. Garrettson was among the most active, zealous, and successful of them all. Indeed, as the Rev. Ezekiel Cooper, who, after his awakening and conversion as before mentioned, was intimately acquainted with Mr. Garrettson, observed to me, he seemed to be all devotion, full of prayer and faith; and his preaching was attended with the mighty power of God. Listening multitudes hung on his lips with the most fixed attention, while the Spirit of God, which so eminently accompanied his word, powerfully wrought upon their hearts, extorting the anxious inquiry, "What must we do to be saved?"

CHAPTER XII.

Attends Conference in Baltimore—Elected superintendent of the societies in British America—Strong solicitations to accept the office—Reasons for declining—Appointed to the Peninsula—Contrast between the present and former state of the people here—Methodism generally prosperous—But some delusions—Their cause—Closes his labours in this place.

WE have traced the life of our venerable father in the gospel thus far, having been guided by his printed and manuscript journals. We have seen him contending with the cold, the snow, the mud and water of the north, and seen him triumphing in the midst of these and other privations of that inhospitable climate, from a consciousness of the divine approbation and the prospect of usefulness to the souls of men; until, having completed his mission in these parts, he found himself once more seated among his beloved brethren in these United States.

To give a faithful narrative of the events of his life, it is necessary to detail some of the transactions of this conference, which was held in Baltimore, May 1, 1787. It seems that Mr. Wesley having witnessed the sincerity, zeal, and devotedness of Mr. Garrettson in the work of the ministry, had designated him as the future superintendent in the British dominions in America. Dr. Coke, on his arrival to this conference, made known the wishes of Mr. Wesley in this respect, and the subject was submitted to the conference, and was by that body "unanimously sanctioned." Mr. Garrettson, with a view to correct an erroneous statement which had been made of this affair, gives in his "semi-centennial sermon" a fair and candid narration of the facts in the case. He says that after the conference had approved of his appointment to this office by Mr. Wesley, "Dr. Coke, as Mr. Wesley's delegate and representative, asked me if I would accept of the appointment. I requested the liberty of deferring my answer until the next day. I think on the next day the Dr. came to my room and asked me if I had made up my mind to accept of my appointment: I told him I had upon certain conditions. I observed to him that I was willing to go on a tour, and visit those parts to which I was appointed for one year, and if there was a cordiality in the appointment with those whom I was requested to serve, I would return to the next conference, and receive ordination for the office of superintendent. His reply was, 'I am perfectly satisfied,' and he gave me a recommendatory letter to the brethren in the West Indies, &c. I had intended as soon as conference rose, to pursue my voyage to the West India Islands, to visit Newfoundland and Nova Scotia, and in the spring to return. What transpired in the conference during my absence, I know not; but I was astonished when the appointments were read, to hear my name mentioned to preside in the Peninsula."

It would appear from this plain statement of Mr. Garrettson, that some alteration took place in the mind of the conference respecting his appointment to the superintendency of the British provinces in America, and that it was finally agreed among themselves that it was not expedient that he should go at this time. Probably knowing the value of his services in his Lord's vineyard, and being comparatively young as a church, they were unwilling to have him so entirely separated from them. However this may be, it is certain that it was a source of disappointment to himself, of some grief to Mr. Wesley, and contrary to the wishes of many of his brethren in Nova Scotia, as the following extracts of letters will show:—

Mr. Black in a letter dated Cornwallis, March 10, 1787, and presumed—for the inscription is torn off—to be directed to Dr. Coke, says:—" Brother Garrettson has been a great blessing to us in this province. The hearts of the people and preachers are more than ever united to him; and we believe that were he to return to us he would be more extensively useful than heretofore; for the ears of the people are more than ever open to hear his message. He is better acquainted with the peculiar dispositions of the people than any one else, and therefore would be most likely to do them good. Thinking it to be his duty to attend the conference in the United States, we fear when he finds so many urgent calls for help in that extensive country, that he will be tempted to forget us in this dark corner of the world. At the same time we cannot but think it to be his duty to return. We are truly sorry that he refused the superintendency,* but hope when he sees you he may receive that honour. These lines are to request you to use your influence in persuading him to do so."

In a letter to Mr. Garrettson himself, dated at Shelburn, June 4, 1788, Mr. Black thus expresses himself:—"I have heard nothing from you these six months. We have been expecting you a long time, but in vain. Do, my dear brother, make all the speed you can. Let none persuade you to the contrary. Do, my dear brother, come away directly." In another of June 30, 1788, he thus earnestly addresses Mr. Garrettson:—"O my dear brother, do come away as soon as possible. The hearts of the people are knit to you in a peculiar manner, and I believe you would be more useful than ever; and you know your labours were before blessed to many precious souls. Come away! come away, my dear brother, come away! O do not let any persuade you to stay. You know you have Bishop Asbury's consent to come: besides the people are ready to think you are forgetful of your words, as they expected you long since."† Once more under date of

* This must have reference to his appointment to that office by Mr. Wesley, as at the date of this letter Mr. Garrettson had not been elected by the conference.

† Perhaps these expressions were founded on a letter which Mr.

August 14, of the same year, Mr. Black says, "O! my dear brother, do make haste and come away to Nova Scotia. The friends long to see you, and our circumstances call for you. Come once more and help us."

Mr. James Mann, another preacher who was travelling in Nova Scotia at this time, under date of Feb. 2, 1788, after detailing some of the embarrassments under which they laboured, says to Mr. Garrettson, "O brother! pray for us. Heaven bless and prosper you in the vineyard of the Lord. I long to see you, and we have been looking for you, and hope we shall not be disappointed of your coming in the spring."

Mr. Alexander Anderson, likewise a travelling preacher in that country, writes to Mr. Garrettson under date of June 17, 1788, thus:—"We have ardently longed for your return to this province; and have expected you for some time past. We trust, however, that the charge you have received in the United States is for the glory of God and the good of souls."

Surely no testimonies could be more honourable, or invitations more pressing. The idea, however, was finally abandoned by Mr. Garrettson of returning to Nova Scotia, or of accepting the superintendency of the work in the Garrettson had written some time previously to Mr. Baxter of Antigua, of which the following is an extract.

"*Maryland, Sept.* 10, 1787.

"*My very dear brother*,—I have been earnestly solicited by Dr. Coke and others to become a member of the British conference in British America. I expect to meet Mr. Asbury in a few weeks, and know not but I shall be with you late in the fall. I want to act in that sphere in which I shall the most glorify my dear Lord. The cause of God lies near my heart: though my connexions here are very near to me, yet at the call of my God I could cheerfully leave them.

"I expected to be in Halifax before this, but there was none to take charge of the work in this quarter, so that necessity called me to stay. I fear lest our societies should decline in that country. The work is very great in the States."

British provinces, for which he assigns the following reasons:—" 1. I was not acquainted with all the preachers, especially with those who were lately from England. 2. I felt unqualified for the charge. 3. I was not clear that I had a call to leave the United States." Of whatever use he might have been to the people in that country, subsequent events have justified the belief that his labours were both highly prized and eminently useful in the United States, and the whole tenor of his life proves that he strove to move in the order of Divine providence.

Having thus relinquished the thought of returning to Nova Scotia, and having received his appointment to preside in the Peninsula as above stated, he entered upon his work with his accustomed diligence, though not without some pressure of spirit, as he had reason to suspect that some unfriendliness had been manifested towards him, though he knew not by whom. To Dr. Coke he felt a strong attachment and the sincerest affection, and says that they " mingled their tears together at this conference."

Perhaps no place on the continent could have been more agreeable to him as the field of his labour, than the Peninsula. It was here that he had spent the first days of his ministry, where the Lord had given him signal displays of his approbation, and where he had suffered beating and imprisonment for the cause of his adorable Master. The effect of his former labours, however, was now most visible. The storm of human passion was hushed to silence—tranquillity reigned—and he now felt himself in more danger from the caresses of his friends, than he before had done from the peltings of his enemies. Being now among his old friends, many of whom were his spiritual children, the ardour of his soul burst forth, as it were, anew, and he found himself, in some sense, unexpectedly in the midst of every thing calculated to make life agreeable. He continued in this part of the country about twelve months, during which time he visited every circuit, and almost every congregation, and was greatly refreshed and strengthened in his work. Multitudes flocked to hear the word, some excited from curiosity to see the man of whom so much had been said in former days, some from a desire to "learn the way of the Lord more perfectly," and numbers more to hear again from the lips of this flaming messenger of Christ, those precious truths which they had found to be "the power of God to their salvation." So great, indeed, was the attention given to the "words of this life," that Mr. Garrettson observes, "that it seemed as if they would all become Methodists."

Though this was the general aspect of affairs in this favoured region of country, there were some exceptions. In Dorset county, which he visited on the third of June, he was glad to meet a large congregation of attentive hearers, to whom he preached under the shade of a grove, as the house could not contain so numerous an audience. On this occasion he observes, that some time since there was a great work of God on this neck of land, but now it seems the work is quite stationary, if not on the decline. As a reason for this he remarks that "those preachers whose labours had been particularly blessed in this revival were lively and powerful in their ministrations, so that some thought there was much of what is called wild fire among the people. Indeed the cries of the distressed were frequently so loud, that the voice of the preacher was drowned. I was informed that these people had been visited by some who had but little fellowship for what they called *noisy meetings*, in consequence of which the work began to decline. Extremes are always dangerous; and happy the man who knows how to keep in the golden mean. I am never offended in hearing convinced sinners cry aloud for mercy; neither do I doubt but that the children of God are so happy at times, that they are constrained to shout the praises of God."

To distinguish between the mere excitement of human

passions, and the operations of the Spirit of God, is highly important, though sometimes difficult, to the promotion of the work of grace. When the Spirit of God operates upon the human heart, the passions are less or more excited, either to sorrow or joy, according to the moral state of the heart. To suppose, therefore, a work of grace without the excitement of the human passions, is as great an absurdity as it would be to expect a man to breathe without any movement of the lungs, the organs of respiration. That the passions may be under strong excitement where there is no genuine work of the Holy Spirit forms no valid objection to this position. In the first case the " fruits of the Spirit" follow; in the latter not; and "by their fruits ye shall know them."

He continued in the Peninsula until May 1788, during which time a day seldom passed but that he preached at least once, and sometimes twice or three times with great freedom. Though there was not so large an increase to the societies as in former days when he laboured there, many were edified in the church, in the several counties on the eastern shore of Maryland, through all of which he travelled during the year.

CHAPTER XIII.

Proposes visiting New-England—Stops in New-York—Takes charge of the northern district—Enters on his work with twelve young preachers under his oversight—General state of the country—Correspondence with Mr. Wesley—Second tour through his district—Death of Mr. Cook—Curious conversation—Origin of Methodism in Ashgrove—Dangerously wounded—Commencement of Methodism on Long Island—Mr. Garrettson visits there—Obstacles to the progress of truth—Attends the first Council in Baltimore—Journal of a tour through a part of New England to Boston—Attends conference in New-York—Comparative view of the work in this part of the country.

HAVING completed his labours in the Peninsula, and being very solicitous to visit the New-England states, where the Methodists had made yet but a feeble impression, by the request and approbation of Bishop Asbury, Mr. Garrettson left this scene of his successful toil in May 1788, and came to the north, having Boston particularly in his view. Arriving at New-York, the stationed preacher, Mr. Hickson, being at the point of death, and Mr. Dickins, the other preacher, in ill health, he was solicited by the people to remain with them, and supply the pulpits. Believing the call to be urgent, he complied with their request, and continued in the city, except some occasional excursions on Long Island and the New Rochelle circuits, until the ensuing conference. Having received several invitations from a variety of places, backed by similar ones directed to the conference, Mr. Garrettson relinquished the idea of visiting Boston for the present, and took charge of the northern district of country bordering on the Hudson river.

It seems that since the year 1785, in consequence of there being but few preachers ordained to the office of elder, a number of deacons and preachers were placed under the special oversight of some one of the elders, that the people might be the better supplied with the ordinances of the gospel. These elders were instructed to travel at large through the bounds of their respective districts, hold quarterly meetings, preach and administer the ordinances, assist and direct the preachers under their care in their work. This is the origin among us of presiding elders, though they were not designated by that name in the minutes of conference until the year 1797. Mr. Garrettson had been appointed to this charge on the Peninsula, and indeed he had exercised a similar oversight while in Nova Scotia, as well as during part of his labours before he went to that country. To this office he was more especially appointed at this conference, with a view to open new circuits, for which he seems to have been peculiarly qualified, and in which he was remarkably successful.

He observes that as it had pleased the Lord to thrust out a number of young men in the New-York conference, Bishop Asbury, our venerable father in the gospel, "requested me to take charge of them, and do the best I could. I was very uneasy in my mind, being unacquainted with the country, an entire stranger to its inhabitants, there being no Methodist societies farther north than West Chester; but I gave myself to earnest prayer for direction. I knew that the Lord was with me. In the night season, in a dream, it seemed as if the whole country up the North river, as far as lake Champlain, east and west, was open to my view.

"After the conference adjourned I requested the young men to meet me. Light seemed so reflected on my path, that I gave them directions where to begin, and which way to form their circuits. I also appointed the time for each quarterly meeting, requested them to take up a collection in every place where they preached, and told them that I should go up the north river to the extreme parts of the work, visiting the towns and cities on the way, and in my return I should visit them all, and hold their quarterly meetings. I had no doubt but that the Lord would do wonders, for the young men were pious, zealous, and laborious."

Having thus laid down the plan for their work, he set out for the north on his intended tour. A great portion of the country through which he was appointed to labour, especially the northern part of New-York state, and Vermont, was in a very barren state as it respects religion. Some scattering congregations, consisting of Lutherans, and Dutch Reformed, and some others, were established along the eastern and western sides of the Hudson; but even in these the distinguishing doctrines of the gospel were but feebly supported, and rarely made the subject of experience. The settlements on the west side of the river, at a small distance from its margin, were quite new, the roads bad, and accommodations for preachers very poor. The same may be said of all the country north of Lansingburg. In respect to that portion of New England which was included in the district of country allotted to Mr. Garrettson as the scene of his present labours, though it was regularly divided into parishes, each of which generally had a settled pastor, yet experimental religion was at a low ebb. The theological tenets also, chiefly inculcated in this country, were diametrically opposed to some points of doctrine promulgated by the Methodists. The former embraced all the peculiarities of the Calvinistic system, while the latter embraced those of the Arminian. On this account I suppose that in no place did the Methodist preachers meet with more decided opponents or more forward disputants than in New England. Though the preachers laboured principally to inculcate experimental and practical godliness, as being the most essential to man's happiness and salvation, yet to promote this object the most effectually, they found it necessary frequently to bring before their hearers those peculiarities of their theological system by which it was distinguished from Calvinism. This gave offence to the clergy who tenaciously held to the latter, and provoked them to controversy. From them a disputatious spirit descended to their hearers, many of whom considered themselves fully competent to defend those abstruse points of divinity, and thus mingled their ignorance with a love of controversy, often involving themselves in a labyrinth of intricate reasonings which they could neither understand themselves nor explain to others, much less defend against the plain declarations of inspired Scripture. These circumstances often obliged the Methodist preachers, after delivering their discourses, to encounter a spirit of opposition as irksome to an ingenuous mind, as it is unprofitable to a hardened heart. Frequently, however, the pointed question, "Have you been converted to God?" put by one of these flaming messengers of God, would silence debate, and produce a conviction, at least in the minds of some of the hearers, of the superior advantage of experimental over a merely theoretical knowledge of divine things.

This was the general state of the country, and of the people where Mr. Garrettson was appointed at this time to labour. He entered, however, upon his task with the same ardour of soul, and applied himself to the work with the same indefatigable and untiring zeal by which he had before been distinguished. Passing up the country on the east side of the Hudson, through New Rochelle, North Castle, Bedford, Peekskill, in all of which places he stopped to administer the word of life, he arrived at Rhinebeck, where he lodged with Thomas Tillotson, Esq., and the next day preached in a barn, on, "We preach Christ Jesus, unto the Jews a stumbling block, and unto the Greeks foolishness." Before he left the place he preached several sermons, and the number of hearers continually increased. He was generally received in this, as well as other places, as a commissioned messenger of God, and "one said he need not change his appearance to be received as an angel."

After having passed through the northern part of his district, he returned and found that the Lord had abundantly blessed the labours of the preachers in almost every place. "Many houses," says he, "and hands, and hearts were opened; and before the commencement of the winter, we had several large circuits formed; and the most of the preachers were comfortably situated, sinners in a variety of places began to enquire what they should do to be saved.

"Satan and his children were much alarmed, and began on every hand to threaten us. Some said, 'They are good men;' others said, 'Nay, they are deceivers of the people.' A stranger from Vermont, on his way down the country, informed the people that we were spread all through the country through which he came. This sudden spread of our preachers caused some person to say, 'I know not from whence they all come, unless from the clouds.' Others said, 'The king of England hath sent them to disaffect the people; and they did not doubt but they would bring on another war:' while others gave it as their opinion that we were the false prophets spoken of in Scripture, who should come in the last days, and deceive, if it were possible, the very elect. Among others, the ministers of the different denominations were alarmed, fearing lest we should break up their congregations; and frequently coming to hear, some of them openly opposed, declaring publicly that the doctrine was false. The power of the Lord attended the word, and a great reformation was seen among the people; and many were enabled to speak freely and feelingly of what God had done for their souls. My custom was to go round the district every three months, and then return to New-York; where I commonly stayed about two weeks. In going once round I usually travelled about a thousand miles, and preached upwards of a hundred sermons."

During the above tour, he informs us of his being frequently occupied, when not engaged in travelling and preaching, in writing. It seems that Mr. Wesley, having heard much of Mr. Garrettson's experience, activity, and success in his Lord's work, had been very desirous of receiving a written account of these things from himself. After considerable hesitancy, he concluded to gratify the wishes of Mr. Wesley in this respect, and accordingly set himself to transcribing such parts of his journal as he thought would be most beneficial to give to the public. Fearing, however, that he should not live to receive it unless sent immediately, and that Mr. Garrettson was unnecessarily scrupulous on this subject, Mr. Wesley addressed to him the following letter:—

"FROM MR. WESLEY TO MR. GARRETTSON.

"*London, Jan.* 24, 1789.

"*My dear brother,*—It signifies but little where we are, so we are but fully employed for our good Master. Whether you went, therefore, to the east, it is all one, so you were labouring to promote his work. You are following the order of his providence wherever it appeared, as a holy man strongly expressed it, in a kind of holy disordered order. But there is one expression that occurs twice or thrice in yours, which gives me some concern: you speak of finding *freedom* to do this or that. This is a word much liable to be abused. If I have plain Scripture or plain reason for doing a thing, well. These are my rules, and my only rules. I regard not whether I had freedom or no. This is an unscriptural expression, and a very fallacious rule. I wish to be in every point, great and small, a scriptural rational Christian.

"In one instance, formerly, you promised to send me your journal. Will you break your word, because you do not find freedom to keep it! Is not this enthusiasm? O be not of this way of thinking. You know not whither it may lead you. You are called to square your useful life below by reason and by grace. But whatever you do with regard to me, you must do quickly, or you will no more in this world.

"Your affectionate friend and brother,

"J. WESLEY."

The journal was sent, but in consequence of the loss of the ship in which it was despatched, it never arrived. Of this circumstance Mr. Garrettson was not apprized until the following letters from Mr. Wesley gave him the information.

"*Chester, July* 15, 1789.

"*My dear brother,*—You are entirely in the right. There can be no manner of doubt that it was the enemy of souls that hindered your sending me your experience. Many parts of both of your inward and outward experience ought by no means to be suppressed. But if you are minded to send any thing to me, you have no time to lose. Whatever you do for me you must do quickly lest death have quicker wings than love. A great man observes that there is a three fold leading of the Spirit: some he leads by giving them on every occasion apposite texts of *Scripture*; some by suggesting *reasons* for every step they take, (the way by which he chiefly leads me,) and some by *impressions*; but he judges the last to be the least desirable way, as it is often impossible to distinguish dark impressions from divine, or even diabolical.

"I hope you will not long delay to write more particularly to your affectionate friend and brother,

"J. WESLEY."

"FROM MR. WESLEY TO MR. GARRETTSON.

"*London, Feb.* 3, 1790.

"*My dear brother,*—Two or three weeks ago I had the pleasure of a letter from you, dated August 23, 1789, giving me a comfortable account of the swift and extensive progress of the work of God in America. You likewise informed me that you had written an account of your life, and directed it should be sent to me; and I have been expecting it, from day to day, ever since, but have now almost given over my expectation; for, unless it comes soon it will hardly overtake me in the present world. You see time has shaken me by the hand, and death is not far behind. While we live let us work our Lord's work betimes, and in his time he will give us our full reward.

"I am your affectionate friend and brother,

"J. WESLEY."

While Mr. Garrettson was finishing a letter in which he designed to enclose another copy of his journal, the public prints announced to him the death of that great man of God, the Rev. John Wesley. Being thus disappointed of gratifying the desires of his venerable friend, Mr. Garrettson concluded to print the journal, somewhat enlarged, in America. It was republished in Europe, both in the English and French languages, and has no doubt proved a blessing to very many souls.

June 9, 1789, Mr. Garrettson set off on another tour to the north. According to his usual custom, as he passed through the towns, he stopped and preached to the people, and generally found much attention to the word. On Sunday the 14th, he preached in the town of Bedford, and formed a society. Though the people in this place had been educated in the Calvinistic faith, many of them became convinced of its errors, and were glad to hear a system of doctrines exhibited more consistent with the divine perfections, and better adapted to the condition of man. Both at the Stony-street church on the morning of the 16th, and at the English church in the evening at Peekskill, he found much freedom in preaching the word of truth; and at General Van Cortlandt's, where he lodged for the night, he found an agreeable and an affectionate family.

After passing through the highlands, and preaching at Mr. Jackson's, where he found a people apparently struggling after the liberty of God's children, he paid a visit to Mr. Cook, an exemplary and zealous preacher, whom he found near death, but his soul was happy in the enjoyment of his God. He died in peace soon after. He had been fifteen years in the work of the ministry, was a son of affliction, naturally subject to great dejection of spirits, too modest to complain, and in the midst of his sufferings evinced by his patient submission to the allotments of providence his constant faith in God. "The last words I heard him utter," says Mr. Garrettson, were, "I feel myself an unprofitable servant, but Jesus is precious to my soul. I am now reminded of what I have often told the people in my preaching of the happiness of dying saints. I now see angels around my bed, waiting to convey my happy soul to heaven." At Dr. Bartlett's he met Bishop Asbury, in company with one of the preachers, with whom he took sweet counsel, heard him preach, and then passed on to Rhinebeck, where he preached, and found a few whose hearts the Lord had touched, but felt somewhat distressed on account of the indifference manifested by most of the people to the things of eternity. Perhaps he little thought at that time that this place was to become his future residence, connected with a partner in life so admirably qualified to participate in his joys and sorrows. From Rhinebeck he went to Hudson, and thence to Albany, (visiting the intermediate places,) where he preached in the assembly room, but found much opposition among the citizens generally to the truths he delivered. A few, however, bowed a willing obedience to the word, and a small society seemed to be in a flourishing state. In Schenectady also he found a strong current of prejudice setting in against his endeavours to do good, though he was permitted to preach in the English church. The good seed, however, sown in these places, did not entirely " fall by the way side," as some are yet living who received their first religious impressions under Mr. Garrettson's preaching, and how many will be found " in that day," who can tell?

The following conversation which Mr. Garrettson relates shows the pernicious influence which an erroneous doctrine has over the hearts and practices of some people. " Monday, July 6," he says, "I set out on a journey to the north, and on my way I overtook an old gentleman, who said, ' I expect you are a minister. O! it is a blessed work if you are called to it. I am a follower of Christ, and know my peace made with God.' How, said I, do you know that? ' By the spirit which he has given me.' Do you, said I, know that your sins are forgiven? 'O yes.' Do you, said I, live in sin? 'Yes, we are all sinners.' Pray, said I, how can you know your sins forgiven, if you live in sin? 'I have the imputed righteousness of Christ, and it is no more I that do it, but sin that dwells in me.' Don't you, said I, swear sometimes? 'Swear, yes, and I have been drunk too, many times since I was made a new creature, but my comfort is, I cannot fall.' What, said I, would become of your soul if you were to die drunk? 'Die drunk! what would you think to see the sun fall? was it ever known that a saint died drunk? Impossible!' Well, said I, according to your doctrine, if you always keep yourself intoxicated with strong liquor, you will never die. Sin made man mortal; but I cannot find from Scripture that drunkenness makes him immortal. 'Sir,' said he, 'I perceive you are a rank Arminian, and I would not go the length of my foot to hear you preach, for you are an accuser of the brethren; and hold out a very uncomfortable doctrine to God's dear children.' Pray, said I, to what denomination do you profess to belong? 'I am an old Englishman, and a convert of Mr. Whitefield's, and a New Light by profession, from the sole of my foot to the crown of my head.' After I endeavoured to set his danger before him, I wished him well; and riding thirty miles I found great liberty to preach my dear Lord's gospel, from the language of the jailer, 'What shall I do to be saved?'"

Passing through the country, and preaching to attentive congregations, he came to Ashgrove, where he found a number of kind friends, members of society, who had erected a house of worship. He observes that when he first visited that place, he found some Methodist emigrants from Ireland, most of whom, however, had become quite lukewarm in religion, but who were reanimated by his preaching, and quite a number of others were awakened to a sense of the importance of religion. On this circuit Mr. Darius Dunham had been instrumental in the conversion of a number of souls, so that on the present visit Mr. Garrettson found a thriving society.

Perhaps the following sketch of the rise of the society in Ashgrove may not be uninteresting to the reader. It is taken chiefly from a communication from the Rev. D. Brayton, published in the Methodist Magazine for 1827. Before the revolutionary war, a Mr. Ashton emigrated from Ireland to this place, who, in conjunction with Mr. Philip Embury—the same Embury who had been instrumental in raising the society in New-York—formed a society at Ashgrove. It seems that after the arrival of the regular preachers from England, Mr. Embury not finding his services needed in New-York, in company with some others of the society, removed to this placé. They had no help until the arrival of Mr. John Baker, also an Irish emigrant, in the year 1786. After his arrival, he made several efforts to obtain the assistance of some travelling preacher, but was not successful, on account of the paucity of their number, until 1788, when, in answer to a petition sent to the conference, Mr. Lemuel Smith was sent to take charge of the society, under the direction of Mr. Garrettson. He brought the society into regular order, and extended his labours with effect into other places. He was succeeded by Mr. Dunham before mentioned. This society may be considered as the centre of Methodism in this northern part of the country.

After holding a quarterly meeting at Ashgrove, which was attended with signal displays of the power of God, Mr. Garrettson returned to Albany, where he met the little society. The next day he rode to Dr. H.'s. His horse being so lame as not to be able to carry him, he set off on foot, and after travelling nearly twenty miles, he came to Spencertown, where he preached with much satisfaction. Notwithstanding much opposition had been made here against the work of God, he found it in a prosperous state. In Sheffield, also, he found some souls brought to the knowledge of the truth. In Canaan he was permitted to preach in the Presbyterian meeting house, and found the minister and people of a very catholic spirit, and willing to promote the cause in which he was engaged. Here, also, he found the work of God prospering under the labours of Messrs. Bloodgood and Wigton. Though the people in these parts, he says, had been much troubled with Antinomianism, he found the gloomy doctrine receding before the rising beams of the sun of truth.

July 23, he came to the town of Sharon, in Connecticut, where he found a number of precious souls, to whom he preached in the open air, there being so many assembled that no house could accommodate them. After remarking that he believed the Lord had a work to do in this place, he records the following incidents :—

"I was sweetly drawn out in writing till about two o'clock. As the man of the house was gone out early in the morning, I went into the meadow to catch my horse. He was tied with a long rope to feed in the edge of the meadow, and as I had hold of the rope gathering him to me, he gave a sudden jirk, and by some means the rope got around my arms and body so that in less than half a minute I was thrown, and entirely bereft of my senses. How long I lay in this situation, I know not; for no person was near me. I knew not who I was, nor where I was. After lying, for a considerable time, in as much pain as if I had been on a rack or wheel, I suppose rolling from side to side, I made an attempt to lay my head on my hat for a pillow, and saw the two first letters of my name in my hat, and immediately I knew myself, and cried out, *is this poor Garrettson?* where is he, and what is the matter? I received a small degree of knowledge, and arose from the earth, walked to the house, and was laid apon a bed. Providentially a skilful surgeon was at hand, who came to me and found my right shoulder dislocated,* and my

* From the effects of this accident he never fully recovered.

left wrist, thumb, and shoulder, and several fingers, much strained, my body severely bruised, and several contusions on my head. Several assisted, and my shoulder was replaced, blood was let, and my other wounds bound up. Immediately after I was bled I recovered my senses as perfectly as ever, and was enabled to look up by faith to my beloved Saviour and received a strong confidence in him. Many of the inhabitants of the town came in to see me, and my soul was so happy that I was constrained with tears to exhort all that came near. I think I never had so strong a witness of perfect love. I was enabled to bless God for the affliction, and would not have had it otherwise. I do believe it was rendered a blessing to the place. I desired a person to borrow a carriage; he did, and carried me as far as Oblong, and the next day to Dover, where I received strength to preach to a large congregation in the church, to administer the sacrament to about twenty, and it was a powerful time. The two following days I rode about forty miles across mountains almost impassable for a carriage, and suffered much pain; but my mind was sweetly calm and happy.

"Wednesday I rode to Mr. Braiday's, still accompanied by my kind friend, A. Lion, who took tender care of me, for I was not able to comb my head, to dress myself, or to get in or out of the carriage without much pain, and yet I was enabled to preach with strength and freedom."

From thence he passed on through Newcastle, where he held a meeting and witnessed a great display of the power of God; but finding himself very feeble from his recent wounds, he took a passage by water, and on Tuesday arrived safely at New-York, where he remained seven days to recruit his strength. The ardour of his soul in his Master's work would not permit him longer to remain in the city. Though still suffering from the effects of his recent bruises, he left New-York, in company with a friend, to attend some appointments on Long Island. On Tuesday evening he preached by candle light in Newtown, and the next day at the court house in the town of Hempstead.

Long Island has become somewhat famous in the history of our country, as being the theatre of much individual suffering in consequence of its having been occupied for a considerable time by the invading armies of Great Britain. But before this event, it was visited by some of the Wesleyan Methodist missionaries. Captain Webb, the efficient helper of Mr. Embury in New-York, as early as 1768, passed over to Long Island, preached in Jamaica, Newtown, and some other places, with considerable success, many souls being awakened and converted as seals to his ministry. The political troubles, however, which soon succeeded these incipient attempts at planting Methodism in this place, checked its progress for a season, and the whole island was almost entirely abandoned, during the war, by ministers of all denominations. On the return of peace, in 1783, the way was opened for spreading the gospel of the grace of God among the people. The Rev. Philip Cox was the first regular preacher stationed on Long Island. This was in 1784. He found many who had not forgotten the preaching of Captain Webb. He was succeeded in 1785 by the Rev. Ezekiel Cooper, who preached extensively on the island. Many to this day remember his zealous efforts with gratitude. In 1786 Mr. Cooper was succeeded by the Rev. Thomas Ware. Great attention to the things of religion was excited by these men of God. Mr. Ware was followed by the Rev. Messrs. Moriarty and Cloud, whose labours were greatly owned of God. In 1789, the time Mr. Garrettson visited the island, the Rev. Messrs. Phœbus and John Lee were stationed there. At this time there were two hundred and twenty-four members in the church in the several societies which had been formed.* Mr. Garrettson visited most of the

* The following account, so illustrative of the particular care which God exercises over his people, respecting the introduction of

principal places in the island where the Methodist preachers could gain access, but says that though he found some precious souls who were breathing after God, there was a

Methodism into the town of Southhold, is related on the best authority; having been taken from the lips of those who were witnesses of the facts.

In 1794 Methodism was brought into Southhold, and the manner of its introduction is worthy to be recorded, as it will show the efficacy of prayer and the peculiar agency of the Holy Spirit in the spread of the gospel. A Mrs. Moore, who had been converted to God through the instrumentality of the Methodists, removed to this place; and although there were churches and ministers not very remote from it, yet no very efficient means had been used to build up the cause of God, or to arrest the spread of iniquity. Living at too great a distance from that ministry which had been the means of her conversion, and finding in her village two females like minded with herself, they agreed to meet together every Monday evening, to pray that God would send such a minister among them as would feed their own souls, and be made the means of awakening the wicked inhabitants of the place. They met accordingly two evenings at the house of Mr. P. Vail, who, at that time, was not a member of any church, but so far favourable as to gratify his wife in bringing her female friends to his house for prayer meeting. On the third night of their meeting, Mr. V., returning home weary from the business of the day, had retired about the time they usually met, which rendered it inconvenient to hold it that evening. This circumstance almost discouraged them, fearing that it arose from his dislike to the exercises, and that they should be deprived of this means of grace. However, they agreed to return home, and remember individually before God the great object for which they had met together. During the exercises of this evening they felt an unusual spirit of prayer. Sister Moore in particular, who continued until near midnight; her whole soul was drawn out to the Lord, nor could she be denied: the wickedness of the place and the want of an engaged ministry were continually before her. At the close of this struggle she felt an assurance that God had heard them, attended with these words, "I have heard their cry, and I am come down to deliver them;" and so strong was this conviction that she began to praise God for what she knew he would do.

At this very time Wilson Lee, a Methodist minister, was in New-London, and had his trunk on board a vessel to go to his appointment in New-York. Waiting for a passage over night, the wind lamentable spirit of indifference to the things of religion manifested by most of the people, and a determined opposition evinced by others.

Among other things which have tended to retard the progress of Methodism on this island, is the prevalence of Quakerism as held and propagated by Elias Hicks. Whether his peculiar principles were much developed at the time of which we are now speaking, I cannot say, but as he is now one of the oldest ministers of that society, and as he was raised up on Long Island, and devoted much of his time to the propagation of his principles, it is highly probable that the minds of the people over which he has had influence, have been for a long time tinctured, I might perhaps say poisoned, with his peculiar notions. It is not from hearsay that I assert that he undervalues the sacred Scriptures, sets aside the proper Deity and atonement of

being contrary, he felt an unusual struggle for the salvation of souls, attended with a constant impression to cross the sound to Long Island. Never having been there, and having his work in another direction, he endeavoured for some time to dismiss it, but perceiving that it still followed him, resolved, if his way were opened, to proceed. It should be observed that his peculiar exercises in New-London were on the same night, and almost at the same hour, in which these pious females were engaged in prayer on Long Island.

Next morning on going to the wharf, he found a sloop ready to sail for Southhold, and believing his call now to be from the Lord, immediately went on board. Making inquiry on his landing if there were any praying people in the place, he was immediately directed to the house of Mrs. Moore, who seeing him coming, and knowing a Methodist minister from his appearance, she, without a personal acquaintance or previous introduction, came out to the door, and said, "Thou blessed of the Lord, come in!" He then told the end for which he came, and related the peculiar providence which had directed him on his way, and she, in turn, the circumstance of their prayer meeting, and the assurance they received that God had heard them. A congregation was soon collected, and he who had felt such a desire for the salvation of souls, found here a ready people to whom the word of the Lord was attended with power. Shortly afterwards a class was formed, and from that period to this Methodism has continued in this place.

Christ, and openly denounces all other ministers as hirelings, their modes of worship as the offspring of superstition, Bible, Missionary, and other benevolent societies as mischievous in their design and tendency. These prejudices, to be sure, are mingled with an apparent spirit of piety, and a commendable zeal for the operation and indwelling of the Holy Spirit, thereby facilitating the progress of his pernicious errors.* At an early period of the settlement of the island, these people established societies, and so far as their influence extended, they presented a powerful barrier to the progress of the distinguishing doctrines preached by Mr. Garrettson and his associates. The east end and interior of the island were settled principally by emigrants from New-England, most of whom had their minds strongly imbued with the peculiarities of the Calvinistic creed, and were of course averse to those points of Methodism which came in contact with unconditional election and reprobation. And perhaps there are no people to be found on our continent who manifest a stronger tenacity in adhering to the traditions of their fathers than the inhabitants of Long Island. To this rigid adherence to what they had early been taught, they in general, especially in the interior of the island, join great simplicity of manners, an unostentatious show of piety, and great economy in their household affairs, together with a regular exterior deportment. These appear to have been, and are at the present day, the characteristic peculiarities of the inhabitants of Long Island. Some of these traits of character are undoubtedly favourable to the reception of the gospel, unless when accompanied with a pharisaical righteousness, while some of their tenets are no less unfavourable. The power of God, however, in many places,

* It is but justice to remark that a great portion of the societies of this denomination denounce the peculiarities of Elias Hicks, and have made strenuous efforts to check the progress of his doctrines. These are now distinguished from him and his followers by being called the "Orthodox Friends."

accompanied the delivery of his word by the Methodist preachers, and made it the instrument of salvation to the souls of sinners.

After the third tour around this district, in which he found a gradual spread of the work of God, and increase to the several societies which had been formed, Mr. Garrettson set off to attend "The Council," as it was called. It seems that in consequence of the great increase of preachers, and their extending themselves over so large a tract of country, measures had been devised to supersede the necessity of their assembling altogether in one place annually. It had been the practice of Mr. Wesley from the time he commenced calling the preachers together in conference, to assemble them once a year in the same place. At the beginning of Methodism in this country, a similar plan was adopted; but in consequence of the great extent of country over which the preachers spread themselves, it was soon found inconvenient for them all to convene annually at the same place. To remedy this inconvenience several conferences were held in the same year, but the acts of one conference were not considered binding unless they were sanctioned by them all; and as this could not be generally expected, it was plainly seen that this method of doing things tended to the dissolution of the body.

Such was the state of things when it was resolved to have a Council. It was to consist of the bishops and presiding elders, provided that it should never consist of a less number than nine. The following members composed the first Council, which met in Baltimore the first day of December, 1789:—

Francis Asbury, bishop; Philip Bruce, Freeborn Garrettson, Joseph Everitt, John Dickins, Nelson Reed, Richard Ivey, Reuben Ellis, Edward Morris, James O'Kelly, Lemuel Green, James O. Cromwell, elders.

It was soon perceived that this method of conducting

the affairs of the church was very far from being satisfactory, and hence the Council assembled only the second time. After attending this first Council, Mr. Garrettson observes, "I was resolved, God being my helper, to be more than ever engaged in the blessed work of God, it being my earnest prayer that the flame in the north might equal what I had witnessed in the south. On my return I felt something of it in Philadelphia, and when I came to New-York, I preached with an enlargement of soul which I had never before experienced in that city. I believed that the brethren would have glorious times, and so it came to pass, for in a few days after I left the city a most gracious work commenced first in a prayer meeting, extending itself to the congregation; and I saw and felt something of the same flame in many places on the district, in my winter visitations."

Soon after this Mr. Garrettson set off on a tour through some parts of Connecticut and Massachusetts on his way to Boston. In order to show the diligence and zeal with which he usually discharged his duty, and the manner in which he was received in this part of the country, the following extracts from his journal are given:—

"Having stayed a few days in the city, on Wednesday, June the 2d, accompanied by Harry who is to travel with me this summer, I rode as far as Miles's Square, and preached to more people than could get into the house. In the evening I rode to brother M.'s, at East Chester, and felt myself not so much drawn out as I could have wished.

"Thursday 3d, the appointment was in New Rochelle church, where I preached from, 'O my dove which art in the clefts of the rock,' &c. I had a degree of freedom while comparing the church to a dove; but more while speaking of the rock and the secret places of the stairs; and when I came to speak on the latter part of the text, 'Let me see thy countenance, let me hear thy voice; for sweet is thy voice and thy countenance is comely,' I was much drawn out, and a small moving ran through the people. In the evening I retired to brother S.'s and was very comfortable in a kind family, and blessed be God I felt my soul somewhat refreshed.

"Friday 4th, we had a solemn meeting at the Plains. Though it was a wet day many came to hear the word; and gave great attention. My mind is sweetly drawn to love the ways of the Lord. I found great freedom to describe the pure in heart.

"Saturday 5th, we met in King-street: more people gathered than the house could contain, and I found great enlargement in speaking. Harry exhorted after me to the admiration of the people. When I came into the house I found a man extremely ill with the colic. I ordered him to drink a pint of cold water, and he was relieved in less than three minutes. I returned to brother C.'s and was very comfortable.

"On the Lord's day we met in North Castle church, where I was surrounded by a listening multitude while I explained, 'A King shall reign in righteousness,' &c. I found great freedom to speak the word, and we had much of the divine presence. Again in the afternoon I was enabled to expatiate on Matt. xxii, 12, 'Friend, how camest thou hither not having on a wedding garment?' I think there were more people than I had ever seen together in this place. I suppose Bedford court house would not have contained half the people, so that I was obliged to stand under the trees: many of the rougher kind of people attended, some of whom did not behave very orderly. It is not common to be threatened with stoning in this country; the children of the devil would threaten a long time before they would venture on such a work, for the laws are very strict and the greater part of the people favour religion. In the evening I retired to brother L.'s and I trust enjoyed the company of my blessed Master.

"Monday 7th, preached at brother B.'s in the manor

to a crowded audience from, 'All Scripture is given by inspiration of God,' &c. I had great liberty to point out the benefit of our glorious dispensation. Our dear Lord owned his blessed word, and my spirit did rejoice in God my Saviour.

"Thursday 8th, many more came together at brother H.'s than could crowd into the house : we had a joyful season ; my own spirit is filled with sweetness. The people of this circuit are amazingly fond of hearing Harry.

"Wednesday 9th, I rode to Sing Sing and had an attentive audience while I enforced, ' Now the just shall live by faith,' &c. I have not preached a sermon with more sweetness since I left New-York. In the afternoon, at General Van Courtlandt's, near Croton river, I had great comfort while declaring , ' It is God that justifieth, who is he that condemneth ?'

"Thursday 10th, though a wet day, the church at ——— was well filled and I had much pleasure in describing the walk and prosperity of the blessed man, Psalm i, 1, 2, 3, and in the afternoon the old English church was nearly filled. I showed that, ' He that is born of God doth not commit sin,' &c. Harry, though it was a heavy cross, exhorted afterwards. I lodged at the old governor's, where I was comfortable with a kind family. The governor was gone far to the west to make a treaty with the Indians.

"I highly approve of the conduct of our statesmen respecting the poor Indians. On the frontiers of other states they encroach on the Indians' property ; here they have made a large purchase from them, and it is a rare thing to hear of an Indian's killing a white person.

"Friday 11th, I rode over the highlands and at three o'clock preached to a large congregation among the mountains : in this place our gracious Lord has raised many from the dead. I felt my heart much alive among the people while I explained St. John's advice to and account of the church of Philadelphia.

"Sunday 13th, our horses gave us the slip, so that we had to send five miles after them, and just as I was determining to set out on foot the man brought them to the door. We got to the place in good time; but the day was very wet and the house so very leaky that we had a disagreeable time at Fishkill. In this place the Lord hath given us a few good souls, and I trust that we shall have a precious gathering.

"Monday, early in the morning we set out and called on the son of the widow at whose house preaching was the day before: he was in deep distress of soul, and I trust it will not be long before he shall be set at liberty. In the afternoon I preached to a crowd of people from Ezekiel's vision of the dry bones, and I trust there was a shaking among the people who came from almost all parts of Oswego, some perhaps from curiosity to hear Harry.

"Tuesday 15th, I had but a small congregation assembled in a barn at a new place among the Presbyterians: the next day I preached at Rhinebeck, and spent the day following comfortably with my old friend, R. Sands, Esq.

"Friday 18th, I advanced towards the Cold spring, and preached at my good friend Rowe's from, 'Loose him and let him go.' Spent an hour with Dr. Bartlett and had a comfortable meeting at Mr. Lewis's. Jesus is precious to me; his ways are delightful.

"Saturday 19th, I rode to Mr. Herrick's, where I preached in the afternoon. I had great freedom to preach from 'In hell he lifted up his eyes,' &c. Harry exhorted after me with much freedom.

"June 20th. This day I was met by a Churchman who desired me to come and pray with his family: I did so with freedom; then rode on to Sharon, where I preached to about one thousand people under the trees from, 'O my dove that art in the clefts of the rock,' &c. I was much drawn out and great attention was paid to the word. The devil strives very hard to hinder the spreading of the gospel in this town: but blessed be God, many are under awakenings and I think the kingdom of Satan will be greatly shaken.

"Monday 21st. This was a day of great trial to me arising from a very plausible story told of one who I believe was entirely innocent of the charge. My heart was pained within me, but I could not convince those who were the accusers of his innocence. In the afternoon I was obliged to preach in the open air again for want of room in the house.

"22d. This morning I called a few together and examined into that strange affair, and am convinced of the innocence of the accused. I rode about fifteen miles and preached in the Presbyterian meeting house to some hundreds from, 'If the righteous scarcely be saved, where shall the ungodly and sinner appear.' It is encouraging to see such hearers affected under the word I am informed that when I preached in this meeting house last spring Mr. G., who was one of my hearers, was very much touched, and a few weeks ago died a penitent. I have great hope for the people of this town. I had a comfortable time at R——, Esq. who has a friendship for us.

"Wednesday 23d, I rode about twelve miles to Litchfield, and was surprised to find the doors of the Episcopal church open and a large congregation waiting for me. I preached from, 'Enoch walked with God,' and I believe good was done. I left Harry to preach another sermon and went on to the centre of the town; the bell rang and I preached to a few in the Presbyterian meeting house, and lodged with a kind Churchman.

"I preached in the skirts of the town where I was opposed by —— who made a great disturbance. I told him the enemy had sent him to pick up the good seed, turned my back on him, and went on my way accompanied by brother W. and H. where I found another waiting company, in another part of the town, to whom I declared, 'Except ye repent ye shall all likewise perish.' In this town we have given the devil and the wicked much trouble; we have a few good friends.

"Friday 25th, we rode fourteen miles through the rain, many people gathered, and I found freedom to declare, 'If we say that we have no sin we deceive ourselves:' several were in tears, and there was a shaking among the people. The squire and several other Calvinists came out to converse on the disputed points of unconditional election and reprobation, the freedom of the will, and the perseverance of the saints. I had to discourse with them until nearly midnight, and I believe some of them were much shaken. We have hard work to plant what they call Arminianism in this county: we stand in need of the wisdom of the serpent and the harmlessness of the dove.

"Saturday 26th, I rode a few miles and preached to a company of people assembled in a barn; my text was, ' But deliver us from evil.' I had a considerable degree of freedom in enforcing the necessity of being delivered from all sin; some believed it and some did not; among the rest one good old man who came a considerable distance on foot, said the Lord is with us and I am satisfied. A few weeks ago he was a warm pleader for the unconditional decrees; but now he sees differently.

"Sunday 27th, I preached in Farmington to about three hundred people, and had great freedom in showing that Christ tasted death for every man, and that as the way was open, if they did not repent they would justly be damned. There are a few precious souls here who cleave to our doctrine and have united to our society.

"28th, we set out for Boston, rode fifteen miles, stopped at Hartford, and preached in the court house to five or six hundred people, who seemed to give great heed to the words which were spoken: while Harry gave an exhortation some rude people behaved very uncivilly. The two following days we travelled and arrived at Worcester about four o'clock, where I was kindly entertained by Mr. Chanler, but the people appeared to have a small share of religion: I went from one end of the town to the other and could get no one to open the court house and gather the people. I went to the house of the Rev. Mr. B——. I was asked to take tea. I drew near, and inquired if it was not customary to ask a blessing? No, said he, not over tea: I then drew back from the table: his countenance changed, and he said in a very short manner, 'You may ask a blessing over your dish.' Pinching want might drive me to eat and drink in such a case. I had an hour's conversation with him. It is lamentable for masters in Israel to deny the power of religion.

"Tuesday July 1st, we rode through a very pleasant country; I never saw more elegant buildings in a country place than those that surround Cambridge, and the college has an imposing appearance. I got into Boston, about seven o'clock, after riding forty-eight miles. I boarded Harry at the master Mason for the Africans, and I took my own lodgings with a private gentleman, who had been a Methodist in England, but has, I fear, fallen from the spirit of Methodism.

"Sunday 4th, I attended church in the morning, and gave great uneasiness to the people with whom I lodged on account of my not communing. I never in my life saw such a set of communicants, dressed in the height of the mode, and with all the frippery of fashion—so much of the world in their manners and appearance that my mind was most easy to look on. In the afternoon I preached in a meeting house which had formerly belonged to Dr. Mather. Monday evening likewise in the same place. Tuesday I went from end to end of the town and visited several who were friendly, a few of whom were formerly Methodists, but I fear they are not such in practice. I engaged the use of the meeting house, and a place for a preacher to board, and on Wednesday set out for Providence. I had rode but about thirty miles when I met brother Lee, and while we were sitting on our horses talking, an old gentleman rode up and asked us to go to his house and preach that night: we went and had a comfortable meeting, and I also preached the next morning: after dinner we parted; brother Lee consented to go to Boston and make a trial there until I could send another preacher. I reached Providence about five o'clock; the bell rang, and I had an opportunity of preaching in good old Mr. Snow's meeting house.

"Friday 9th, I had a sweet time in retirement, and in the evening addressed a larger congregation than I had the night before.

"Sunday 11th, with freedom I preached in the morning at six o'clock. I officiated all day for good Mr. Snow, and at six Harry preached in the meeting house to more than one thousand people. I appointed to preach the next morning at five o'clock, and I suppose three hundred people attended to hear my last sermon. I had a sweet time in Providence. I have no doubt but the Lord begun a good work in many hearts. I left many in tears. I left town about nine o'clock, rode about thirty-five miles, and lodged at Colonel P——'s, whom I found to be a very kind man, and I trust the family were stirred up: the daughter seemed to be much affected.

"Tuesday 13th, I rode forty-five miles to Hartford, and preached the next evening to as ill behaved an audience as I have ever seen in New-England. The people of this place, with a few exceptions, seem to be fast asleep in the arms of the wicked one. The following night I preached again, and some of what are called the gentry behaved so ill that I was under the necessity of breaking up the meeting and declining to preach by candlelight.

"Sunday 18th, I preached again in the state house, to

a few who gave attention. I rode to Weathersfield and preached at eleven o'clock and likewise at two o'clock, and then returned and preached at Hartford at five o'clock to about two hundred people. I am apprehensive from the state of religion in this place that the ministers do not enjoy the life and power of religion; they seem to be so smoothed over that they cannot with any degree of patience bear to hear of the carnal mind, or any mention of hell.

"Thursday, I preached with freedom at Farmington, and on Tuesday morning I gave an exhortation on the subject of baptism, and baptized fourteen adults and children, and we had a sweet time, and then rode to Litchfield and preached to a serious company. I have no doubt that the Lord has begun a good work in this town. Brother W—— is a very acceptable preacher in this new circuit, and the Lord owns his labours.

"I lodged at Mr. O——'s, and had a long conversation with him and his brother, who related a very singular circumstance, which was as follows:—The brother (as they both informed me) was intended for a Presbyterian minister; he had gone through his course of study, and as a probationer he had begun to preach, and I doubt not from what he informed me but that he was acquainted with inward religion. He fancied that if he was called to preach the Lord would endue him with a gift of miracles, and he concluded that he would preach no more until he obtained that gift. He began to fast, and after he had fasted eight or nine days, ministers, people and physicians came around him, telling him that he would shortly be a dead man unless he took some nourishment—at another time they endeavoured to force him to eat, but to no purpose. He told me that he did not eat a mouthful of victuals during forty days, and only drank water and a few times a little small beer. He likewise told me that nothing went through him for forty days. His brother, who I trust is a man who fears the Lord, professed to be an eye witness of the truth of this statement; he was with him most of the time, and said that during the forty days he did as much work as he himself was able to do, who eat four or five times a day. When we would come in from work, said he, he would take nothing but a little water or a little small beer, and then go to work again. From the tenth to the nineteenth day of his fast, he seemed somewhat feeble, but after that he grew strong and looked nearly as fresh and well as he ever did, and continued to labour hard during that time: after the forty days were ended, he eat as hearty as usual, and found no injury from it, though the physicians warned him that in so doing he risked his life. Before this he was much exercised about the doctrines peculiar to Calvinism, and had renounced them. When I saw him I found him a believer in the same system of free salvation which the Methodists hold out, and he has begun boldly to preach again.

"Saturday I rode as far as Cornwall, and preached at Squire Rogers's. I found that the Lord had begun a blessed work in this town when I preached here before, so I rode to Canaan, where I was comfortable.

"Sunday 25th, I preached in Canaan to about five hundred people, from Matt. xxv, 14, 15, the parable of the talents. The Lord was with us: the work in this place is moving on. I have circulated a subscription for the building of a church here. Brother Bloodgood was with me; as it was too warm in the house I preached in the open air. Harry preached after me with much applause. I rode in the afternoon and preached in Salisbury, in a part of the town in which I had never before preached, and I think I have never seen so tender a meeting in this town before, for a general weeping ran through the assembly, especially while Harry gave an exhortation. The Lord is carrying on a blessed work in this town.

"Monday July 26th, I preached on the whole armour of God, with freedom, and in the afternoon at brother Haywood's from, 'If our gospel be hid it is hid to them that are lost.' One careless woman was brought under concern, so that shortly after she went home she returned and opened to me the state of her mind, and appeared to be in great distress indeed.

"Tuesday July 27th, between two huge mountains the morning appeared very beautiful, and I was very much delighted with the prospect when the natural sun had arisen and illuminated the earth with his bright beams, but one much brighter Sun doth arise to cheer the mind, even the Sun of righteousness. At four o'clock I preached on another beautiful mountain, in a Presbyterian meeting house, to about three hundred people who gave heed to the things spoken. The people on this mountain are so far convinced that they appear to receive the gospel. When we first came to this mountain the people were much prejudiced, but are now more reconciled, and there is a prospect of a society.

"Wednesday July 28th, I had a sweet time at the furnace, and sent on Harry to supply my afternoon's appointment. I rode twelve miles with two disciples, and had an opportunity to see a distressed woman, Mrs. L——n, who has almost lost her reason. I endeavoured to converse with her, but I was too late. They are very much engaged to give her medical aid, but a revelation of the love and favour of God alone can relieve her.

"July 29th, I rode to Hudson, where I found the people very curious to hear Harry. I therefore declined preaching that their curiosity might be satisfied. The different denominations heard him with much admiration, and the Quakers thought that as he was unlearned he must preach by immediate inspiration.

"Friday 30th, I spent part of the day in planning a new church in this city, and in the evening preached to several hundred people with considerable freedom from, 'Him that honoureth me I will honour,' &c, and I think I never witnessed a more solemn time in this place. The people of this city drive away their convictions by the love of the world. I have frequently seen fine prospects here which were soon gone.

"Saturday 31st, crossed the north river, rode twelve miles, and preached among the mountains. The Lord is deepening his work among these poor people. The society is young, but growing."

In the month of October he attended the conference in the city of New-York.

We may form some idea of the extent and usefulness of the labours of Mr. Garrettson and those associated with him, from the fact that there had been an increase of two thousand five hundred and forty-seven church members during the three years of hard toil in this part of the country. When he commenced his labours here in 1788 there were only four circuits, namely, New-York, Long Island, New Rochelle, and Dutchess; but in 1791 there were twelve circuits, namely, New-York, Long Island, New Rochelle, Dutchess, Columbia, New Britain, Cambridge, Albany, Saratoga, Otsego, Newburg, and Wyoming. This one district at that time comprehended nearly the whole territory now included in the New-York conference, consisting of seven districts, numbering eighty circuits and stations, and one hundred and sixty-three effective preachers.

By this estimate those who now come among us may see what their fathers in the gospel had to encounter, the immense labours they performed, and the consequent privations they must have endured, as well as the astonishing success which accompanied their exertions in the cause of their Master.

CHAPTER XIV.

End of the printed journal—Division of his district—Visits Albany—Meets with Bishop Asbury—Attends conference—His testimony of Bishop Asbury's excellencies—Account of the Shakers—Tour into the new settlements—State of the country—Work of God revives—Providential escape from danger—Visits the eastern part of his district—Meets Bishop Asbury, and converses with him on church government—Attends general conference in Baltimore—Mr. O'Kelly's division—Its effects—Visits his friends in Maryland—Returns to New-York—Passes through his district—His marriage.

The printed journal of Mr. Garrettson, by which I have been so much assisted thus far, ends with the contents of the preceding chapter; and his manuscripts from this period are not very voluminous, although he continued occasional notices of the exercises of his mind, as well as of his public labours. From these and from other documents within reach, I shall endeavour to fill up the remainder of the years of his devoted life—devoted exclusively to the best of all causes, the cause of man's salvation.

At the conference of 1791, the district over which Mr. Garrettson had presided with so much honour to himself and usefulness to others, was divided into two: the southern part, including Newburg, Wyoming, New-York, New Rochelle and Long Island circuits, was placed under the oversight of the Rev. Robert Cloud; Dutchess, Columbia, New Britain, Cambridge, Albany, Saratoga, and Otsego, formed the district of Mr. Garrettson. On the 11th of June he arrived in the city of Albany, found the labours of the preacher had been much blessed, and that he had succeeded in erecting a house of worship, which Mr. Garrettson dedicated to the service of Almighty God; after which, in company with the preacher, he went through the city from house to house, soliciting contributions to aid in paying for their newly-built house. They collected, however, in the whole, only forty pounds or one hundred dollars. From Albany he travelled west as far as Johnstown, where he contracted for a lot of ground and engaged the workmen to build a house of worship.

In consequence of the division of his district, Mr. Garrettson was enabled to fill up more of the intermediate places, and to spend more time in regulating the societies and setting things in order. Having done all he could for the "little flock" in Johnstown, he returned to Albany, and from thence passed on the Hudson and visited the western part of Connecticut, preaching in all the towns through which he passed where he could obtain a place to preach in until he came to Farmington, where he met Bishop Asbury.

From the time Mr. Asbury had been consecrated to the office of a bishop, according to the rules of the Discipline, he had travelled at large through the country, meeting the preachers in their several conferences at times and places most convenient for them and advantageous to the work in which they were engaged. It was customary when he came within the bounds of a presiding elder's district, for the elder to accompany him from place to place, that from a personal inspection of the work, he might be able to oversee the whole work to the better advantage. And this personal and efficient superintendency devolved principally upon Bishop Asbury, as Dr. Coke, though denominated a joint superintendent with him, was generally in Europe during the interval of the conferences. To Bishop Asbury, therefore, the preachers looked for direction in all important matters, and next to him to the presiding elders of the districts. At this time Mr. Asbury came into this district, and accompanied Mr. Garrettson through Litchfield and Cornwall to Canaan, where they held a quarterly meeting, and thence to Albany, where Mr. Asbury preached five times in the new meeting house. Here the preachers assembled and "held," says Mr. Garrettson, "a little conference," and one of the brethren was set apart to the office of a deacon. From thence they "travelled through Coeyman's, Hudson, Rhinebeck, and Nine Partners, and on Saturday and Sunday held a quarterly meeting not far from Oblong, where a vast concourse of people assembled, so that the meeting house, though large, would not contain one third of the people; they therefore withdrew to the woods, and many seemed to receive the word with joy." From thence they went on south to Peekskill and lodged at Governor Courtlandt's. In the "morning," says Mr. Garrettson, "I was under the necessity of parting with Bishop Asbury. We had had a pleasant time together, and I felt a continual calm in my soul, and could not leave him without reluctance. I am satisfied that he possesses the qualifications of a primitive bishop." This testimony to the qualifications of Mr. Asbury as a bishop in the Methodist Episcopal Church is the more valuable as it comes from one who had been for a considerable time his intimate friend, had frequently heard him preach, been in his private and public councils, and who knew how to estimate true worth of character. And it is no little recommendation of Mr. Garrettson that such a man as Bishop Asbury reposed the most unlimited confidence in his integrity and faithfulness in the cause of his divine Master.

Mr. Garrettson continued his itinerary visits through his district, often cheered by crowded congregations hanging upon his lips for instruction, and sometimes depressed by the indifference with which the word was received. On Monday, Sept. 3, he entered the state of Massachusetts, and met Mr. Robert Green, one of the preachers who travelled on the Albany circuit, and he found the commencement of a glorious work of religion in that part of the country.

The faithful minister of Jesus Christ who has proclaimed an irreconcilable war against sin and Satan, will very much deceive himself if he thinks to pass on smoothly without opposition from his grand adversary. Not only are the wicked and the openly profane leagued against him, but also the merely formal professor, as well as all those whose peculiarities of belief are brought into contact with the pure truths of the gospel. Among other evils in our country, where an unrestrained liberty of thought and action in religious matters is guaranteed to its citizens, numerous heresies, some of the most wild and extravagant nature, have sprung up, and thriven as in a luxuriant soil. These, often more destructive in their consequences than an undisguised opposition to the gospel, are to be encountered, their influence as far as possible counteracted, that those who are carried away by their fatal delusions may be reclaimed to the "good and right way." Among others by which the age has been distinguished, and in many instances disgraced, is that of Shakerism. Though quite local in its character and influence, it has been considered of sufficient importance to be noticed in the records of the day as a distinct denomination. This spurious offspring of an adulterated Christianity, has deluded and blinded the minds of a very considerable number of our citizens, and ought doubtless to be stamped with a seal of disapprobation by all sober-minded and orthodox Christians.

These remarks have arisen from the following notice of this deluded sect by Mr. Garrettson, under date of September 3: "I met a sensible man who had been a Shaker, but has left them and joined us. Of this person I received the most full and satisfactory account of the people called Shakers that I have ever had. I had been at a loss to know how or from whence they sprang. He tells me they are the relics of Bell, who was formerly a Methodist preacher in England, but was excommunicated by Mr. Wesley for his enthusiastic notions. He held to our being as perfect as angels, or as Adam was in paradise; and was so wild as to prophesy that on such a day a part of London should be destroyed to the great harm of thousands in that city. Once he was a man of great faith; but where is poor deluded Bell now! His followers were dispersed, and after a time a few of them came over and settled at Niskayuna, where they remained peaceably for some time, until the *mother*, as she was called, ANN LEE, professed to pass through an uncommon change; and a few entered upon their new work, which consisted mostly in dancing, shaking, turning round, and talking, as they call it, in the unknown tongues. This new system was for a time carried on with great rapidity, so that persons of respectability joined them, and among the rest several ministers. I have conversed with several sensible men who have left them, who told me that while among them they hated every thing they thought to be sinful, and verily thought they were doing right."

The following extracts from his journal will show the progress of the gospel in some of the new settlements on the west side of the Hudson river.

"Saturday, Sept. 24, I left Albany and attended a quarterly meeting at Captain Groosbeck's twenty miles to the north. I found great freedom to speak. Several of the preachers spoke feelingly and freely.

"Sunday 25th, our love feast began at nine o'clock. Several of our friends spoke their experience well. One of our pious sisters gave the following account:—' I was convinced all was not well with me; but knew not what I wanted, (this was previous to hearing the Methodists.) One day I took my Bible and went into the woods to read and seek the Lord. I sat down under a large tree, and was reading and weeping, and desirous to know what I should do to be saved: I at length listened and heard a voice saying unto me, Remove from that place. I knew not but it might be imagination, and read on till I heard it again a second and a third time. I at length removed from the place and sat down about twenty feet off. No sooner had I done this than a part of the tree fell on the place where I had been sitting. I looked up and saw the hand of God in my preservation, and was enabled to look to my blessed Redeemer, and he gave me to know that all my sins were blotted out, and I returned to the house happy in the Lord. After this I had the pleasure of casting in my lot among the Methodists, and I feel thankful to the Lord, and am now happy in the love of God.' I preached after the love feast on St. John's account of the Laodiceans, for I feared they were in a lukewarm state. After meeting ended we settled a dispute between two brethren, and I trust some are brought to mourn on account of their backsliding.

"Monday 26th, I crossed the north river accompanied by brother C——c, and preached at Newtown, and administered the sacrament. I had a sweet season, and considerable enlargement in the society by the instrumentality of brother Candle. I rode ten or twelve miles to Saratoga, where I was to preach at four o'clock, but could not begin till five: the congregation was so numerous that the house would not contain them; so I preached under a tree with great freedom. I had several of the settled clergy to hear. On the whole we had a weeping time. I was much pleased with the good behaviour of the people. By candle light I administered the sacrament to nearly twenty of our young converts, and as many waited to see it as could crowd in, and we had a happy and an affecting time. I feel myself happy among the poor children of God.

"Tuesday 27th, I was to preach at Fish creek: a man met us in the road. 'Stop, sir,' said he, 'and clear up one thing. Is it right for you to part man and wife? My wife joined your church last night. We are parted, we are parted!' The woman was in a flood of tears, and he raving like a madman. We passed along, and I preached again to upwards of two hundred, and communed with a few of our young converts. The people in this place seems as hard as rocks. I lodged at the house of a kind friend, and had some conversation with a religiously disposed Presbyterian.

"Wednesday 28th, we rode to Saratoga springs, where I preached. The larger part of the congregation behaved well, but some were rude. This was a mixed company from different parts of the union. In the afternoon I preached at Cadersoy's creek, and was much discomposed by noisy children. I stand in need of patience. O God! give every grace of thy Holy Spirit.

"Thursday 29th. This morning my mind is comfortable in the Lord. I travelled about twenty miles through a country thinly inhabited, the road new and exceedingly bad, to Broadalbin, where I had an opportunity of preaching to a well-behaved congregation, part of whom had moved from Rhode Island. Among the rest I met with Mr. Snow, son to the Rev. Mr. Snow of Providence, at whose house I preached. He emulates the piety of his good old father. In this place we have a growing society. Among them my spirit was much refreshed.

"Friday 30th, I rode to Mayfield, a town settled since the revolution. When in this place four months since I was much encouraged; but they appear to be greatly retarded in the *race*. O! the world and the sublunary things thereof are a great hindrance to vital piety.

"Saturday 31st, I rode to Johnstown. In time of preaching the children made much disturbance. After sermon two of our brethren exhorted. About four months ago I visited this town, agreed for a lot, and encouraged our few friends to build the Lord a house, which is now in order for worship.

"Sunday, Nov. 1st. As it was quarter day, as many people came together as our new building would contain, made up of a variety of denominations: I preached from, 'Now the end of the commandment is charity, out of a pure heart, a good conscience, and faith unfeigned.'"

In 1792 we find him travelling over the same ground, and extending his labours even farther west. The principal part of the country, after going a short distance from the banks of the Hudson, at this time was but recently settled; the people, though industrious, were generally poor, living in log houses, enjoying merely the *necessaries* of life. On this account the preachers who first visited them were subjected to privations and inconveniences to which those who have since "entered into their labours" are strangers. How often have the pioneers in the gospel field been found to preach, eat, and sleep in the same room, live on the coarsest fare, and at their quarterly meetings either assemble in a barn or in a grove! In the warm season of the year, however, it is not unpleasant to worship Him who "hangeth the earth upon nothing and stretcheth the north over the empty space" under the foliage of a pleasant grove.

On the last of June Mr. Garrettson held a quarterly meeting at Broadalbin, and on the second day of the meeting, July 1, he says that about four hundred people assembled, and they had a moving profitable time:— "There were," says he, "a large number at the communion, and many, I trust, will bless God in eternity for this day. We lodged at the house of brother Snow, son of the Rev. Mr. Snow of Providence, R. I., before mentioned, and I am happy to add that I think the son emulates his pious father. I am much pleased with the people of this town, as they appear well disposed, and the Lord is carrying on a glorious work among them. It is not enough for me, O my God! to bear a public testimony to the truth, and to labour heartily and cheerfully in thy vineyard: I must be holy or I cannot have a seat in thy kingdom."

It was in this spirit of ardent devotion, with his mind constantly bent and all his powers of soul and body consecrated to the advancement of the Redeemer's glory, that

Mr. Garrettson pursued his way through this newly-settled country, encouraging the hearts and strengthening the hands of his junior brethren in the ministry, as well as dispensing the word of life to all whom he could reach with the sound of his voice. After he returned to the city of Albany, a place of great spiritual dearth, though much of his labour had been bestowed upon it, he was cheered with the following intelligence from the preacher who had charge of the societies where he had preached the preceding Wednesday and Thursday near old Schoharie: "The day after you left us I began to visit from house to house. Many in deep distress followed me, and cried aloud for mercy, so that before we went to rest *ten* souls were set at liberty." Soon after another letter from the same person and place informed him that "the blessed work was going on, and that twenty souls had found peace with God." On recording this joyful news, he exclaims, "O Albany! when will God arise in power and shake thy dry bones! Gracious God! thou canst work and none can hinder."

On Monday he left Albany to attend some appointments on his district, when, "on crossing a creek," says he, "my horse suddenly plunged into a deep hole entirely over his head in water; but though I was much wet, I was brought through unhurt; and after travelling upwards of twenty miles, I was abundantly compensated by those refreshing streams of which the world knows not, while preaching to a company of the poor gathered from their cottages. This to me is much sweeter employment than to dwell at ease in affluence, while the poor are perishing for lack of knowledge. O that all the ministers of God would consider this and carefully look after Christ's sheep in the wilderness." In this tour around his district he extended his labours still farther into the new settlements, and derived great satisfaction from witnessing the blessed effects of those faithful preachers over whom he watched with paternal tenderness and care, and whose assurance of a divine call to this important work was rendered still more satisfactory in the awakening and conversion of souls. To satisfy himself more fully respecting their qualifications and call to this work, he tells us that he "took particular pains to examine them, as well as to hear them preach as often as practicable; and also to give them those cautions and directions which I considered suitable and necessary; for which many of them manifest their thankfulness." After traversing through several parts of this new country, and witnessing the blessed effects of their ministrations, he says, "God will do a great work in this country." How prophetic! Since that time the blessed work has spread through all this western country to the lakes, and into Upper and Lower Canada.

Under date of Saturday 28th, he gives the following remarkable account:—"On looking back I see the hand of a good God in my preservation last Thursday. I came to Mr ——— weary and thirsty. I asked for something to drink, and my kind friend's wife went to fetch it; after staying about fifteen minutes she returned with some small beer: as she advanced towards me I was as sensibly impressed as if some one had told me, *That woman is not too good to put poison in the drink.* As I was putting it to my lips the same impression was so strong, that immediately I refused, and put it down on the table untouched. Shortly after dinner was brought on the table; but I could eat very little. The next morning she poisoned her husband and two others with the meat which had been set before me. I was informed not long since that she had said she would put an end to all the d——d Methodists. A skilful physician was at hand, or in all probability they would have lost their lives. She was immediately sent to the jail in Albany."

He then came to Rhinebeck, where he enjoyed sweet consolation in communion with God in secret, and with his Christian friends. Thence he passed on through the eastern part of York state into Connecticut and Massachusetts to Pittsfield, where he had the pleasure of again meeting Bishop Asbury, as he was returning from the conference at Lynn, Mass. "I can truly say," observes Mr. Garrettson, "I was never more happy to see him." They then went in company to Albany, where the preachers in these parts, twenty in number, were assembling for conference, which was opened on Wednesday 15th, by Bishop Asbury, "with an excellent sermon." This conference, it seems, was attended with much of the presence of God, and the preachers went to their several stations with glad hearts and renewed courage, knowing their work was with God.

From this conference he accompanied Bishop Asbury to Rhinebeck, where he had the happiness of hearing him preach a "very useful sermon." On the way Mr. Garrettson says, "we had some close conversation on church government. On this subject there is not a perfect unanimity of sentiment." What particular point of church government it was concerning which they discoursed, we are not told; but it is presumed that it related to the general superintendency, as Mr. Garrettson was of the opinion, that instead of having the whole continent under one general superintendency, it would have been better if it had been divided among several, making each superintendent responsible for his own particular district to the general conference. To this opinion I believe he adhered to the last, though he calmly acquiesced in the decisions of a majority of his brethren in this as well as in all matters relating to the regulations of the discipline of the church.

From Rhinebeck he passed on to New-York, and from thence through Philadelphia to Baltimore in order to attend the general conference which assembled October 31, 1792. It was at this conference that the subject of an appeal from the appointment of the bishop to the annual conference was brought forward by Mr. O'Kelly, and largely debated. That all may understand the nature of this subject, it is necessary to remark that according to the regulations of the discipline, the bishop attending an annual conference has the sole power of appointing all the preachers to their several stations. Mr. O'Kelly wished to put what he considered a salutary check upon this power, by providing that if a preacher felt himself aggrieved or oppressed in his appointment, he should have the privilege of appealing to the conference, which should consider and finally determine the matter. After a long and animated discussion, the question was decided in the negative, and Mr. O'Kelly withdrew from the Methodist Episcopal Church. In reference to these things, Mr. Garrettson observes that "Mr. O'Kelly's distress was so great on account of the late decision, that he informed us by letter that he no longer considered himself one of us. This gave great grief to the whole conference. Two persons were appointed with me as a committee to treat with him. Many tears were shed, but we were not able to reconcile him to the decision of the conference. His wound was deep, and apparently incurable."

The tenderness thus manifested towards an erring brother, so characteristic of Mr. Garrettson, reminds one of the apostolic direction, "If a man be overtaken in a fault, ye which are spiritual restore such a one in the spirit of meekness, considering thyself, lest thou also be tempted." When an act of excision becomes necessary, from the stubbornness of an offending member, the character of the church sustains no injury, but acquires much credit, by performing this duty in the spirit of tenderness, evincing a love to the person she is constrained to disown. I believe this spirit was strikingly exemplified in the present instance towards Mr. O'Kelly, not only by Mr. Garrettson, who mourned over his fallen brother with the sympathy of a Christian, but also by the whole conference.

This was the first schism of any considerable magnitude which had been made in the Methodist Episcopal Church. Mr. O'Kelly was a preacher of some talent and influence; he had been employed as a presiding elder, according to Bishop Asbury's account, " in the south district of Virginia for about ten succeeding years." Mr. Lee, in his History of the Methodists, affirms that O'Kelly was not sound in the doctrine of the Trinity, and thinks that a fear of being called to an account for his heterodoxy in this particular, was the principal cause of his withdrawing from the church. Whatever truth there may be in this, his proceedings raised very considerable disturbance in the societies, particularly in some parts of Virginia, as three of the travelling preachers withdrew with him; and as they immediately commenced a warfare against the people they had left, several thousands of the people were induced to join their standard. They at first called themselves "republican Methodists," uttered many harsh and uncharitable censures against the Methodist Episcopal Church, particularly against Bishop Asbury, and endeavoured to inflame the passions of the people so as to induce them to revolt against their former pastors. Their success for a while stimulated them to increased exertions, but they soon began to decline, until finally their influence was annihilated, and at the present time they are not known as a distinct denomination. Pure religion, however, in the region of country where they prevailed most, suffered a sad declension, and perhaps in some instances, it has scarcely recovered its wonted vigour and activity to this day; so deleterious are the effects of " dissensions among brethren."

It is not doubted but that a man may withdraw himself from the Methodist Church from conscientious motives; but it is a remarkable fact in the history of this church that nearly all those who have withdrawn have distinguished themselves more by the virulence of their invectives against their old friends, than by their zeal to " convert sinners from the error of their ways." This was particularly the case with Mr. O'Kelly and his party, as well as others who have taken similar steps. The consequence has been a diminution of that loving zeal by which the sincere and devout Christian is characterized, and an increase of party animosity, of strife and many evil works, which have ultimately led to the overthrow and entire prostration of the party. Let but the Methodist Episcopal Church persevere in its career of " doing good of every possible sort to the souls and bodies of men," manifesting a spirit of forbearance and brotherly affection among its members, and of Christian moderation towards all men, and " no weapon that is formed against her shall prosper."

At the close of this conference Mr. Garrettson has the following reflections:—" O what a wonder to see so large a body of preachers gathered from all parts of the continent, and, like little children sitting at each other's feet, united as the heart of one man, and all engaged in one common cause, namely, to demolish the kingdom of Satan and to build up that of the Redeemer! I retired to my room, not indeed alone, for I trust my blessed Saviour was with me. O my God, let me rather die than cease to love thee."

From this conference Mr. Garrettson returned to Cokesbury college, where he preached, and then paid a visit to his relations on the eastern shore of Maryland, and was much comforted in their society. After preaching a number of times with great satisfaction to those with whom he formerly " took sweet counsel" in this part of the country, he pursued his journey to New-York, and immediately entered upon the labour of his district with his usual zeal and success, every where hailed as a messenger of God.

He continued in this work, extending his excursions still farther and farther into the western settlements, until June 30, 1793, when he was united in marriage to Miss Catherine Livingston, daughter of Judge Livingston, of Clermont, manor of Livingston, a woman every way qualified to be to him "a help meet indeed," and whose pious efforts to promote the Redeemer's kingdom were ever after, during his life, affectionately united with those of her devoted husband. They were married by the Rev. Peter Moriarty in the first Methodist church in Rhinebeck, and afterwards partook of the blessed Supper of our Lord and Saviour Jesus Christ.

On this occasion he makes the following reflections: "I am now happy in the society of my dear friend, and find the two families, Sands's and Schuyler's, as kind and as attentive as ever. I hope always to live as God would have me both for time and eternity. I am happy, and hope to be more and more so. Lord, we are thine. Thou hast united our spirits to thyself and to each other. Do with us as seemeth thee good, only let us be wholly thine: let us live to thy glory, and grant that our union may be for the furtherance of each other in the way to the kingdom of heaven."

CHAPTER XV.

Mr. Garrettson stationed in Philadelphia—On the New-York District—Settles his family in Rhinebeck—Prosecutes his labours—Erects a house—Goodness of God displayed towards him—Situation of his mansion—His cares multiply—Dedicates his new house to the Lord—Several stations he filled—In 1809 visits his old friends at the south—His account of this tour—Remarkable preservation—Visits Baltimore, Washington city, and various places on the Peninsula of Md.—Attends camp meetings, &c.

FROM the time of Mr. Garrettson's marriage in 1793, until 1809, I find no regular account of his travels and labours. It appears, however, from the minutes of the conference, that he was this year stationed as *elder* in the city of Philadelphia, and likewise had charge of Bristol, Chester, and Wilmington circuits. This was a season of peculiar affliction to the citizens of Philadelphia. The yellow fever raged; and as Mr. Garrettson was going into the city, thousands were coming out, to escape this fell destroyer of human life. His labours here were greatly blessed. In 1794 he was stationed in what has since been called the New-York district, which included Pittsfield, Cambridge, Dutchess, Columbia, Croton, New Rochelle, Long Island, New-York, and Brooklyn circuits. With a view to his temporal accommodation, he purchased a farm in Rhinebeck, and settled his small family. This, however, did not interrupt his ministerial labours, nor circumscribe the sphere of his usefulness. In this place his family resided five years, during which time Mr. Garrettson continued his exertions in the sacred cause of his divine Master with his usual zeal and devotedness, chiefly in that part of the country. In 1799 we find him stationed as a presiding elder within the bounds of the Philadelphia conference, having Salem, Burlington, Bethel, Trenton, Freehold, Elizabethtown, Flanders, and Newburgh circuits for his district.

In the year 1800 he was returned to the New-York district. Having made an exchange of the place he had occupied for another on the eastern bank of the Hudson, in 1799 he commenced building a dwelling house. The following incident is related on the best authority: The day on which the house was raised, while Mr. Garrettson stood admiring with what facility the frame went up, the power and goodness of God were so gloriously manifested, that he was constrained to retire to the lime house to give vent to his tears. After composing himself he returned. While another part of the frame was going up, the Lord so smiled from heaven upon him, that he retired to give an expression of his joys, of glory and thanks to his Redeemer. On returning home, he related these things with evident satisfaction to Mrs. Garrettson, and they rejoiced together "for the consolation." The next day they were visited by their much beloved friend, Bishop Asbury.

In this mansion the family of Mr. Garrettson, consisting of his wife, an only daughter, and a few pious domestics, resided until his death, and here the widow and daughter still reside. Here was every thing to make life comfortable. The house stands on a high bank on the eastern side of the noble Hudson, whose waters are perpetually enlivened by numerous sloops transporting the produce of the country to New-York and carrying up in exchange the necessaries and luxuries of life, as well as by steam boats loaded with passengers. A commanding view down the river for several miles is afforded to the eye of the inmates of the house and their numerous visiters. Trees of various sorts, apple, peach, and a variety of other fruit-bearing trees, shrubbery, &c, surround the dwelling, and combine together to render it a most delightful residence. But what tended to make it a much more desirable retreat to the pious of all denominations, was the Christian urbanity, the pious example, and the amiable spirit manifested at all times by the inmates of a mansion which had been dedicated to God from its foundation.

Having become the head of a family, and very soon made responsible for the use and management of a very considerable estate, Mr. Garrettson began to feel his cares multiply upon him, and was often distressed at the thought of being called by these means, in any measure from his more immediate vocation; and sometimes he would with tears in his eyes say, that God had designed a brighter crown for him. "One night," says Mrs. Garrettson, "I heard him conversing in a low voice, with tears and groans. Soon after he turned to me and said, that he had been pleading with the Lord not to take his crown from him on account of his unfaithfulness; and that the Lord had assured him, that *No man should take his crown;* and that what he *could do* in his present situation should be accepted. At which he rejoiced, and was greatly comforted."

The following is the account given by Mrs. Garrettson of the manner in which they took possession of their new house. Were all newly married persons thus to enter on life, thus to dedicate themselves and their house to God, how many blessings now unhappily lost would be secured! "Our house being nearly finished, in October, 1799, we moved into it, and the first night in family prayer, while my blessed husband was dedicating it to the Lord, the place was filled with his presence, who in days of old filled the temple with his glory. Every heart rejoiced, and felt that God was with us of a truth. Such was our introduction into our new habitation;—and had we not reason to say with Joshua, *As for me and my house, we will serve the Lord.*" The pious order, great simplicity, and regularity ever after observed in this house, evince how sincerely it was thus dedicated to God's holy honour and service.

Mr. Garrettson continued to fill the office of presiding elder on the New-York district, until the conference of 1804, when we find him stationed in Rhinebeck. In 1805 and 1806 he was stationed in the city of New-York. In 1807 Mr. Garrettson received the appointment of a missionary within the bounds of the New-York conference, having Seth Crowell, a young preacher of zeal and enterprise, and Robert Dillon, a man at that time equally zealous, as helpers in the mission. In 1808 he was again stationed at Rhinebeck; and in 1809 and 1810 a missionary. These appointments may be considered as an accommodation to Mr. Garrettson, that he might feel himself at liberty to preach at large, visit the churches in different places, and *confirm the souls of the disciples.*

In the year 1809 he paid a visit to his old friends on the eastern shore of Maryland, a place where in former days he had been greatly owned of the Lord.

Under date of June 12, 1809, he relates the following occurrence:—

"Last Saturday about two o'clock, I went to the ferry to cross at Powles Hook, and drove near where the boat lay; a crowd of people being around. The horse began to back;

and convinced I could not recover him, I leaped immediately out of the chair, and within the twentieth part of a minute after, horse, chair, and baggage, were all in the water. The horse was active, and swam with the carriage for life. Many people were engaged with boats, and got off the harness with only cutting the girt; so that the harness was not injured; the horse was extricated unhurt, and shortly after the chair was taken up, and every individual thing, without the smallest damage, except getting wet, and the small end of the shaft broken. I crossed on to Newark, and got there by the middle of the afternoon, and found none of my baggage seriously injured, excepting my precious little Bible. It was a heavy jar jumping out of the chair, but I am nearly as well as ever. The affair was most remarkable; first—one hour before it happened I said to a friend, I will put this pocket book into my packet, lest something should happen, in which were notes and valuable papers. Second—my escaping the tenth or twentieth part of a minute before the chair and horse went over. Third—the horse, chair, baggage, and harness unhurt, except the shaft. Fourth—my mind was kept as calm and collected as at this moment. All these things considered, we may see the superintending hand of God, and be led to adore his holy name. No doubt it was permitted for good, and I believe I shall profit by it."

From thence Mr. Garrettson passed on to Bellville, from that to Newark and Trenton, in which places he preached, and thence to Philadelphia. Here he preached with much liberty and satisfaction, and was greatly refreshed in the society of his old friends. After spending some time in this place, preaching and visiting, he passed on to Wilmington and to Elkton, where he had the happiness to find his niece, Mrs. Taylor, in the fear and love of God. Under date of June 22, he makes the following reflections:—

"In the afternoon I met a large society, after which I inquired if any were alive who were members thirty years ago, when I rode that circuit. They told me not one. 'O! my friends,' said I, 'probably all of you will be in eternity before the end of thirty years more. You see the necessity of training up your children for the church, in order to keep a succession of faithful members, as our children and children's children must perpetuate the memory of Christ on earth; and so from generation to generation be transplanted from the militant to the church triumphant, that the upper region may be peopled with blessed millions to adore the Saviour eternally.'"

The following account of this tour was communicated to Mrs. Garrettson in a series of letters which he wrote during his absence. It will doubtless be read with interest by those especially of his surviving friends in that part of the country, as well as by all others who delight in seeing "the good hand of God" on his servants.

"Friday 23. I leave my horse to rest, and Mr. Presbury accompanies me to Baltimore. My sister Elizabeth died about thirty years ago, and left an only child. I saw her about a twelvemonth ago, but she is now gone.

"Saturday I spent mostly in retirement, except to visit some friends.

"Sunday 25. This morning I preached at Old Town, in the afternoon at Light-street, and in the evening was to be at the Point; but as the weather was so excessively warm, I thought I could not go in justice to myself. The congregation here do not increase much; indeed they are rather smaller. The extravagance of some of our people has had a greater tendency to fill other churches than their own. Mr. D——d's congregation they say increases very much; it seems a half way house. I am willing God should work when, where, and by whom he pleases. I have met brother Jesse, and he sent on my appointments to Washington and Georgetown.

"Monday 26. I took the stage, and in the evening arrived at Georgetown; had a large congregation. Our friends are much engaged. Brother Roszel is the stationed minister. The weather remains very warm. 'Tis well I got a loose thin garment before I left New-York. I lodge at Mr. Elison's, a very worthy family. Here I have a large cool room. They are some of my old Eastern Shore friends.

"Tuesday 27. To-day Mrs. Foxal sent her carriage for me, and kindly gave me the use of it while I stay. In the afternoon I went to town, and stopped at Captain Lewis's, where I found Jesse Lee, the chaplain, nursing his leg. On his way from Baltimore the day before, his horse fell, broke the shaft of his gig, threw him out, and one of the screws bruised and cut his leg very much. I am fearful it will go hard with him if the hot weather continues. I preached in the evening to many people with a degree of freedom.

"Wednesday 28. This morning brother Smith, the city preacher, went with me to the navy yard, and I thought well of the improvements. Dined at Captain Lewis's. He is not a member of society, but his daughters are. I was well pleased with the family. In the afternoon brother Elison came for me; I intended to go and hear the debates in congress, but they had adjourned for dinner sooner than usual. This evening I preached in Georgetown again; here we have a respectable society; and had I been an apostle they could not have treated me much better.

"Thursday 29. I went to breakfast with an old Eastern Shore friend, brother Gruntree. He is an old Methodist preacher. Here brother Parrot and his lady, my earliest friends, came to see me, and took me to Mrs. Foxall's.

"Friday 30. I left my hospitable friends, and came on in the stage, laden with members of congress and others, to Baltimore.

"Saturday 31. Mr. Hollingsworth gave me a kind invitation to stay with him; so that I am now most comfortably retired in a large airy room. This afternoon I had an interview with Richard Garrettson, my nephew. He gave me a particular account of his father's landed estate, which has been for years involved in law. Their title was thought by the first lawyers to be good, and there was no probability of their losing the suit. He tells me the first person that entered a claim died very suddenly before the trial came on, and likewise the second; and lately a third person renewed the suit, and died suddenly, and left his pretended right to no one. The suit is fallen.

"July 2. My to-day's appointment was announced last week in the public paper. I had much freedom to preach in the new church this morning. Mr. Colvil, with his five motherless children in deep mourning, came around me in tears; it was an affecting sight. In the afternoon I preached in good old Mr. Otterbine's church. I am not in Rhinebeck now, but where thousands think it a privilege to hear an old Methodist preacher. Mrs. Gough drank tea with us at Mr. Hollingsworth's, and talks of taking me to my appointment at Mr. Presbury's, where I left my horse. It was published in all the churches to-day for my last sermon in the new chapel. On Tuesday evening I heard brother Shin preach. He is a good preacher, and is stationed here, and appears deeply devoted to God.

"July 4. This is the day of great parade in the city. Some of the Methodists were warmly engaged in it. From what I understand, it was conducted with as much decency as the nature of the thing would admit. The language of my heart was, Turn away thine eyes from beholding vanity. In the evening I preached in the new church to a large congregation, and we had a time of power. I have known the society here in a more flourishing state. I fear politics has done hurt to the cause of religion.

"Wednesday 5. This morning I left my kind friends,

accompanied by brother Hagerty, in his gig, to Presbury's church, where I left my horse, and had an agreeable time and freedom to preach. This is a blessed family; his mother was my father's niece, and I knew her thirty years ago deep in piety; but she has long since gone to glory. Her son is now treading in her steps.

"Thursday 6. Accompanied by my cousin Presbury and other relatives, we repaired to what is called the Camp Meeting Chapel. It is beautifully situated in a forest, at a distance from any house. As I rode up, my mind was solemnly impressed when I saw such a number of horses and carriages fastened to the trees, and the people waiting to hear the word. I had a sweet time in speaking from 1 Cor. vii, 21. While the gracious Lord was visiting the people with his heavenly grace, we had a little shower to refresh the vegetable creation. It seems this chapel is one of Mr. Gough's last acts of kindness to the poor. I went home with Mrs. Gough. There are some handsome improvements about this venerable mansion, and the garden excels any thing I have seen. At present the parlour family is very large, there being much company. While they enjoyed themselves in the hall, Mrs. Gough and myself sat in the parlour, talking over old times. At nine o'clock the bell rung, and about fifty of the family assembled for prayer in the chapel. All the gentlemen and ladies were present morning and evening. The riches of the world are good, if made a good use of. Who can tell how these pretty things will be employed a few years hence?" (Mrs. Carrol and her mother were both out of health; and since both are dead.)

"Friday 7. My appointment to-day is in Hartford, at Belle Air court house. I came to the place a little after 3 o'clock, and found there had been a misunderstanding. A large gathering had been there at 11, and were gone. We went to Mrs. Montgomery's, and had a little gathering at five. Dined to-day at my oldest brother's widow's.

Brother Galespy, the circuit preacher, met me there, and he and my nephew came with me to my niece Mrs. Norris's, and spent the night. She and her daughters are very friendly, and desire to enjoy religion.

"Saturday 8. This day the preacher and my nephew, F. Garrettson, left me. Here I have one sister living; she is old, and her memory is so totally gone, that she does not know her own children; but gives no trouble whatever; and sits and knits without speaking a word, unless spoken to. A few nights ago she called her daughter, and told her she should die soon, and requested her to bury her by her dear husband. I think I never saw a greater picture of innocence. This afternoon I go to Abington.

"Sunday 9. This morning a very large congregation assembled from almost all quarters. My mind was sweetly drawn out. The church was much crowded, and many of my relatives were present. Preached from Psalm xlviii, 12, 13. I told them I had come several hundred miles to invite them to come to Jesus, and to inform them that after following the Lord between thirty and forty years, I found religion better and better. I preached about an hour and a half, and scarcely knew when to give over. There was no loud noise, but the whole assembly were melted into tenderness; while I entreated them to meet me in heaven, for thither I was bound. In the afternoon I rode seven miles, to what is called Bush chapel; but it would not contain the people; so I preached in a grove with freedom. Glory to God, I have lived to convince friends and foes that I am sincere at least.

"Many descendants of my ancestors were present. Some of you have wondered where I have been, and what I have been about. Excuse me if I make a small digression to inform you. When the sermon was ended, many gave the hand; among the rest was good old brother Watters, 80 years of age, and brother Herbert, 90, who had made an effort to come out. Indeed they looked like ripe shocks, fit to be gathered home. Mr. Allen, minister of Specucia church, who was a hearer, said he wanted some conversation. I requested him to fall in with me at some other place, where we could have more time together. He said he would. I went home with my cousin R. Garrettson, and found my mind sweetly composed after the labours of the day. There are very few families in this country, at least in the interior part of it, to whom I might not have access. Indeed if I were an angel I could not be treated with a greater degree of kindness. I rejoice to find Dr. Hall, who is stationed in this circuit, very much followed. It is in his power to do much good through the blessing of God.

"Monday 10. I preached in a church in Bush River Neck, near the Chesapeake Bay, and not a mile from the place in which I was born, and within half a mile of where I believe the first church in Maryland was built. From what I can learn, it was built by an ancestor of mine more than two hundred years ago. It was the height of harvest, or there would have been more hearers than the church could contain; however, it was pretty well filled. I had some freedom to preach from James i, 24. A Colonel Mathews was present, whom I have not seen since we were boys. I requested him to go with me to Mr. Chancy's, where I was to lodge. I wanted to talk with him about new things and old; he gave me his company some hours. He is not acquainted with Jesus, but seems to have a respect for religion.

"Tuesday 11. This day I spent in visiting my relations in the Neck. None of them oppose religion, and they generally think well of Methodism. They are, I believe, moral and industrious, and have a fulness of this world's goods. I told them freely my errand among them, and that they wanted but one thing to make them a happy people.

"I appointed to preach at Miss Griffiths. One of the young ladies went to give an invitation to our relatives there; they said they should be glad to see me, but they had not time to attend the meeting. I sent a message to them, begging if they would not meet me on earth, they would strive to meet me in heaven. In this place I had but a small congregation. Here parson Allen met me again, and stayed all night. When alone, I inquired with regard to his knowledge of divine things experimentally, and the manner of his preaching. I told him he was appointed to serve a people who were near to me by natural ties, as the greater part of his congregation were my family connexions. I begged of him to declare the counsel of God faithfully, to attend to regular church discipline, to visit from house to house, to have meetings in different parts of the congregation, and to exercise extemporaneously, both in prayer and exhortation, and show the people that there is something wanting besides profession and morality. He said he would do the best he could, that he wished my time was not so short, and would be glad I would stay some days at his house.

"Thursday 13. This morning I parted with Mr. Allen, and yesterday I parted with brother Galespy, (who had faithfully attended me to every place,) and my affectionate Harford friends, and was accompanied by some relatives to the ferry. I crossed, and went on to the head of north-east **********. I have just received a letter from brother Cooper; he says he must leave the Peninsula soon, and I must by all means come on and help him. I shall, God willing, be at Smyrna, Del., the 27th of this month.

"July 14. This morning I left North East, came to Elkton, and preached at five o'clock to a small congregation. My niece and her husband were very kind to me, and my mind was easy and free. I am not of that service to people as I wish to be. *This* always was, and I fear always will be, a poor place for religion.

"Saturday 15. I rode to Mr. Canaan's, where I found several of my old friends and acquaintances still in the profession, and I trust happy in the enjoyment, of religion. We had a comfortable time together; the conversation turned mostly on the subject of falling, jumping, shouting, and clapping. I made free to speak my sentiments. Mr. Canaan was with me; but Mrs. Canaan had her fears, and asked if I had ever been at a camp meeting.

"Sunday 16. A large congregation assembled in Bethel chapel. While we were singing the first hymn, a woman shouted and jumped amazingly. Before I gave out my text to prepare the assembly for an attentive hearing, I told them I had come a great way to communicate gospel truths to them, and I requested a patient hearing. I was led to give a display of the wisdom and goodness of God, and to open to view our duty in resigning up our all to him, to the evidencing the power of religion experimentally, and likewise to display the external marks of inward religion. I told them a ministry of this kind was necessary to keep up a pure flame; without it they could not expect to prosper, and that there would be an evaporation that would leave them a mere sound, without the vital flame. The congregation was still and attentive till I ended the sermon, and then one jumped and shouted. I thought it a great favour that there was stillness and attention till I ended my sermon. Mr. Basset dined with us, and in the afternoon I rode home with him, and spent an agreeable evening; but I find my friends are growing old like myself. Mrs. B. is a pious woman, and he is full of zeal and love. He would have gone with me, but his many concerns prevented. He told me that wherever his influence extended he did not suffer a drop of distilled liquor to be used. His house and table are very plain; and he says he feels it to be his duty to do every thing in his power for the cause of God.

"Tuesday 18. I rode after dinner 22 miles to Smyrna.

preached with freedom, and lodged at Dr. Ridgley's. His wife was daughter to parson Harris, and was among some of my first spiritual children about Chestertown, 30 years ago. Here I met an old friend, one of Judge White's daughters, who has stood fast in the Lord more than thirty years. In the vicinity they are making great preparation for a camp meeting, to begin next week. I went to the spot, where I suppose fifty men were employed in seating the ground. They thought it would take fifteen thousand feet of plank, and there seemed to be great anticipations of glorious times.

"Wednesday 19. I rode to Queen Ann's. When I rode up to my old friend's, brother Segar's, I told him to take a full view of me, and try to recognise some features; but he could not. I made myself known, and we had a season of much happiness.

"Thursday 20. This dear friend intends travelling with me till I return from Smyrna. We went on, and dined at Thomas Wright's, and after dinner lodged at Mr. Fediman's. He did know me, and that was all, for he had to consider a long time. Several friends came over this afternoon, and we had some religious conversation, and some politics. Upon the whole it was an agreeable time. Brother Segar is a pillar in the temple.

"Friday 21. We came to Centreville, and in the evening the church was nearly filled. I preached, and then went on to Mr. Kanard's to lodge. This is a respectable and kind family.

"Saturday 22. I spent the day retired, and had an opportunity to read and write.

"Sunday 23. I had hearers from five to twenty miles, and should have had a great congregation had there been general notice. However, the church was filled morning and afternoon. There is a large, respectable congregation in and about this place. I can say, glory to God, this was a high day. I had the privilege to see many of my old friends and their children. Some of the blacks were in raptures. My intention was to go down the Peninsula for about three or four weeks, on the Chesapeake side, and up on the other side, and I had my appointments about fifteen or twenty miles apart, by which means I might have an opportunity of speaking to thousands and tens of thousands, perhaps for the last time, and seeing many of my old friends; but I found the country filled with notices for camp meetings. I was pressed by Mr. Basset and others by all means to attend them. I am now going on my way to Smyrna, where the first begins.

"Monday 24. I leave my kind Centreville friends, and am to preach in the English church, which is almost an unheard of favour in this country; but it was the desire of the vestry. In this neighbourhood I was beaten by Mr. Brown years ago, and now a near relation of his is the principal vestryman. My appointment was at four o'clock, and though a wet afternoon, the church was crowded above and below with Methodist and church folks, white and black, and we had a moving time. This meeting was at Church Hill. I do indeed love the Lord Jesus.

"Tuesday 25. At four o'clock, in the Methodist church near Saddler's cross roads, I had uncommon freedom to preach. A large church was filled above and below. Indeed it looked a little like quarterly meeting. I preached on Peter's denying Christ. We had a very powerful time; but the enemy took advantage of a weak minded black man in the front gallery, who cried aloud, stripped, and struck his fists together, and declared he would not see his blessed Master treated in that sort;—that he would fight for him till he died on the spot. I desired them to take him out, and not let him return till the meeting closed; which they did in less than two minutes. My soul is happy; Lord, keep me humble. The children and grandchildren of old friends show me the same respect that their parents would if alive.

"Wednesday 26. I had great freedom to preach to-day. I left you at Smyrna; I again resume my detail:—There were about thirty preachers present, local and travelling, and seats provided for about three thousand. There were two hundred and sixty tents. I lodged every night on the ground, in Dr. Ridgley's tent. We had fourteen sermons in the course of the meeting, and very powerful speaking. I preached with great freedom on Friday, from Isaiah's vision, vi, 8; and on Sunday, from 'I am not ashamed of the gospel,' &c, Rom. i, 16. M'Claskey, Chambers, and M'Combs, delivered some able discourses. The meeting increased every day till Sunday, when there were about five thousand people. I did not see one disorderly person on the ground from first to last; scarcely a single thing to drink except water, and sometimes a little milk with it, or molasses and vinegar. They had tables, beds, curtains, carpets, and provisions, and servants, in great order. We had a solemn, profitable season, but no particular outpouring of the Spirit, and very few converted, awakened, or sanctified. The people in this country must be either Methodist or nothing, for there is scarcely a minister of any other name. At this meeting I saw a great many of my old friends with pleasure, and I trust with profit. Good Mr. Basset seems taken up with divine things. At parting they had a manœuvre, which some of us old men did not feel free to join in, marching round the camp, blowing five or six trumpets, and singing by turns.

"Tuesday, Aug. 2. At eight o'clock the meeting closed. O! what a blessed day it will be when friends meet to part no more for ever! Brother Chambers, a respectable old preacher from Baltimore, travels with me. My appointment at night was in Dover church, and it was well filled. My text was, 'Grow in grace.' Brother Chambers exhorted, and we had a good time. Lodged at Mr. Basset's.

"Wednesday 3. My appointment was at Barret's chapel,

at three o'clock. About three hundred people were assembled, many more than I expected, as they had but short notice. I spoke from, 'But one thing is needful.' Brother Chambers exhorted, and the Lord was with us. I am still among my children and old friends. A woman belonging to the community of Quakers was present in a state of desperation; whom her friends sent in hope of relief. I conversed and prayed with her, but left her in the same state, despairing of the mercy of God. Here I met with many kind friends I had not seen for four or five and twenty years. Many of my old associates are gone to glory, but their children and grandchildren have taken their seats in the church. We stayed at Judge Barret's. His brother was a dear friend of mine, and a spiritual child, but long since gone to rest. I hope the children will tread in the steps of their pious parents.

"Thursday 4. We went on to Milford, and got on the camp ground by ten o'clock. Seats were prepared for about two thousand. Meeting opened at three—a small congregation, and a small sermon. Friday the congregation increased. I preached from Peter's denial of Christ. Saturday the congregation increased. Brother Chambers preached a good sermon :—not a great many, and mostly young. Sunday about three thousand. I preached from 'Walk about Zion,' &c, Psalm xlviii, 12, 13. Had much freedom;—about one hundred and fifty tents. Here I met many dear old friends from fifty and sixty miles round, and we were happy together. We had three sermons each day, but I cannot say we had any extraordinary work either in conviction or conversion. Those who do not profess religion behaved well. No intoxicated person, nor even the smell of liquor, on the ground. A few noisy, jumping, dancing Methodists, did, I fear, more hurt than good. An empty head is very disagreeable to me; a shout, when the power of God is in it, is sweet to me. I have never been at a meeting where there were more fruitless human exertions, though I did what I could to prevent them. I begged them to wait for the Master, and let him take the lead. Extravagance was carried to the greatest height among the blacks, for many of them continued it for hours together. Such things, when the power of God is not in the camp, tend to dissipate the mind. The most I can say of this meeting is, there was great attention paid to the word preached. During my stay I got accommodations at my friend Shockley's—a rich friend, who was within call of the camp ground, where my friend Chambers and I retired for lodging. It is a blessing to have able, wise, and prudent rulers in the church; but to my grief, I say we have some whose zeal and imprudence go far beyond their knowledge; but, thanks be to God, there are men of piety and knowledge to check their precipitancy, or we might soon bid farewell to good old Methodism. Glory to God, I think it will stand, though encumbered with many disagreeables. There are thousands in this country deeply pious. The Methodists have the whole business to themselves in this country. There is scarcely a minister of any other denomination.

"Monday 7. I had an appointment at Dover to-day at three o'clock. We started early this morning, rode twenty-two miles, and got in by twelve o'clock. I feel a little weary. The church was nearly filled. I discussed two heads of doctrine—the lowest and the highest degree of Christian experience. Brother Chambers made the application, and we had a precious season. This town looks old;—in fact, there are very small improvements made in any part of this country, except in matters of religion. We stayed at Mr. White's, brother to Dr. White, an old friend. We had a number of my good friends to tea.

"Tuesday 8. To-day I preached at Blackstone's chapel. Dined at Ringold's. At three we had a large congregation. After speaking more than an hour on the various parts of prayer with great freedom, while the power of God was graciously displayed, and I was much spent, I asked brother Chambers to speak on the duty and benefit of prayer, which I had promised to do if strength permitted. He did so in a very pertinent manner, for he is an excellent preacher. He began travelling when he was sixteen, about twenty years ago, but has been located several years. Brother Whitby, a worthy man, where we now lodge, (who was once a travelling, but is now a local preacher,) said, For your encouragement I can tell you that under the sermon you preached in our chapel, as you went down, a poor sinner was awakened, who has since found pardon, and is now happy in God.

"Wednesday 9. My appointment is at Chestertown in the evening. My good friend Chambers leaves me this morning. As Basset's camp meeting begins to-day, and he expects to meet his wife from Baltimore, I have no other chance to see my old friend, Dr. Anderson, who is very ill from a fall from his carriage. I think it a small thing to go twenty-five miles out of my way to see so worthy a member of the church, and the fruit of my poor little labours more than thirty years ago. I rode twenty-five miles, and dined at Chestertown, at brother Harris's. In the evening I had the church full of serious hearers, and to my agreeable surprise the Doctor was among my audience. I had a most sweet season among my friends. My sermon was from Psalm xlviii, 12, 13. 1, I spoke of the church ministry, beauty, and order; 2, her strength and fortitude; 3, her privileges; 4, her testimony.

"Thursday 10. Our worthy brother Burniston accompanied me to the camp ground.

"Friday 11. A very rainy day. I preached in a large tent, on the necessity of holiness. Mr. Harris fell under the word, cried for mercy, and found peace. He is not a member of our church. Brother Chambers got under such a deep travail of soul for holiness, that he fell under the power of God, and lay for hours; and when he came to, rejoiced in the perfect love of God. I was requested by some of my old friends to call this meeting; among others was Mrs. Bruff and her sister Ward. These holy women are full of the perfect love of God. This meeting held several hours. I likewise called a meeting in the preachers' tent at the same time;—the tents rung with the praises of God. The poor blacks seemed almost ready to fly. There is, nevertheless, a probability we shall have a great meeting. Many of our good friends have come from Baltimore. I must leave you. This minute I have been conversing with Mrs. Bruff;—she tells me, at the above-mentioned meeting three besides Mr. Chambers were brought out, and several led to feel the necessity of holiness. My dear love, there is a struggle in the camp. I will tell you more when we meet. God bless you and yours. I am in the cause of God; nothing else would reconcile me to so long an absence from you. I remember you at the throne of grace;—there also remember me;—I can only stand by grace. While I am writing, prayer, praise, and shouting are all around me."

CHAPTER XVI.

Appointed to the New-York district—Some account of his duties—His sermon on the union of fear, hope, and love—General Conference in 1808—Attends the first delegated Conference in 1812—His views on some parts of our ecclesiastical economy—Appointed a conference missionary—His letter to the Rev. Lyman Beecher—State of that controversy—Mr. Garrettson's views of the subject—His charity sermon—Not pleased with being returned a supernumerary—Domestic enjoyments—Makes a journey to Albany, Schenectady, Troy, &c.—Returns home—Solemn reflections—Makes another southern tour—Visits New-York, Trenton, Burlington, Philadelphia, Wilmington, Abington, and his native place—Reflections on the state of the people—Goes to Baltimore, and participates in a revival of the work of God in that city—Returns to Rhinebeck.

In the year 1811 Mr. Garrettson was appointed again to the New-York district, over which he presided with dignity and usefulness four years. He was every where received, both by preachers and people, as a father in the gospel, and his word was often attended with power to the hearts of his hearers. It was at this time that the writer became more intimately acquainted with this venerable servant of God; and still remembers with pleasure and gratitude the tenderness with which he was treated by him. With what delight have I accompanied him to some of his quarterly meetings, and witnessed the devotedness of his soul to the service of his divine Master.

Mr. Garrettson occasionally employed the hours which were not otherwise devoted to the services of the sanctuary, in writing. Though his publications are by no means numerous, yet they are sufficient to speak for him, since his voice is hushed in the silence of the grave.

The first publication was an account of his experience and travels, from which copious extracts have been made in the first part of this memoir. The second was on the evils of slavery, a copy of which I have not been able to find.

It was about this time that he published his sermon " On the union of fear, hope, and love in the believer." The object of Mr. Garrettson in this sermon was to show how fear, hope, and love, coexist in the heart of a true believer in Christ, balancing and regulating each other. "Fear and hope to the soul of a Christian," says he, "are like the cork and lead to the net; the cork keeps it from sinking, and the lead from too much floating;—so it is in a spiritual sense; fear keeps hope from rising into presumption, and hope keeps fear from sinking into despair." —"There is also a union in the souls of believers between fear and love. Love without fear would become secure, and fear without love would be slavish. Love is the dearest companion of filial fear. There is nothing more fearful than genuine love, and nothing more loving than filial fear. These two graces sweetly draw the soul to God. Love is the grace that unites the soul to God, and fear keeps from departing from him."*

At the general conference held in the city of Baltimore in 1808, on account of the great increase of our work, extending over so large a territory, the number of travelling preachers continually multiplying, it was resolved to establish a delegated general conference, to be composed of a certain number of delegates to be elected by the several annual conferences. This measure, so necessary for the well being of the church, had been in contemplation by Bishop Asbury and others, elders in the ministry, for several years. When it was first proposed at this general conference, it met with a determined opposition, and was finally lost by a very considerable majority. Towards the close of the conference, however, it was reconsidered, and presented in a somewhat modified form, and very unanimously adopted.

The first delegated general conference was held in the city of New-York, in May, 1812. Among others, as delegates from the New-York conference, was Mr. Garrettson; and such were the respect and confidence manifested towards him by his brethren, that at every subsequent general conference he was selected as one of their delegates. In this character, though he often differed with some of his brethren on certain points of church government, he always manifested the most stern and inflexible opposition to any innovation upon the established doctrines of the church; at the same time cheerfully bowing to the will of the majority on matters of indifference.

In respect to the question on which the general conference have long been divided in sentiment, namely, whether the presiding elders should continue to be appointed as they now are by the bishops, or be elected by the annual conferences, it is well known that Mr. Garrettson

* Those who wish to see the whole discourse may find it in the Methodist Magazine (in which it was republished) for July, 1825.

was in favour of their election by the conferences. This is mentioned merely as an historical fact, without entering into the merits of the question, pro or con, or intending even to express an opinion in relation to it, any farther than to say that, whether right or wrong, no doubt can be entertained but that Mr. Garrettson acted from the purest motives, and according to the best dictates of his judgment.

At the close of his service as presiding elder of the New-York district, in the year 1816, he was again appointed as a missionary within the bounds of the New-York conference. This appointment was also designed, as is believed, to give him an opportunity to travel at large, as his inclination, age, and circumstances might dictate; the conference and bishops having full confidence that he would employ all his time and talent in the best way he could for the glory of God and the good of souls.

It was during this year that he published "A Letter to the Rev. Lyman Beecher, containing animadversions on a pamphlet" written by that gentleman, entitled "An Address of the Charitable Society for the education of pious young men for the ministry of the Gospel." This pamphlet of Mr. Beecher gave great offence to most of those denominations of Christians not connected with that charitable society. To awaken a spirit of liberality among Christians for the support of that institution, Mr. Beecher gave a most pitiful description of the spiritual and moral desolations of our country, the paucity of "competent ministers" to afford moral and religious instruction to the people; and likewise made a powerful appeal to the community, to induce them to exert themselves by every possible means, and especially by pecuniary contributions, to assist in educating and sending forth these "indigent, pious young men."

It was generally thought, and I believe very justly, that Mr. Beecher, in his descriptions of the spiritual destitutions of many parts of our country, was not fully borne out by facts, and that in his estimate of the number of "qualified ministers," he had excluded nearly all except those of his own denomination. He calculated the population of the country at that time to be 8,000,000, and says, that from the best information he could obtain, there were not over 3,000 "educated ministers of the gospel in our land; leaving a deficiency of 5,000 ministers, and a population of 5,000,000, destitute of proper religious instruction:"—that is, on the ratio of one minister for every 1,000 of the population, which he supposes to be necessary to afford that quantum of religious instruction which the wants of society demanded.

It was said above that it was supposed that Mr. Beecher designed to exclude nearly all other denominations except those of his own order—meaning thereby the Congregational, Presbyterian, and Dutch Reformed orders,—from being competent to preach the gospel. According to the best data within our reach, there were not less than 6,000 ministers at that time belonging to the Presbyterian, Congregational, Dutch Reformed, Lutheran, Baptist, and Protestant Episcopal churches; and allowing only 2,000 for the Methodists and all other sects, which it is believed is very considerably below the actual number, we had even then one minister for every one thousand inhabitants. From this computation it will appear that the supposition is fully sustained; at least there were at that time not less than 3,000 ministers belonging to the three denominations of Presbyterians, Congregationalists, and Dutch Reformed, all of which hold fast the distinguishing doctrines of Calvinism.

Allowing the accuracy of these remarks, what could have been Mr. Beecher's design in sounding the note of alarm on such a high key? Did he not mean to insinuate among his brethren of New-England, to whom the Address was especially directed, that all other ministers must be superseded, as not being qualified to impart religious instruction? It is not intended to impeach the motives of the author of this Address. Such is the power of prejudice, operating under the impulse of strong, local feelings, that he might have persuaded himself that the salvation of the nation depended upon a well-organized Calvinistic ministry, marching forward in firm phalanx against the host of Arminians, and all others whom they might consider to be heterodox in their religious opinions. Allowing this to have been the case, the means resorted to on this occasion were highly proper. But if any choose to say that this was not the belief of Mr. Beecher and his associates, then they must allow that the assumptions contained in their Address were entirely unwarranted by facts,—that a false and highly exaggerated description was given of the moral and spiritual destitution of our country.

The inevitable result of this investigation is this:—
1. If Mr. Beecher's statement, that there were but "3,000 competent religious instructers" at that time, were true, none were considered such except Calvinistic ministers, and not even all of these, for most of the Baptists are such. 2. By supplying the deficiency of 5,000 ministers with such as Mr. Beecher had described, then all other ministers must be put down as incompetent to instruct the people in religious things. 3. To accomplish this object, entirely sectarian in its character, the Address was written and circulated, in which it was stated that

"To produce such a combination and such efforts, the wretched state of our country must be made known. The information contained in this Address may, with propriety, it is believed, be communicated on the sabbaths to all our worshipping assemblies, and the investigation commenced in it, with propriety be continued, until a regular and minute account can be given of the religious state of our land. The newspaper, the tract, and magazines, must disclose to our slumbering countrymen their danger. The press must groan in the communication of our wretchedness; and from every pulpit in the land the trumpet must sound long and loud. The nation must be awaked to save itself by its own energies, or we are undone!"

Such was the language of the Address. Such were the mighty efforts to be made to annihilate the influence of all the ministers in the land, but such as should be marshalled under the Geneva standard, and answer to the watchword taught in the theological school under the charge of this charitable society. Is it therefore any wonder that other denominations took the alarm?

Among those whose zeal was kindled on this occasion, Mr. Garrettson showed himself in the foremost ranks. Excepting the bishops of our church, perhaps no man living was better qualified from his personal observation, to make a true estimate of the religious state of the country. For more than forty years he had travelled in various parts of the United States, and preached the everlasting gospel with a rare success. Believing that Mr. Beecher's representations were calculated to make an erroneous impression on the public mind; that he unjustly depreciated the talent, the piety, and usefulness of ministers of other denominations, and that his remarks tended to promote a spirit of sectarian zeal incompatible with those liberal views and feelings inculcated in the gospel of Jesus, Mr. Garrettson addressed himself directly to Mr. Beecher on these subjects, in a printed letter of 28 pages, 12mo.

He commences by telling Mr. Beecher, that he had "been endeavouring to promote the Redeemer's kingdom through various parts of this continent for more than forty years," and that during that time he had witnessed the displays of the convincing and regenerating power of God from one end of the country to the other. But it "appears to me," says he, "that you and your associates have given a very unfair and uncharitable representation of the religious state of our nation, whether designedly or for want of better information, I leave for your readers to determine."

The remainder of the first part of the letter is devoted to the refutation of what were considered to be Mr. Beecher's injurious imputations of other ministers; but the author confines himself principally to the vindication of his own brethren of the Methodist ministry, leaving it to others to answer for themselves. The following paragraph will show how adroitly and successfully Mr. Garrettson meets his antagonist in one item of his calculations:—

"You have placed your church in Connecticut on the highest scale among the several states in the Union. You have given a short history of it, and have, in your way, prostrated the southern part of our country. Probably you are a native of Connecticut; I was born in Maryland; and as you have, among other southern states, undertaken to degrade the religious character of the people of this state, I am willing to compare them with those of your state. I am well acquainted with almost every part of both; and as you have fixed your eye on the Congregational Church in Connecticut, I shall fix mine on the Methodist Episcopal Church in Maryland.

"You say that you have upwards of 200 congregations, averaging 50 members each, making about 10,000 church members. I have looked over our church records, and find that we have in Maryland* more than 25,000 church

---

* Mr. Beecher had represented the state of Maryland as being in a most deplorable condition. After having stated that Virginia, with a population of 974,622, needed 900 ministers in addition to the 60 it already had to make up the 1 for every 1,000 of the inhabitants, he says, "Of the state of Maryland we cannot speak particularly. But from general information on the subject, we have no reason to believe the supply any better than that of Virginia;" that is, as 60 to 900. He must therefore have considered either that the Methodists were not worthy to be included among Christian ministers and members of the church, or otherwise greatly depreciated the religious character of the state of Maryland.

members, who have the pure word of God preached, and the sacraments duly administered." This certainly was a triumphant refutation of Mr. Beecher's statement.

In addition to its being the professed object of this Address to awaken the slumbering energies of this nation to the religious state of the people, it was believed by many, and indeed I believe by most who read the Address, that it had a political object to accomplish. This belief, in connexion with the general movements of the Congregational churches in New-England, was founded on the following passage. After intimating that our general government was very defective as to its provisions for its own permanency, the Address says:

"A remedy must be applied to this vital defect of our national organization. But what shall that remedy be? There can be but one. The consolidation of the state governments would make a despotism. But the prevalence of pious, intelligent, enterprising ministers, through the nation, at the ratio of one for a thousand, would establish schools, and academies, and colleges, and habits, and institutions of homogeneous influence. These would produce a sameness of views, and feelings, and interests, which would lay the foundation of our empire on a rock. Religion is the central attraction which must supply the deficiency of political affinity and interest. Religion is the bond of charity, which in storms must undergird the ship,"—meaning evidently the national ship.

Whether Mr. Beecher really designed to produce a political revolution, by effecting a change in the national constitution, or merely to produce such homogeneousness of views, and feelings, and concentration of action, as would enable those who should be under the influence of these views and feelings to control the national elections and councils, we pretend not to determine. It is, however, manifest, I think, to all dispassionate minds, that could he place one minister of his own order over every one thousand of the inhabitants of these states—and his calculations went to that object—for by including ministers of all other orders, there was more than that proportion even then,—they might exert a most powerful influence on the national legislature. At any rate, many serious people fully believed this was one object of the Address. That this was the opinion of Mr. Garrettson is evident from the following sentence:— "The glimmering light beaming through your performance leads us to suppose that as you are the privileged order in the eastern states, so you wish to be through the whole Union." Whatever may be thought of the merits of this controversy, such was the general burst of indignation manifested from almost all quarters against the assumptions of the Address, the evident proscriptions it uttered against other denominations of Christians, that the friends of Mr. Beecher it is said called in and destroyed the Address.* It was, however, reprinted by those who were inimical to its principles, thinking that probably the most effectual way to prevent them from being carried into effect was to have them generally understood.

Mr. Garrettson finishes his strictures in the following words:—" I hope in future that you and your associates will be more wise and pious. You will then be less self-confident, and will find it easier to exercise Christian

---

* But though the Address was called in, the principles set forth and advocated in it, have never, so far as I have understood, been disavowed, either by Mr. Beecher or any of his friends. Had this been done, so much notice would not have been taken of this affair in this place. On the contrary, subsequent measures have only tended to strengthen the belief expressed by Mr. Garrettson and others, that something more than a mere desire to propagate pure religion, had mingled itself with the councils of that society, and those who were pledged for its support. Sorry indeed should we be to attribute any improper motive to any body of men; but we can no more close our eyes to the history of events, than we can refrain from rejoicing that the "Lord God omnipotent reigneth," and granteth to his people rest in this happy land.

charity toward those who do not think in every particular as you do. I have during my ministry laboured for peace, and I desire as far as it is admissible to have a charitable feeling for all. It was with a degree of reluctance that I undertook to write upon this occasion; but a sense of duty overruled my inclination. I desire neither the honours, riches, nor pleasures of the world, but only to be a follower of the Lord Jesus, whom I have loved from an early part of my life. Indeed for more than fifty years I have studied the Holy Scriptures with pleasure." All who were acquainted with the author of the above extract, will readily perceive that it is perfectly characteristic of his manner of writing, as well as expressive of the prevailing sentiment of his heart.

In the year 1815, Mr. Garrettson published a *Sermon which he had preached in John-street Church, N. Y., for the benefit of the Methodist Charity School*. This school has been in existence for more than forty years. It is designed for the special benefit of the poor children under the care of our church, orphans and others, and is supported by the voluntary contributions of the community. For this purpose a sermon is preached annually in each church in the city, and a collection taken up for the benefit of the school, at which time the children are present.

After stating the objects of the institution, the nature of true charity, and the arguments by which the duty is enforced, Mr. Garrettson says, "I have brought forward these strong testimonials, my beloved friends, to strengthen and animate your faith in this glorious work. Call to your remembrance the prayers and alms of Cornelius, which ascended to heaven as a sweet memorial before the Lord. You now have it in your power to bring blessings on yourselves, and to entail them on your posterity to the latest generation."——"You see these tender lambs rising from their seats to express their gratitude for what their kind benefactors have done for them, and to implore farther aid."——" You see their little hands stretched out, while their eyes are fixed on you, as their fostering fathers and mothers, and to all who are willing to reach to them a friendly hand."——" Brethren, if you want barren souls and slender fortunes, give sparingly to the poor; but if you want to be rich in grace, and your ability to do good to be increased, then give liberally, accordingly as God has bestowed upon you." In this way did Mr. Garrettson plead in behalf of poor children; and through his and the influence of others who have from time to time lent their aid to the support of this benevolent institution, it has gladdened the heart of many a widowed mother and many a helpless orphan.

At the conference of 1817, which was held in Middlebury, Vermont, Mr. Garrettson was returned as a supernumerary. This appointment by no means pleased him, as he fully believed himself competent to do effective service. The appointment, however, was made by the conference with a view to his accommodation, that he might be at liberty to labour when and where he might think he would be most useful; and the assurance of this respectful and friendly feeling gave him satisfaction.

It is manifest that his growing infirmities made it somewhat difficult for him to travel very extensively. Blessed with a pious and agreeable family, possessing every thing calculated to make retirement or domestic life desirable and happy, Mr. Garrettson had every inducement which an indulgent Providence could afford to remain at home. Yet in the midst of all these enjoyments, he sighed for another sort of repose, for that repose which resulted from a consciousness of having done his best to bring sinners into the fold of Christ. "My mind," says he, "is after precious souls."

To gratify this prevailing desire of his heart, after remaining for a few weeks in the circle of domestic and social enjoyment at his mansion in Rhinebeck, and preaching as occasion offered in the chapel, in company with Mrs. Garrettson and his daughter he set off on a tour to the north, "hoping," says he, "I might do some little good to the churches." Leaving Mrs. Garrettson at Kinderhook, at the house of his friend, Judge Van Ness, whose pious consort formed an agreeable associate for Mrs. Garrettson, his daughter accompanied him to Schenectady. They stayed with Dr. Nott, the president of Union College. "This institution," says Mr. Garrettson, "is blessed with a worthy president and professors, and will, I trust, be a blessing to society, and give much pleasure to its patrons." Here the Methodists, though few in number, and far from being generally wealthy, had recently, by great exertion, built a convenient house of worship, in which Mr. Garrettson preached with lively satisfaction. From thence they returned to Troy, and put up at the house of the Hon. George Tibbetts, whose hospitable mansion is delightfully situated on the side of a sloping hill ascending from the eastern part of the city, denominated Mount Ida. On the sabbath Mr. Garrettson preached in the Methodist church in this city, morning, afternoon, and evening, to an attentive congregation; and "truly," says he, "it was a good day." He remarks, that when he first visited this place about thirty years before, there were only a few scattering houses, and no Methodist society; but that now he was rejoiced to find a flourishing little city, in which were four houses of worship, and not less than three hundred members of the Methodist Episcopal Church. What seemed to add to his religious enjoyment was the catholic and friendly spirit manifested by the several religious denominations towards each other. On the 30th of June they all returned in safety, blessing and praising God, to their peaceful home.

After his return he makes the following reflections, which perhaps some whom they might concern may read to their benefit:—"The great ones have set themselves against the work of reformation. I have laboured to do them good; but all my efforts seem like water spilt on the ground, which cannot be gathered up. They do not openly oppose; if they did, perhaps I might have more hope. If I would let them alone, they doubtless would bear with me; but how can I, as a messenger of God, let them sleep quietly over the pit of destruction!"

The most part of the summer months of this year he spent about home, preaching only on the sabbaths, except a tour through some parts of Connecticut, and some visits to New-York, Poughkeepsie, and a few other places in the state. During this time he says, "I have had sweet seasons in reading, writing, and family devotion; I feel that God is good, and I will praise him." He observes, "From the 20th of June to the 9th of December, I have travelled about 1,000 miles, and preached whenever and wherever I could find an opening."

Under date of Dec. 9, 1817, he says, "Being pressed in spirit, though a great cross for me to leave my precious wife and daughter, I entered into an examination in regard to my motives in leaving home—whether duty called me in my 66th year to leave a quiet, plentiful habitation, and a most agreeable family, to encounter the cold and storms of winter, at my own expense;—but having made up my mind, a little before sunset I bade adieu to my family, went on board the steam boat, and by sunrise next morning found myself in the city of New-York, one hundred miles on my journey southward." Staying only one night in the city, the next day by steam and stage he went to Trenton, where he spent the sabbath very agreeably, preaching to crowded congregations. From thence he passed on to Burlington, where he preached to a very full house, and lodged with his old friend, Mr. Stirling. Of him Mr. Garrettson observes, "He is a very old man, confined to his bed, appears innocent and happy, and has been a great support to the cause of Methodism in this place." On

Tuesday he rode to Philadelphia, and put up at Mr. Lemuel Green's, a located minister, who had travelled and preached until he was worn down, but whose Christian hospitality invited the servants of God under his peaceful roof. He remained in this city preaching to large and attentive audiences in the several churches, visited many of his old friends, with whom he enjoyed sweet fellowship, until the 6th of January, 1818, when he took the stage for Wilmington, and on the following evening preached to the people with much satisfaction. He passed thence to Abington, where he spent the sabbath, preached three times to the people, and then went on to his native place. Thursday 15th, he says, "I preached within a mile of the spot where I was born: they were chiefly young people and distant relations. They seem," says he, "to be almost an entirely new race of people, there being few in the congregation whom I could recognise as my former acquaintance. I fear," he continues, "that my native county makes but little improvement, and that too much dissipation prevails among the young people especially, for their own good either in temporal or spiritual enjoyments. Though the society at Boosbyhill was not as large as it was 45 years since, I was comforted under the reflection that it had been a nursery from which many plants had been taken, some to heaven, and others transplanted to some of the new settlements, where they have grown into stately trees of righteousness. Here they have established themselves, and been the means of good to the souls of others. Thus the work spreads." Here he was cheered with an account of an aged couple, Mr. Herbert and his wife, the first fruits of Methodism in this place; the woman had recently departed to glory in her 90th year, and the man still lived in the fear of God in the 94th year of his age. Here also he preached in what was called the Bush Church, the second Methodist church which was built on the continent of America, and which had been standing nearly fifty years. Taking an occasion from the decayed state of the church, and the reflection that so many of the old members had gone to their reward, and also fearing that the rising generation were not so zealous for God as they should be, he cried aloud from these words, "Who will rise up, and rebuild the temple?" After which, assisted by Mr. Toy, an aged minister, he administered the sacrament of the Lord's supper to about 60 communicants, with whom he had a solemn and profitable time.

Having finished his labours in these parts, and cleared, as he humbly hoped, his skirts of their blood, he went thence to the city of Baltimore, where he was much refreshed to find a glorious work of religion going forward. With all the vigour of youth he entered into this work, catching, and enkindling in the hearts of others, the fire of Divine love. He preached in the several churches in the city, morning, afternoon, and evening; attended prayer meetings and love feasts; visited from house to house, and in the midst of all enjoyed great peace of mind and health of body. Though he could not approve of all the exercises which were tolerated, thinking that in some things extravagances might have been beneficially checked, yet he rejoiced greatly at witnessing such manifest displays of the awakening and regenerating power of Divine grace. After remaining in this city about two weeks, during which time he preached no less than fourteen sermons, he took his departure for the north, passed through Abington, Philadelphia, Trenton, and New-York, in all which places he stopped long enough to "scatter some of the good seed of the kingdom," and in the latter part of March, after an absence of about four months, he once more saluted his beloved family in peace and health.

CHAPTER XVII.

Attends the New-York Conference—Secession of a number from the church in New-York—His feelings in relation to that unhappy affair—Makes a short tour to the north—Thence to the eastward—Passes through New-York—Thence on to Middletown, Conn.—Thence to New-London, where he enjoys much peace—Visits Norwich and preaches—Conversation with a pious lady—Revival of religion—Grieved with beholding the ravages of Socinianism—Goes to Providence, R. I., and preaches—Probable check to the Socinian heresy—Visits Boston and Lynn—Origin of Methodism in Dorchester, Mass.—Visits Cambridge—Returns to Hartford—Thence to Rhinebeck—Domestic felicity—Makes a second tour—Affliction—Reflections thereon—Ardent desire for the salvation of souls—Returns through New-York city to Rhinebeck—Revival of religion there—Attends Conference.

Mr. Garrettson's relation to the conference, though not altogether such as he wished, remained unchanged, and he continued to employ his time and talent in that way and in those places which he judged might best promote the good of the church. The New-York Conference, which was this year, 1819, held in the city of Troy, was attended with some very serious difficulties, originating from the state of affairs in the city of New-York. These difficulties which terminated in a secession of a number of members with a preacher at their head, were accompanied by measures which made it necessary to bring the affair before the conference; but though some collisions existed among some of the preachers in relation to this unhappy business, in which conflicting interests and feelings were enlisted, it terminated as peaceably as could have been expected under the circumstances.

To these things Mr. Garrettson alludes in his journal with much feeling. Being a man of peace, and having the interests of the church much at heart, he was always deeply affected whenever any thing occurred to disturb the harmony of brethren, or to impede the progress of true religion. But though a momentary gloom was spread over the church in the city of New-York, the clouds were gradually dispersed, truth finally prevailed over error, and great peace has since rested on those who loved our Jerusalem.

After remaining at home a short time, on his return from the conference, Mr. Garrettson set off on a tour for the north. He visited Kinderhook, attended a camp meeting at Niskayuna, a quarterly meeting at Troy, and preached in Pittstown, Lansingburgh, Schenectady, and Albany, and likewise at a quarterly meeting near Spencertown, and then returned to his beloved family at Rhinebeck. "During this tour," he says, "of about two weeks, I had great sweetness in preaching the word, which I did once or more at every place I visited. I am now," he adds, "officiating in my little congregation at Rhinebeck. Here I am pleasantly situated, an agreeable family with every thing necessary to make life desirable. This makes it the greater cross for me to leave home."

On August 18, having engaged a young man to accompany him, he took his departure for an eastern tour. He first, however, passed down through Poughkeepsie, over the highlands to Peekskill, to Tarrytown, in all which places he stopped and preached, and to the White Plains, where he preached on sabbath morning, and in the afternoon at New Rochelle. "I am now," he says, "in a part of Mr. Beecher's *moral wilderness*. We think, however, that the gospel has had a glorious spread in this part of the country. Within eight miles of the place where I now am we can count six or seven Methodist churches, where the word and ordinances of God are administered, and where many persons of undoubted piety assemble for the worship of God." On Monday he rode into the city of New-York, and put up with his old friend, Mr. George Suckley. He observes, "I could have shed tears over the society, on account of their trying situation," alluding to the unhappy division before mentioned, which was now near its consummation.

The Saturday following he left the city on his way eastward. He passed on through Rye, Stamford, Fairfield, Stratford, New Haven, to Middletown, where he spent the sabbath, preaching to a full house of attentive hearers, morning, afternoon, and evening, the last sermon being on the certainty of the resurrection of the body. Thence he passed on to Hebron, where he was happy to find a revival of religion, and to be comfortably situated in the pious family of Mr. Burroughs. On Tuesday he went to New London, where he enjoyed much of the divine presence in secret devotion in the house of God.* This was his first visit to this place. He remained here until Thursday, preaching to a crowded house every evening. On Wednesday evening he gave information that as he expected to depart next day, he would preach at sunrise on the doctrine of Christian perfection. Accordingly he says, "I arose about four o'clock in the morning, and after spending more than an hour in retirement, I repaired to the church at the hour appointed, and preached to about 200 attentive hearers. I enjoyed a solemn, sweet season, while endeavouring to water the souls of God's people."

After these solemn exercises were over, and taking some refreshment, he journeyed about four miles, to a Mr. Miller's, whose daughters and one son had recently experienced a change of heart, during a revival in New London and its vicinity. The father, 78 years of age, though friendly, made no profession of religion. "With him," says Mr. Garrettson, "I conversed on the subject of religion, congratulated him on the happy change wrought in his children, and urged him to seek the same blessing;

* It was a common practice with Mr. Garrettson, whenever he first visited a place where there was a church, to repair thither at the first opportunity for private prayer.

I endeavoured to obviate the common objection he made, that he could not change his own heart, by remarking that although Jesus Christ had merited every thing for us by his passion and death, yet we may not expect to be saved unless we seek by repentance, prayer, and faith. After spending several hours with this kind family, and praying with them, we took our departure, and rode ten miles to Norwich, and preached in the church, which was nearly filled. After service a pious woman asked me if any one had requested me to explain the Lord's prayer. I answered in the negative. She then informed me that she had prayed to God that I might be led to make that prayer the subject of my discourse. I answered, that when I went into the pulpit, as well as before, it lay with much weight on my mind, so much so that I dare not refuse taking it as the foundation of my sermon. She received it as an answer to prayer. She had been particularly exercised on the petition, *Thy will be done in earth as it is in heaven.* It seems that her husband was under an impression that it was his duty to become a travelling preacher, and her mind was deeply exercised in respect to consenting to give him up to the work." While in this place the stationed preacher gave him a reviving account of the spread of God's work in the conversion of souls, which had commenced at camp-meetings. It had extended gloriously through several of the neighbouring towns, and some hundreds had been brought to the knowledge of the truth.

Having finished his work here, he passed into the state of Rhode Island, and was much annoyed in one place where he preached, with the Socinians. With the Socinian doctrine Mr. Garrettson held no fellowship. Perhaps his zeal never showed itself more intensely on any subject than when he came in contact with a system that to support itself, the real Divinity, the proper, unoriginated, and eternal Deity of Christ, must be called in question. His tract on this subject, which was published in the Methodist Magazine, and by the Tract Society of the Methodist Episcopal Church, evinces the deep interest he felt in the support of this cardinal doctrine of Christianity. He could not, therefore, but behold with sorrow and indignation the ravages which the Socinian scheme was now, and had for some time past, been making among the churches in New England, particularly in the metropolis of Massachusetts, as well as in some parts of Rhode Island.

After preaching with much satisfaction in Providence, both in the Methodist church, and by request, in the one occupied by the Rev. Mr. Wilson, a pious Presbyterian clergyman, Mr. Garrettson rode forward to Bristol, where he preached to a large congregation on the doctrine of Christian Perfection, a favourite theme with him. Here he found a large society of pious members, whose devout behaviour and delightful singing pleased him much. Of the bishop of the Protestant Episcopal Church, residing in this place, Mr. Garrettson speaks in terms of high commendation, as a man deeply devoted to the interests of Christ, and expresses an ardent hope that he with his clergy and the Methodist preachers, between whom there appears no difference in their doctrinal views, will be able to check the progress of the Socinian heresy, and stem the tide of Hopkinsian refinements on the liberty of the human will, or their metaphysical speculations concerning a *moral* inability and *natural* ability. From Bristol he went on to Warren, and preached on "Now the just shall live by faith; but if any man draw back, my soul shall have no pleasure in him." Among others, the Unitarian minister made one of his hearers. May he not have heard in vain! "I feel," says he, "for this loving society." In Somerset he also preached to an attentive congregation, with much satisfaction.

He then passed on to Easton, and thence to Dorchester, and thence through Boston, in company with the Rev.

Elijah Hedding and wife, to Lynn, where he preached on a short notice to a large congregation, on "Put ye in the sickle, for the harvest is ripe."

Mr. Garrettson gives the following account of the rise and progress of the Methodist Church in the town of Dorchester. He says, "I lodged with a Mr. Otheman, a pious, wealthy gentleman from France, who a few years since removed from Boston to this place. Some time previously to his leaving Boston, he had embraced religion, and had become a member of our church. After removing to Dorchester, he invited preaching at his house. Though but few attended at first, and much opposition was excited, so much so that the thoughtless multitude frequently stoned the house, the Lord soon began to work on the hearts of the people, and in a short time a considerable society was established. Soon after, more room being wanted, Mr. Otheman built a handsome church at his own expense. It was in this house that I preached."

From Lynn Mr. Garrettson went to Cambridge, where he lodged with his old friend, Mr. Black, under whose hospitable roof, and in the society of whose pious family, he felt himself much at home. The Sunday following he preached three sermons in the city of Boston to very large congregations. From thence he journeyed through the several towns, in most of which he officiated, to Hartford, where he preached with great freedom. Sunday he preached in Goshen (Connecticut) in the morning, and in the afternoon in Cornwall, and on the Tuesday following he was permitted once more to embrace his family in health and peace. "In this tour," says he, "I was absent six weeks, travelled 600 miles, and preached about 60 sermons. I thank God for his presence, which was with me every day. I do not wish to be employed in a better work."

We have already seen, that notwithstanding Mr. Garrettson enjoyed at home every thing that could make domestic life agreeable—that though age and its attendant infirmities might plead a reasonable excuse for his remaining in such a pleasant retreat, free from the cares and fatigues of travelling—yet the ardour of his soul would prompt him to break through all these restraints, and brave the inclemency of seasons, contemning equally the indulgences of this life and the peltings of the storms, when they stood in the way of his duty to God and man.

Accordingly, in the latter part of December, in the year 1820, we find him bidding adieu to his family again, for another tour to the south. As he travelled over nearly the same ground as that traced out in a former chapter, passed through similar exercises of mind, and preached with equal ardour, displaying for his old friends and near relatives the same affectionate attachment, as well as evincing the same devotedness to the cause of his divine Master, it is thought not necessary to give a detailed account of this journey. The following reflections, however, which he wrote down in Philadelphia, under date of Jan. 21, will be read by every pious reader with satisfaction. It seems that before he left New-York, walking out one evening, he slipped down in the street, and severely bruised his leg. Notwithstanding he was able to pursue his journey to Philadelphia, when he arrived there, his leg was so much swollen that he was obliged to keep his room, and to put himself under the care of a physician. To Dr. Sargeant he expresses much gratitude for his kind attentions. While confined here, unable for active service, he thus writes:—

"All is right, being in the order of God. He knows what is best for his creatures. For three sabbaths I have been deprived of the privilege of the sanctuary; but while thus solitary, I have been contemplating on the wonders of redeeming love, and the various beauties of the sacred Scriptures. O redemption! How deep! How unsearchable the Deity! Eternally existing in three hypostases, yet one glorious, incomprehensible Deity, coequal, consubstantial, and coeternal!

"During the week past I have had a great travail of soul. My exercises were various, but the most weighty concerned myself. I saw indeed in God infinite perfection; but in myself merely I am but a fallen speck of the creation. I inquired what motive could have led me at this period of my life, and at this inclement season of the year, to leave my quiet home. Was it for money? No. Was it for ease or honour? No. Was it because I thought myself a great preacher? No. I was, as I believed, called of God, forty-six years ago, to be a minister of Jesus Christ; and the blessed God has frequently suggested to me that he had called me for life, or as long as I should be able to work in his vineyard. I did some years since plead with the Lord that I was growing old and infirm, and begged that I might be permitted to stay at home, and labour there occasionally as I was able. The blessed God restored me to my hearing almost as perfectly as ever, strengthened my intellect, renewed me in soul and body, and told me I must go and do his work. To be sure it is a great cross for me to leave one of the most agreeable families with which a man can be blessed; but for Christ's sake I can stagger under even this cross, and cheerfully cast in my mite to promote the interests of his kingdom."

As a proof of the high estimation in which his labours were held by the citizens of Philadelphia, we may remark, that unknown to him, the official members appointed a committee to wait on him, and request his longer continuance with them. To which he replied, "I receive the voice of the church as the voice of God to me, and therefore agree to remain a few weeks longer."

To the same fact, the following letter, directed to Mrs. Garrettson, will bear testimony:—

"DEAR SISTER,—We accept with much esteem the

tender yourself and daughter have been pleased to make us in your Christian respects.

"Your good husband has been detained among us, for some time, partly by affliction, and partly by a general or official request. Some of us see, or think we see, a providence in his affliction. It opened the way in part for his useful labour among us, which possibly might not have been the case, had he passed through on his original plan. He will now leave us. His leg has got well, and he has delivered his message to thousands; many of whom, we trust, in the embrace of the truth, will praise God in time and eternity for his Christian visit. We have, with others, strove to make his situation as agreeable as was conveniently in our power, and have been blessed in having him with us under our roof. Many thousands of precious vessels has Jesus scattered through this vale of tears, of whom we now know nothing; but he will bring them with him, when he 'comes to be glorified in his saints, and in all those who look for his appearing.'

"Please accept in return, a reciprocity of our Christian esteem; and make acceptable a tender of our love to your dear daughter.

"Believe us in simplicity,
"Dear sister, affectionately,
"WM. and MARY CHANDLER."

Here is the true secret whence originated that restlessness of spirit whenever he had been long at home. He felt that the vows of his God were upon him, and that he must perform them. Often when I have been favoured with a visit to his friendly and peaceful mansion, have I witnessed, even in the midst of every thing calculated to make life desirable, the anxiety of his mind to be in the field, labouring for his Lord and Master; and I verily believe that he enjoyed himself far better in an humble cottage on coarse fare, when thus employed in the Lord's vineyard, especially if he could have one or two of his brethren in the ministry with him, whom he always loved with the tenderest affection, than he otherwise could, surrounded with all that this world can afford. This work was the aliment of his soul, it being "his meat and his drink to do his Master's will," as a public servant of the church.

After recovering in some measure from his lameness, and preaching several times in the different churches in the city of Philadelphia, he went thence to Baltimore, to the Eastern Shore of Maryland, &c, every where being received as a father in the gospel, preaching to overflowing congregations, until April 26, 1821, when he returned to the city of New-York, where he spent a day or two, and then arrived once more at Rhinebeck, after an absence of a little more than four months. On finding himself again in his domestic circle, he says, "O Lord, how shall I praise thee for thy loving kindness to me, thy poor, unworthy servant!"

It seems that during his absence there had commenced a gracious revival of religion in Rhinebeck. This was most cheering news to him. "Thank God," says he, "a great change has taken place here within five or six weeks. About 50 have joined the church, and the greater proportion of them profess experimental religion, most of whom are young people. Our little church is crowded with attentive hearers, and if the work continues we must enlarge it. The blessed God began and carried on this work in his own way, and the stationed preacher and several of the most gifted members in prayer and exhortation, were engaged as *workers together with God*. Frequently the meetings continued until twelve o'clock at night, and sometimes until two o'clock in the morning. I have met with them almost every night in the week, and have no doubt of the genuineness of the work."

The harmony of those who were the subjects of this work was somewhat disturbed by the introduction of a spirit of proselytism to the peculiar sentiments of the Anabaptists. This led Mr. Garrettson once more into the field of controversy; and in a sermon he undertook a defence of infant baptism, in order to prevent the young converts from being drawn aside by the efforts of those who insisted on adult baptism by immersion as the only gospel mode. This had the desired effect, and the good work continued to prosper. The quarterly meeting, which was attended on the 26th and 27th, was a time of great power, and "I trust," says he, "much good was done."

On Monday he took the steam boat for Troy, in order to attend the conference. "We had," says Mr. Garrettson, "an agreeable time through the whole session, with the exception of feeling much sorrow for two members whom we were obliged to expel. I fear poor J. C. is gone for ever. O how awful! A professed labourer in our Lord's vineyard for more than twenty years, finally disgraced by his own evil conduct, and cast off. Thus the cause of Christ suffers."

CHAPTER XVIII.

Mr. Garrettson holds on his way—Engaged in building a house of worship at Rhinebeck—Sets off to attend General Conference—Last visit to his native place—Some of the transactions of the conference—English delegates—Friendly intercourse and correspondence between the English and American conferences—His views on some points of church government—Attends the New-York conference—Makes a western tour—Reflections—Novation schism—Testimony against sabbath breaking—Solemn reflections—Attends a camp meeting—Retires to his mansion—Private meditations—Visits some of his old friends in Westchester county—Notice of Governor Jay—Death of Mrs. Carpenter—Her character—Visits Kingston—Death and character of Mr. Sands—Death of Mr. C—— S—— Death of old friends in New-York—Reflections on a call to the ministry—Death and character of Mrs. Suckley—Visits Philadelphia—His zeal for missions—Deadness to the world—Attends the New-York conference—Preaches and publishes his semi-centennial sermon—Extracts from the sermon—Returns to Rhinebeck—Last entry in his journal.

I do not find any particular account in the papers left by Mr. Garrettson of his exercises and travels for the years 1822 and 1823. It is, however, well known that he held on his way, in the same undeviating course of exemplary piety, and, as far as his growing infirmities would permit, in the active services of the sanctuary.

It was during this interval that he was very active in building a house of worship at Rhinebeck. It will be recollected that in the preceding chapter, when speaking of the revival then prevailing in that place, he remarked that if it continued, they must have a larger house to accommodate the hearers. This was soon found to be the fact; and Mr. Garrettson heartily engaged in the work, contributing largely himself, and ceased not until it was accomplished. Such a work was not only needed, but very befitting the exertions of one who expected at no distant period, to be an inhabitant of that "house not made with hands, eternal in the heavens."

Having been elected a delegate to the general conference to be held in the city of Baltimore in the year 1824, in company with Mrs. Garrettson and his daughter he left home in the month of March, came to the city of New-York, where he remained about three weeks, labouring in the city and in Brooklyn, and then, April 1, in company with Mr. Reece, and some others, he took his departure for Philadelphia. Here he lodged with his friend, Dr. Sargeant. He remained in the city, visiting his old friends, and preaching in the several churches with much feeling and satisfaction, until Monday the 12th, when he went on to Wilmington, Del., where he preached the next day to a full house, and "God," says he, "was with us of a truth."

On leaving Wilmington for Elkton, he says, "A young countryman and his wife took the back seat, paying no respect to age or any thing else, so that I had to ride on the front seat with my back toward the driver, which so fatigued me that I had to remain a day at Elkton to rest. This, however, gave me the opportunity of an interview with the Rev. Mr. Drake, an aged, intelligent minister, with whom I formed an acquaintance nearly fifty years since. On Tuesday I took the steam boat at 8 o'clock, P. M., and was in Baltimore before daybreak next morning. I took lodgings with my good friend, Dr. Baker, who married the daughter of Mrs. Dickins, the present widow of the late excellent Rev. John Dickins. She sat under my ministry more than 45 years ago, when she was Miss Yancy. I rejoiced to find her so pleasantly situated, with such a pious, intelligent Christian, as I believe Dr. Baker to be. Here also I met with my good brother Reece and others.

On Tuesday, April 20, at the request of his nephew, Capt. Norris, who came for the purpose of taking him in his carriage, Mr. Garrettson left Baltimore to visit once more his native place. As this was his last visit to that part of the country, I shall present his own account of it chiefly in his own words. "We rode," says he, "about 20 miles to Capt. N.'s sister's, near Bellair. I find a great vacancy in this house. When I was here a few years since, the mother and her daughter Clarissa, two lovely females, received me with smiles;—but where are they now? First the sister, and then the mother, took their flight to glory, leaving four brothers and three sisters to mourn their loss. Mrs. Norris and her daughter Clarissa were both blessed women, and I cannot doubt but that they have gone safe home.

"Friday 23. We set off—my nephew kindly tendering his services to conduct me wherever I wished to go—to traverse that part of the country called Bush River Neck, my native place. I saw many places which I used to frequent in the days of my boyhood, and among others the old church in which I was baptized. By this means many circumstances were brought to my recollection which transpired more than sixty years since. I was glad to find that the people had recently repaired the old church, and that a good fence was kept around the graves of our ancestors. They have, however, no settled minister in what is called the Old Parish; neither do they want one; for the Methodists have societies and houses of worship in every direction. We lodged at Mr. Ruthen Garrettson's, who has one of the richest farms in the Neck. His mother was my mother's sister, and my father was his father's brother, and he married my eldest sister's daughter. They both have a respect for religion, and I hope they will yet be saved.

"On the Lord's day morning I preached with much satisfaction in the Abington church, and then rode six miles, and preached in a neat church lately built in the forest under the direction of old Mr. Webster, who at this time was dangerously ill. I was sent for to visit him, and found him *nigh unto death*, joyfully waiting until his time should come. He was among the first who embraced religion when the Methodist preachers made their entrance into this part of the country about *fifty-six* years ago. He is now about *eighty-five* years of age, and has been a preacher more than *forty* years. He has a large family of children and grandchildren settled around him, while he, like a ripe shock of corn, is waiting to be taken to the garner of rest. I had sweet fellowship with him. A few days after I left him he took his departure. I bless God for this opportunity of conversing with him."

After spending a day or two longer in visiting his friends, he returned, on the 27th of April, to Baltimore, the seat of the general conference.

"May 1, 1824," says Mr. Garrettson, "our conference opened at 8 o'clock, A. M. I am, and I hope I always shall be, an old fashioned Methodist, and therefore was not at all pleased that the conference should have been detained so long in fixing rules for the government of its proceedings. So did not the apostles, elders, and brethren, who assembled at the first council at Jerusalem; but being *full of faith and the Holy Ghost*, they acted in the utmost harmony one with another." This extract is introduced not as a censure on the general conference for adopting by-laws for the government of their deliberations, but to show the predilection of Mr. Garrettson for primitive simplicity and order.

At our general conference in 1820, it was resolved to open a more direct intercourse with our brethren in England by an interchange of delegates from one country to the other.* Accordingly in that year, the Rev. John Emory was sent by the bishops as our representative to the British conference. He bore with him the following letter:—

---

* This mutual intercourse had been kept up by the visits of Dr. Coke until the year 1804, since which time until the present it had been suspended, though the conferences continued an official correspondence with each other.

"*Baltimore, May 27, 1820.*

The General Conference of the Methodist Episcopal Church in the United States of America, to the British Conference of Ministers and Preachers, late in connexion with the Rev. John Wesley:

REV. AND DEAR BRETHREN,—Grace, mercy, and peace be multiplied to you, and to the Israel of God under your charge, both at home and in foreign countries. With a sincere and earnest desire to establish and preserve the most perfect harmony and peace with you, our elder brethren, we have adopted measures for opening such friendly intercourse as will, we devoutly pray, tend to the accomplishment of this desirable end.

Situated so remotely from each other, and under different forms of civil government, it is believed that no mode of correspondence will so effectually unite the European and American Methodists as an interchange of delegates from our respective conferences.

We are encouraged to hope that such correspondence will be acceptable to you, from the consideration of the visit of Messrs. Black and Bennett at our last session, and from the friendly opinion of our dear brother, the Rev. William Black, who has been with us during our present sitting in this city.

Should such a friendly intercourse be approved, we shall receive with cordiality your representative at our succeeding sessions, and, with the most sincere friendship and affection, reciprocate the visit.

The prosperity of your missions, both at home and in foreign countries, is matter of praise and thanksgiving to the great Head of the church; and our unceasing prayer is, that they still may increase more and more.

The last four years have been distinguished by no ordinary success within the field of our labour: our borders have been greatly enlarged, and the wilderness has budded and blossomed as the rose. The last year especially has been attended with an abundant outpouring of the

Holy Spirit, and the increase of our numbers has exceeded that of any former year.

The field of missionary labours is opening and extending before us, and the Divine providence appears to be preparing the way for the conversion of the Indian tribes on this vast continent.

The bearer, the Rev. John Emory, has been appointed our delegate to your body, and will be able to give you a more particular account of the work under our charge, and especially of our commencement and progress in the missionary cause.

Most earnestly praying that the Methodists may be identified in their doctrine, experience, and practice, in every part of the world, and that the Father of lights may pour upon you, and upon us, the Spirit of grace, and preserve us in the unity of faith, and in the fellowship and peace of his Son Jesus Christ, we remain, Rev. and dear brethren, yours in the gospel of our common Lord.

Signed, by order and in behalf of the Methodist Episcopal Church,

ENOCH GEORGE, *President*,
ALEXANDER M'CAINE, *Secretary*."

To which the British conference returned the following answer:—

"To the General Superintendents of the Methodist Episcopal Church in the United States of America:

DEAR BRETHREN,—We enclose to your care the resolutions passed by the conference, after the letters addressed to us by the *American General Conference*, and delivered by the Rev. John Emory, had been read and considered.

In addition to the expression of our sentiments contained in those resolutions, on the renewal of intercourse between the two conferences, we are directed to request you to convey to your next general conference our warmest thanks for those declarations of unabated brotherly affection toward us and the connexion, which your letters contain, and for the appointment of Mr. Emory as your representative.

In him we have recognised the purity of your doctrine, and the fervour and simplicity of your piety. We have received him not as a stranger, but as a "brother beloved." Our hearts are as his heart, and it will be remembered as one of the most pleasing circumstances connected with the conference held in this town, that our personal intercourse with you was here restored, and that this "work of love" was committed to so able and excellent a brother, whose public ministrations and addresses in our conference, have been equally gratifying and instructive to us and to our people.

From the statements made by Mr. Emory as to the progress of the work of God in the United States, we have received the greatest satisfaction. We offered our united thanksgivings to God, that the doctrines of primitive Methodism, the preaching of which God has so eminently owned in the salvation of men, and the edification of believers, are not only continued among you in their purity, but have been so widely extended by your great and persevering efforts, and that the same holy discipline, in all its essential parts, continues, whenever you form societies, to guard and confirm the work which God has made to prosper in your hands.

For the state of our affairs in Great Britain and Ireland, and in our missionary stations, we refer you to Mr. Emory, who, as health would allow, has attended our sittings, and to those publications with which, before his departure, we shall be happy to furnish him, to be laid before you.

You will see that we have had to rejoice with you in the great extension of the work of God into the various parts of the British empire, and that the institutions of Methodism, which we have proved to be so well adapted to promote and to preserve true religion, are known and valued in every quarter of the globe. May we, with you, be the honoured instruments of turning the disobedient to the wisdom of the just in every place, and of hastening the universal kingdom of our Lord.

The resolutions on the disputes in the Canadas, were adopted after a calm and patient consideration of the case, in which we were greatly assisted by Mr. Emory. We hope they will lead to a full adjustment of those disputes, and that the affection which exists between the two connexions generally, will extend itself to the brethren and societies in the Canadas. This is the disposition which we shall earnestly inculcate upon those under our care in those provinces; and we have full confidence that the same care will be taken by you to extinguish every feeling contrary to love, among those over whom you have control and influence.

With earnest prayers for you, dear and honoured brethren, in particular, on whom devolves the general direction of the affairs of the great body of Methodists in the western world, and whose labours are so severe, but so glorious,—that you may be filled with wisdom for counsel, and strength to fulfil the duties of your great office;— and also for all your churches that they may have rest, and walking in the fear of the Lord, and in the comforts of the Holy Ghost, may be abundantly multiplied,

We are, dear brethren,
Yours most affectionately in Christ Jesus,
JABEZ BUNTING, *President*,
GEORGE MARSDEN, *Secretary*.
Liverpool, Aug. 7, 1820."

The following are the resolutions referred to in the foregoing address:—

"Resolutions of the British Conference in reference to their relation with the American General Conference:

The Rev. John Emory having been introduced to the Conference as the accredited representative in our body of the general conference of the Methodist Episcopal Church in the United States of America, presented a letter from that conference, and gave an interesting and encouraging statement of the prosperity of the work of God in the United States; which account the conference received with much satisfaction, and unanimously agreed to the following resolutions on the occasion, viz.

1. That the conference embrace with pleasure this opportunity of recognising that great principle, which, it is hoped, will be permanently maintained,—that the Wesleyan Methodists are one body in every part of the world.

2. That the British conference have frequently rejoiced in the very favourable accounts which have been received, year after year, of the great and glorious work which God is graciously carrying on in the United States of America; but that it is with *peculiar pleasure* that they receive a *representative* from the general conference in America. The statement given by our beloved brother, Mr. Emory, of the present state of Methodism in America, has been received with much joy; and the conference hereby expresses its high satisfaction, not only in the *declaration*, but in the *proof*, of the love of our American brethren in fully opening the way for a brotherly intercourse between the European and the American societies.

3. That the conference particularly rejoices in the zeal which is manifested by our American brethren, in carrying the gospel of our Lord Jesus Christ to the Indian tribes, and in the success which God has already given to their labours in that natural and moral wilderness; and hopes, that the time is drawing near, when the *aborigines* of that vast continent shall become the mild and gentle followers of our gracious Redeemer.

4. That it is the earnest wish of this conference, that the kind and friendly intercourse which is now opened between the British and American conferences should be continued; and that, prior to the time of the next general conference in America, the British conference will appoint

one or more of their body to visit our brethren in America, and to be present at their general conference.

5. That a letter shall be sent to the American brethren, containing these resolutions, and strongly expressing our high approbation of the selection of our highly esteemed brother, Mr. Emory, as their representative to our conference, and our earnest desire and prayer, that, in the spirit of Christian love, we may ever be one in Christ Jesus.

6. That there shall be a regular exchange of minutes, magazines, missionary reports and notices, and of all new original works, published by the European and American Methodists, from their respective book rooms."

This friendly intercourse being thus opened to the mutual satisfaction of the two great divisions of the Methodist family, this year, 1824, the Rev. Richard Reece was despatched as a representative from the British to the American general conference, accompanied by the Rev. John Hannah as his companion. This is the Mr. Reece to whom Mr. Garrettson alludes in the foregoing extract from his journal, and of whom he frequently speaks in respectful and affectionate terms. On the introduction of Mr. Reece into the conference he presented the following letter, which was read by the secretary, Dr. Emory:—

"To the General Conference of the Methodist Episcopal Church assembled at Baltimore, in the United States of America:

DEAR BRETHREN,—The time has arrived which calls us, in pursuance of a resolution unanimously passed in the conference of 1820, held in Liverpool, to commission a deputation from our body, to attend your ensuing general conference, to convey to you the sentiments of our fraternal regard, and affectionate attachment, and to reciprocate that kind and friendly office, which, on your part, was performed by the visit of one of your esteemed ministers, the Rev. John Emory.

The increased interest in your spiritual welfare, which the establishment of this mode of direct and official communication between the two great bodies of Methodists, has naturally excited in us, and, reciprocally, we believe, in you, is to us the first proof of its beneficial tendency, and a cheering indication of its future advantages. For why should the ocean entirely sever the branches of the same family, or distance of place, and distinct scenes of labour, wholly prevent that interchange of the sympathies of a special spiritual relationship which cannot but be felt by those who, under God, owe their origin to the labours of the same apostolic man;—bear testimony to the same great truths before the world,—and whose efforts to spread the savour of the knowledge of Christ, on our part through the British empire, and on yours through the population of those rising states, which have derived their language, their science, and their protestantism from the same common source,—Almighty God has deigned so abundantly to bless?

We received with heartfelt joy the messenger of your churches, the Rev. John Emory, bearing the grateful news of the progress of the work of God in your societies, and were refreshed by the expressions of your charity. We now commit the same charge to the faithful and beloved brethren whom we have appointed to salute you in the Lord, that nothing may be wanting on our part, to strengthen the bond of brotherly love, and to call forth mutual and united prayers for each other's welfare by a mutual knowledge of each other's state.

We are on the point of closing the sittings of the present conference, in which the perfect harmony of the brethren assembled has afforded matter for the most devout and grateful acknowledgments to God; both as it is the *indication* and the *result* of that entire affection and unity which exist among our societies throughout the united kingdom. Through the mercy of God, we have rest on every side,—the discipline we received from our venerable founder is still enforced with unabated zeal, and under a conviction of its agreement with the word of God, cheerfully observed;—the value of those apostolic doctrines which distinguish us in the old and new world, was never, we believe, more powerfully felt among us, and never were they with greater fidelity exhibited in our public ministry; and, as a crowning blessing, numbers are yearly added to us and to the Lord, and the light and influence of the gospel are yearly extending, by the Divine blessing upon the labours of the brethren, into the still dark and uncultivated parts of our beloved country. 'Not unto us, O Lord, not unto us, but unto thy name give glory, for thy mercy and for thy truth's sake.'

You will also, dear brethren, partake of our joy in the success with which it has pleased God to attend the labours of our brethren in our different foreign missions.

The leading particulars of their state and prospects you will have learned from our Magazine and Annual Reports, and it will therefore suffice to state, that, in this department of the work of God committed to our charge, upwards of one hundred and fifty of our preachers are employed; and that the zeal and liberality with which our people and the friends of religion generally co-operate with us in this hallowed work, answer to every call, and seem only roused to greater activity and enlargement as the sad condition of the pagan world is by new developements displayed before them. In the formation of regular missionary societies in your church, to promote the universal establishment of the kingdom of our adorable Saviour, and 'to make all men see what is the fellowship of the mystery which from the beginning of the world hath been hid in God,' we have greatly rejoiced; and in those encouraging dawnings of large success among the aboriginal tribes of your native continent, which have cheered the early efforts of those devoted men whom you have ordained to this blessed service. In addition to the *doctrines* in which we have been instructed, God has in his mercy given to us, as Methodists, a discipline adapted in a very special manner to missionary operations, to build up and establish infant religious societies among heathens, and to call forth in every place a supply of labourers for extending the work, and enlarging the cultivated field into the untilled and neglected wilderness. In the spirit of our great founder under God, who regarded *the whole world as his parish*, let the Methodists of Great Britain and America regard the whole world as the field of their evangelical labours; and mindful of this our high vocation, let us enter in at every open door, trusting in God to dispose the hearts of our people to provide the means necessary to carry our sacred enterprises into effect; striving together in our prayers that from us the word of the Lord may 'sound forth to nations and kingdoms of men, of all colours and climates, now involved in the ignorance and misery of pagan idolatry, and sitting in darkness and the shadow of death.'

More fully to declare unto you our state, and to be witnesses of 'the grace of God in you,' we have appointed and hereby do accredit as our representative to your approaching general conference, the Rev. Richard Reece, late president of our conference, and have requested the Rev. John Hannah, one of our respected junior preachers, to accompany him on this service. 'Beloved in the Lord and approved in Christ,' we commit them to the grace of God, and to your brotherly affection. We earnestly pray that your approaching assembly may be under the special guidance and benediction of our common Head, and that all your deliberations may issue in the lasting union and prosperity of your numerous and widely extended societies; that you may increase in faith and love; and that your labours may year after year continue to enlarge and establish in the western world the kingdom of our Lord and Saviour Jesus Christ—'to whom be glory in the church throughout all ages, world without end. Amen.''

Signed in behalf of the Conference,

Sheffield, Aug. 11, 1823.   H. MOORE, *President.*"

After which Mr. Reece delivered the following address:—

"Mr. President,—The paper which has just been read is an expression of the sentiments avowed by the British conference,—and in which I heartily concur;—sentiments of affectionate concern for the prosperity and advantage of our brethren on this side of the Atlantic. It afforded us much satisfaction to receive from you, by your excellent deputy, the Rev. John Emory, an overture to more frequent intercourse and closer fellowship of brotherly love. *Wesleyan Methodism* is one every where,— one in its doctrines, its discipline, its usages. We believe it to be the purest, simplest, most efficient form of Christianity that the world has known since the primitive days. Doubtless, it is that which has had the sanction of Almighty God, in its rapid and extended success, beyond any other in modern times. It commenced, nearly a century ago, in the mother country, in one of her universities, with a few young men, 'chosen vessels, meet for the Master's use.' Then, it was the 'cloud little as a human hand :'—now, it has spread widely, and is still spreading, over both hemispheres, while its fertilizing showers are descending upon Europe, America, Africa, and Asia, producing fruit wherever they fall,—the fruit of knowledge and holiness. Methodism is our common property. We are alike interested in its preservation and diffusion. It is a sacred trust committed to us. It is a heavenly treasure which we have to dispense for the benefit of man. Its spirit is not sectarian, but catholic, and embraces Christians of every denomination, who hold the essential truths of the gospel, and 'love our Lord Jesus Christ in sincerity.' Your brethren in England were never more concerned to preach its distinguishing doctrines of justification by faith, the direct witness of the Spirit in the hearts of believers, and salvation from all sin in this life, with simplicity, fidelity, and zeal, than at present;—never more concerned to enforce its discipline with firmness and love, and to 'train up' a people in the 'nurture and admonition of the Lord;'—never more careful that it do not deteriorate in their hands, but that it be transmitted, pure and entire, to 'faithful men,' who shall succeed to their labours: for which purposes they are anxious in their instruction, and strict in their examination of the rising race of preachers, that these may be sound in the faith, and lovers of our discipline. Many of them are all we can hope, young men whose 'profiting' has 'appeared unto all,' and to whom we can commit the deposit, without anxiety, believing that they will 'obtain mercy of the Lord to be faithful.'

The result of this care and pains to preserve a pure and effective ministry, has been, and is seen in the blessing of God upon our labours, in an extension of his work through every part of our country, where 'great and effectual doors' are opening into new places, and the Lord is 'adding to his church daily such as are saved.' The members of our society are also improving in personal holiness, and zeal for good works. They are more ready to concur with us in spreading the gospel abroad among heathen nations, as well as in tightening the 'cords' of our discipline at home. On the whole, our prospects were never more bright, nor had we ever more reason to be encouraged.

My opportunities of intercourse with you since my arrival in this country, together with the satisfaction I have had in attending two of your annual conferences, where I met with many of my American brethren, render this one of the most interesting periods of my life. I have witnessed the disinterested and laborious zeal which distinguishes your character and conduct. I have seen the fruit of your labours in the excellent societies in New-York, Boston, Philadelphia, Winchester, and this city. The doctrines and discipline of Methodism, when rightly applied, do, under the blessing of God, produce a scriptural conversion, and form the genuine Christian character *every where;* and either at home or abroad, I find that a Methodist, who lives according to his profession, is a 'fellow heir' of the same 'grace of life.'" My prayer is, in accordance with the prayers of the body whom I represent, that you may go on and prosper, until, as the honoured instruments of God, you have diffused gospel light and life through every part of this vast continent, and every class of its interesting population;—that the name of our Lord Jesus Christ may be every where glorified in his disciples. Amen."

The deliberations of this conference were protracted beyond the usual time, chiefly in consequence of the numerous petitions and memorials which were sent up by many of our local brethren and other members of the church, requesting a lay representation in the councils of the church, as well as several of an opposite character, praying that all things might remain as they were. Though Mr. Garrettson, in coincidence with the majority of his brethren, thought it inexpedient, under present circumstances, to grant the prayer of the petitioners for a lay representation, yet he seemed to think that some modification in the general outlines of the government might be usefully introduced. From what he has recorded in his journal on this subject, it appears that he adhered to the last to the opinion that each annual conference should have its bishop, to travel annually through its bounds, to preside in its sessions, and to station, with suitable counsel, the preachers. And though I cannot agree with him in all his views in reference to this subject, I thought it due to him and to the readers of his life, to state the fact, without farther comment, than just to say, that the mode of church government involves questions so various and perplexing, on account of the silence of Scripture as to prescribing any *particular* mode in distinction from all others, that writers on this subject should, above all others, avoid a dogmatical spirit, and exercise much forbearance and charity towards each other.

After attending the New-York conference June 1, 1824, in peace and safety he returned once more "to bless his household." He did not, however, remain long in his beloved retirement. In company with Mrs. Garrettson and his daughter he set off on a tour to the north-west. After preaching in Schenectady on sabbath, July 4, 1824, he took a canal boat on Monday for Utica, where he arrived on Tuesday, and in the evening of Wednesday preached to a crowded house, on a favourite subject, from the words of our Saviour to Martha, "But one thing is needful." Here he met Bishops George and Hedding, with whom he took sweet counsel. He makes the following reflections on the changes and improvements in this part of the country:—

"What an astonishing alteration in this country! More than thirty years since, when I was travelling through these parts, preaching and forming circuits, I could find here and there only a log hut to screen me from the blasts of winter, or the scorchings of a summer's sun. But now the country is thickly populated, farms highly cultivated, villages multiplied, and churches erected in every direction, splendid coaches rolling through the streets, &c, &c. I fear, indeed, the people in general think more of the world than they do of their souls. I awfully fear for the inhabitants of this fertile country."

After remaining in Utica eight days, "bearing," as he says, "a faithful testimony against the prevailing vices of the place," and likewise recording his sense of the kindness of his friends, he returned to Schenectady, where "our good friends at the college," says he, "were very attentive, doing every thing in their power to make us comfortable."

After observing that in Utica and some other places, the

Methodists seem to be on the back ground, he says, "What is the cause? O Lord, heal our backslidings, and bring us to our former standing. Some men learn to preach as they would learn any other profession, get a scanty support, and I fear get but few if any *souls for their hire.* The good old plan was to be *thrust* out with the awful words pressing on the soul, *Wo is me if I preach not the gospel!* In all such there is an ardent desire for holiness, a burning zeal for the salvation of perishing sinners, and by their means precious souls are gathered into the fold of Christ.

"I spent the greater part of Thursday 15," says Mr. Garrettson, "at Dr. Nott's, reading Jones's Church History. He certainly views what I call the *Novatian schism*—which happened about the middle of the third century—much more favourably than I can. After the death of the bishop of Rome, when the people were about to elect a successor, *Novatian* wished for that high office in the church; but when he found himself defeated, he formed a party, which elected him, and set him apart as bishop of Rome. If this was not making a *schism* in the church, I am at a loss to know what ought to be called by that name. At that period, under the persecutions of the heathen, Jesus Christ certainly had a living body at Rome. I think it was pride, or some other unholy passion, which excited Novatian and his party, thus to rend the body of Christ, to sow the seeds of discord, the fruits of which were so much deprecated by *Cyprian*, bishop of Carthage. I dare not call the origin of that branch of the church which has come down to us through the Waldenses, by means of the Novatian schism, a pure succession from the apostles." I believe the united testimony of ecclesiastical historians goes to say that although Novatian held fast the essential doctrines of Christianity, he formed his party without justifiable means, being actuated by a spirit of rivalry towards Cornelius, who was chosen in preference to Novatian to the office of a bishop on account of his distinguished virtues. This gave offence to Novatian, who was a severe character, and carried his rigid notions of church discipline so far as to refuse a readmission into the church of any persons who had fallen into sin, however penitent they might be. These things being considered, Mr. Garrettson had good reason to suspect the *pure* origin of that church which proceeded from the schism of Novatian. The history of those times, however, is of that character as to render it extremely difficult to form a correct judgment respecting the true causes of the various sects which from time to time disturbed the tranquillity of the church. All who dissented from the main body were denominated schismatics or heretics, with what degree of justice and truth it is somewhat difficult to decide.

After returning and remaining a few days at home, he took the steam boat for New-York. He here bears a pointed testimony against the immorality recently introduced by an opposition line of steam boats, in starting on the Lord's day. "I fear," says he, "our sins will bring down the judgments of God upon us." Sunday the 25th, he observes, "I preached and had a precious sacramental season in Allen-street church, and in the evening the word was refreshing in the church at Greenwich.

"My blessed God has been good to me for many years, for which I will praise him. I am now bending over eternity, and must soon *go the way of all the earth.* Not being able to walk about much, I am retired in the hospitable family of Mr. Suckley, and have a good time for self-examination, meditation, and prayer. I am under many and the strongest obligations to my heavenly Father, and am fully sensible that I have nothing in myself to recommend me to his favour. Mercy through the merits of Jesus Christ is my only plea. The aged as well as the young must continually say, 'Every moment, Lord, I need the merit of thy death.' In several places he has left upon record sentiments similar to the above. It would appear, therefore, that he was endeavouring to weigh himself in the balance, to cast up his accounts, that he might be ready, when called, to render them up " with joy, and not with grief." He continued labouring in the several churches in the city and in Brooklyn, until August 10, when he set off to attend a camp meeting on Long Island. "I endeavour," says he, "in every sermon I preach, to deliver it as if it were my last. I often think of my dear old friend, Bishop Asbury, who spent the last shred of his valuable life in the service of his great Master. I wish to do good, to be greatly taken up in my blessed Master's work, that my last may be my best days. O! wash me, Lord, and make me clean."

After attending the camp meeting, with which he seemed much pleased, because he thought good was done, he returned to the city, where he spent a few days in visiting and preaching. On Monday he left the city for Rhinebeck. "This week," says he, under date of August 22, "I have spent with my family, and have been frequently in deep exercise of mind. I cannot be fully satisfied, unless employed in the work of the blessed God. On this day, sabbath, I have preached in the mission chapel, morning, afternoon, and evening, with much liberty. May the blessed work revive in Rhinebeck."

A few days after he remarks, "I have been several weeks about home, and sometimes have preached two or three times on the Lord's day. I am sensible that to be happy we must be rationally employed, and not take anxious thoughts for the morrow. The maxim of our divine Saviour is founded in the fitness of things, *Sufficient unto the day is the evil thereof.* I have now in my retirement time for reflection and self examination, and although, blessed be God, I have not designedly erred, yet in many things I discover my imperfections. Sometimes I suffer much depression of spirits, when I should rejoice and praise

God, who has surrounded me with so many mercies. Jesus is my friend, and I will praise him. My dear Mrs. Garrettson is always ready, when a gloom overspreads my mind, to administer a word of comfort; and the affectionate and cheerful conversation of my lovely daughter, is enough to awaken sensibility in the heart of a hermit. 'Why art thou cast down, O my soul!' Nearly half a century since I was happy in the perfect love of God, and my labours were abundant in his service. The blessed God has favoured me with many days, and with a good constitution; but I fear I have come short in doing as much in his cause as I might have done. I have a glorious Advocate; otherwise I must sink. Glory to his name! I will praise him, and yet strive what I can do to promote his cause. Unworthy as I feel myself, I would not part with my hope of glory for a million of worlds." Such were the private meditations of this man of God. Such deep self abasement, accompanied with an unwavering confidence in the infinite merits of the Lord Jesus, indicated a thorough acquaintance with his own heart, and a scriptural view of the Divine plan of redemption and salvation.

On the 21st of September, accompanied by Mrs. Garrettson and his daughter, he paid a visit to some old friends in Westchester county. Among others with whom they participated in a friendly interchange of thought and conversation, was the late Governor Jay and his family. He resided in the town of Bedford. Of him Mr. Garrettson thus speaks :—" Mr. Jay lives in dignified retirement, resembling a patriarch in the midst of his children and grandchildren. As several were there on a visit, there were about twenty persons at the table, and the best of all is, they appear to fear God, and to be engaged in doing good. He is now about eighty years of age, and very feeble. After having filled some of the first civil offices in his country, in this advanced time of life, the American

Bible Society have elected him their president, as the successor of Mr. Boudinot, deceased. He has prayers in his family morning and evening.* After a very pleasant visit here, we set our faces towards home, crossed the mountains, and on Saturday arrived in safety at our quiet habitation. God has been gracious to my family many years, and prayers and praise I trust ascend to heaven daily."

As we advance in life we seem more and more affected with the ravages which death makes in the circle of our acquaintance. Our associates and equals in age we behold one after another dropping into eternity, which reminds us of our own near approach to "the valley and shadow of death." It is, however, a reviving consolation in the midst of these melancholy signals of mortality, that a hope of a better state of existence accompanies the holy Christian through his passage into the other world, while he believingly listens to the voice, "Fear not, for I am with thee"—"my rod and staff shall comfort thee."

It was about this time that one of the early Christian friends of Mr. Garrettson, Mrs. Carpenter of New-York, took her departure for a world of spirits. At the particular request of the family, Mr. Garrettson, October 28th, 1824, left home for New-York to preach her funeral discourse. On this occasion he makes the following reflections:—

"Our dear friend, Mrs. Carpenter, has gone to rest, leaving her husband and family to mourn their bereavement. She was born in the same month and year that I was. She has gone a little before me, but I must soon follow her. For more than fifty years she enjoyed an evidence of her acceptance in the Beloved, and for many years she enjoyed, in an eminent degree, the sanctifying

* This venerable man and eminent statesman, the friend of his country, and a firm believer in Christianity, has since gone the way of all the earth, beloved and lamented by all who knew him.

influences of the Holy Spirit; and after a long and useful life she left the world in the full triumphs of faith, in the seventy-third year of her age. She was beloved by all who knew her; and the church, her family, and acquaintances, have lost in her a valuable friend; but their loss is her eternal gain."

After remaining a few days in the city he returned to Rhinebeck. Here he endeavoured to fill up his time in reading, writing, and meditation, occasionally preaching, particularly on the Lord's day, in the mission chapel at Rhinebeck, and making some excursions to the neighbouring villages, where he was instrumental in watering the souls of God's people. After having visited Kingston, and preached to the people under some depression of spirit, he makes the following remarks:—

"This is a poor soil for Methodism. This is an ancient village, first settled by emigrants from Holland, whose descendants seem to hold fast the religious profession of their ancestors, and think it borders on a crime to depart from it. There is, however, but little to be accomplished without perseverance. The time may come when the hearts of the people even in this place may yield to the touches of God's Spirit."*

"March 8, 1825," he observes, "a messenger brought us the tidings that Mr. Sands had taken his departure from this world of sorrow at about three o'clock this morning. On the Sunday following, March 13, I preached his funeral sermon to a large congregation, on the words of the psalmist, *Many are the afflictions of the righteous, but out of them all the Lord delivereth him.*

* This conjecture has been since realized in the village of Kingston. A very considerable revival during the last year has been witnessed, and a number of souls have been brought to the knowledge of the truth. How much of the good seed which has thus sprung up, was sown by Mr. Garrettson, who can tell? Eternity will unfold it!

"Mr. Sands was among the first who joined the Methodist society in Rhinebeck. He was the second person who invited me to preach at his house in this place. I found him a kind, benevolent friend; and it was not long after I came to the place that he was brought into gospel liberty, and was appointed the leader of the class. He discharged the duties of this office as long as he was able. Many of our preachers who have lived in Rhinebeck, will long remember his cheerful bounties. He was a man of an upright character and conduct, and of great benevolence, against whom nothing could be said, not even by the tongue of envy. I give the following anecdote as a proof. When Mr. Jay, of whom I have before spoken, was governor of the state, party politics ran high between what were then called federalists and republicans. This led them to speak very freely of each other's candidates for office. At this time Mr. Sands was in nomination as a senator. I looked over the newspapers to see if any thing could be said against him. I remember a short paragraph which expressed 'a surprise to see good old Mr. Sands coming forward at the head of his party, and suggested that it would be much better for him to remain at home, and take care of his class!' He lived a useful member of our church about thirty-five years, and in the eighty-second year of his natural life took his departure to glory."

This testimony to the worth of Mr. Sands is by no means exaggerated. He was a most amiable Christian, a philanthropist, deeply devoted to God and the interests of his church, manifesting his regard to the ministers of Christ by repeated acts of liberality.

On sabbath, March 20th, he says, "After the morning service I was called upon to attend the funeral of Mr. C—— S——, a useful citizen, and on whom I had often endeavoured to impress the nature and necessity of our holy religion. I felt much for him during his sickness, and was much gratified to learn there was some alteration in his mind for the better before he died.

"On Monday, by the steam boat, we were in New-York, in about ten hours. Our old friends are dropping off one after another. Brother Paul Hick and brother Arcularius, two of the oldest members of the church in the city, have just gone to heaven, and I fear brother Carpenter will not continue long.* O Lord, sanctify me wholly; and I pray God that my soul, body, and spirit, may be preserved blameless unto the coming of our Lord Jesus Christ."

He continued in the city, preaching in the several churches, visiting the sick and his old friends, until April 5th, when he returned to Rhinebeck. On understanding that one of the preachers was about to locate, Mr. Garrettson has the following reflections:—"Did the blessed God call him to be a minister? If so, how has he disposed of the call? Or did he run before he was sent? Or has he fallen from God? It is a very serious thing to trifle with a work of such vast importance. I awfully fear for the consequences, as I believe a call to the ministry is for life."

He was prevented from making his *fifth* visit to New-York for this season, by receiving information of the death of another of his valued friends, Mrs. Suckley of New-York, and who, according to her wishes made known previously to her death, was to be buried in Rhinebeck. Tuesday, November 28th, he observes, "This was a solemn day. We were waiting to receive the remains of our deceased friend and her mourning family. About 10 o'clock in the evening they arrived, accompanied by two of the preachers from the city, and several other persons. Our habitation is highly honoured."

Mr. Garrettson makes the following remarks respecting Mrs. Suckley:—"She was awakened and brought into

* He did not, but died soon after in great peace.

gospel liberty when in the bloom of youth, soon after the introduction of Methodism into Rhinebeck. She was sweetly drawn by the cords of Divine love, which passion seemed always to govern her heart. She appeared, indeed, to be one of those who *think no evil.* She possessed the tenderest sensibilities of our nature, and these improved by education and grace. Her deeds of charity were always performed in such a private manner, that some might think that she was not liberal; but she was a friend to the poor. She was a woman of much prayer, and her communion with God the Father through our Lord Jesus Christ was intimate and constant. Her modest, humble, and unassuming deportment, shielded her from the censures of the invidious. As a wife and mother, she was affectionate and tender. Many are the prayers which she has lodged in the bosom of God for her children.

"In her last sickness she remarked, 'God has not shown me his will distinctly, whether I am to live or die; but in his good time I shall know. I have much to make life desirable,'—having reference to her children,—' but I cannot form one petition for life, knowing it will be best for *me* to go!' Her sufferings were great, but her peace flowed like a river. She has left a husband, two sons, and three daughters, to mourn their loss. O that they may so live here as to meet her in glory."

Under date of March, 1826, Mr. Garrettson remarks, that he had spent most of the past winter in Rhinebeck and its vicinity, and says, "The more I labour in the good cause, the better I feel in soul and body." On the 12th of April, he left home for Philadelphia, and says, that in twenty-five hours he arrived safely, a distance of about two hundred miles, twenty-five of which was by land. As the Philadelphia conference was in session at the time of his arrival, he speaks of enjoying much consolation in the society of the preachers, as well as in dispensing the word of life. Among other meetings, he says that he attended the anniversary of the missionary society of the Philadelphia conference, and was much pleased and profited with the appropriate addresses which were delivered.

Mr. Garrettson possessed, in an eminent degree, the soul of a missionary. He was one of the founders and active promoters of the Missionary Society of the Methodist Episcopal Church, became a life member by his own contribution, aided its operations, and rejoiced in its prosperity until the day of his death. One of the last acts of his life was to make a bequest of an amount annually sufficient to support a single missionary, as he expressed it, until the millennium.

On his return to Rhinebeck, after giving thanks to God for his goodness to himself and family, he says, "I want to have very little to do with the world. I never feel so well as when employed in the vineyard of the Lord." He was, however, happily relieved from worldly care, by his nephew, an intelligent and pious young man, who had for several years past taken the charge of his venerable uncle's temporal affairs, and managed them to his entire satisfaction. Of his faithfulness in these duties and the great relief which it afforded him, Mr. Garrettson often speaks in terms of gratitude to God. This reminds me of a remark made by a particular friend of Mr. Garrettson, that whenever he meddled with temporal concerns he seemed to be out of his element, it being his calling to move in a spiritual atmosphere, and to labour to build up the church of God. In this respect his peculiar gift and predominant inclination were happily united, as every sentence in his journal abundantly shows.

At the New-York conference, May, 1826, the conference requested Mr. Garrettson, as he had just entered upon the fifty-first year of his ministry, to preach a semi-centennial sermon before the conference. Having complied with this request, a vote was passed in favour of its being published. This was afterwards done. In this sermon, Mr. Garrettson gave a short history of the rise and progress of Methodism from its commencement to that time, interspersing remarks on its general economy, its usefulness, and suggesting some hints by which he thought some of its external features might be improved. He likewise gave a history of some of the most striking parts of his own experience and labours, gave short notices of some of the primitive Methodist preachers, and concluded by a solemn word of advice to his brethren. From this sermon several extracts have been inserted in the preceding parts of this Memoir, and the principal facts therein stated are here incorporated. The following additional extracts will be read with interest:—

"How shall we sufficiently praise God for the many, many thousands, who within the last eighty or ninety years have been brought into gospel liberty, either directly or indirectly, by the instrumentality of John Wesley. In looking over the minutes of our annual conferences, I should conjecture, that more than a thousand names, which have appeared on them since mine was first placed there, no longer appear. What has become of them? Thank God, a goodly number have worn themselves out in the good cause, ripened, and were gathered in. There are now more than ten thousand preachers, travelling and local, in the Wesleyan connexion, in Europe, Asia, Africa, and America, and in the islands of the seas, and more than half a million in membership; and how many, can we reasonably conjecture, have been ripened by grace, and called home, since Mr. Wesley first began to preach salvation by faith, and a direct witness of the Spirit of the forgiveness of sins? Would you say two millions?— or suppose one million—would not even this be a sufficient inducement to encourage us in the great work, especially when we view one soul as of more value than all the wealth and honour that this world can afford? The little treasure which, I trust, I have laid up in heaven, I would not part with for the riches of a thousand such worlds as this.

"I must step without the particular pale of my own church, to speak of that numerous body of Christians who were marshalled under Mr. Whitefield and Lady Huntington. To these in their commencement Mr. Wesley bore the interesting relation of a father. We likewise view with pleasure that body of men, who are called the evangelical clergy of the national church. We hear with joy of their preaching salvation by faith, and of their zeal in promoting Bible, missionary, and Sunday school societies. When did this change take place? Will not even prejudice allow, that the religious excitement, which has been spreading more and more, and awakening the energies of labourers in different sections of the Lord's vineyard, began through the instrumentality of the Wesleys? We see them taking the lead, and then you may observe an Ingham, a Hervey, a Whitefield, a Morgan, a Perronet, a Fletcher, a Coke, and several others, all ministers of the established church, making a powerful stand against the powers of darkness. We should not think it strange to find many hundreds of evangelical ministers in that establishment. My dear brethren, let the work spread to the ends of the earth, and let hundreds of millions be brought into gospel light and liberty.

"Have we done no good in America but among our own people? I have heard it said, and that by those who were not very friendly to us, that we drive more to other churches than we draw to our own. Well, if in the order of God, let it be so: if they are safe housed; if they ripen, and get safe to heaven, there will be but one fold there, and one Shepherd; and though we could not perfectly harmonize on earth, there will be no discord in that sweet world of peace and joy.

"Let us, my dear brethren, take the advice of St. Paul the aged, 'Whereunto we have already attained, let us walk by the same rule, let us mind the same thing:'—let us lay aside every weight, and every besetment, looking to Jesus, who is the author, till he become the finisher of our salvation. I told you that we have way marks, and that it is dangerous to remove any of them. 'Stand ye in the ways,' saith the prophet, 'and see; ask for the old paths; where is the good way, and walk therein, and you shall find rest for your souls.' The prophet Joel saith, 'Put ye in the sickle, for the harvest is ripe.' Remember, the field is very extensive, and the whole human family are ripening either for heaven or hell.

"I have had my time, and must soon leave this world; but I bless God for the great change which has taken place in many parts of Christendom within the last fifty years. The old men have been, and are, dropping off, and the young men will have to bear the ark; and I hope that they will do better than their fathers have done.

"From the first planting of Christianity, to its establishment under Constantine, there were great accessions to the church of Christ; and without doubt, millions of happy Christians, and exulting martyrs, went home to God, and are now rejoicing around the throne.

"From the time that papal Rome began to persecute the church, until the coming of the Protestant reformers, an army of martyrs and professors went triumphantly to glory. In the darker ages the church was said to be in the wilderness, and was at different periods known by various names, such as Albigenses, Waldenses, Lollards, Heretics, &c, &c. The stand which Luther and his coadjutors made against the errors of the church of Rome, was rendered a great blessing to the world; and through that and the succeeding period, which may be called the *puritanic* age, many great men were raised up, and many souls experienced the liberty of the gospel; and since the Wesleys were sent on the ministerial stage of action, and awakened the Protestant world from the slumber into which it had fallen, God has been glorified by the numbers who have lived and died in his fear and favour: but there will be a time, and it is not far distant, when there shall be a more glorious, and a universal gathering to the church, which in the language of revelation shall last a thousand years. Isaiah tells us, that 'the mountain of the Lord's house shall be established on the top of the mountains, and that all nations shall flow unto it.'

"Prior to the accomplishment of the predictions of the Old and New Testaments, respecting the last great outpouring of the Spirit, there must be a shaking among the nations, and the kingdoms of the beast, and of the false prophet, will crumble away. We cannot say at what time the martyrs will rise, and commence their reign with Christ in heaven; but to harmonize several passages of Scripture, we are necessarily led to believe that their resurrection will happen some time after the binding of Satan, and will continue as much longer after he is loosed. This opinion leaves room for the fulfilment of the predictions of our blessed Lord, respecting the general apostasy. But perhaps the inhabitants of the earth will be ignorant of the period of its commencement, or of its ending.

"Christ saith, 'What I say unto you, I say unto all—watch.' The trumpet will be sounded, and the dead, both small and great, will arise. Christ will come in grandeur, and the whole human family will appear at the judgment seat; the pious of every nation, and of every sect, on the right, and the wicked on the left, to be judged according to the deeds done in the body. Sinners will feel awful when they see the Second Person in the Godhead coming in majesty and great power, to pronounce sentence upon the quick and the dead. You that deny the infinite merit of Jesus Christ, tremble! You that have set up idols in your hearts, and have rejected the Son of God, let fearfulness take hold upon you.

"I fully believe that the doctrines taught by Mr. John Wesley are scriptural, and will stand the test; but what his people will be a hundred years hence we cannot say. They may be a numerous and a learned people; but it is possible, that by slow degrees they may retrograde, until they have very little of the spirit of old Methodism; and this certainly will be the case, without a steady and conscientious perseverance in the good old paths. The letter is good in its place; but we shall be, comparatively, nothing without the life and power of godliness. We must look well to our doctrines and discipline, and guard the sacred ministry. 'Lay hands suddenly on no man:'—look more to genuine piety, and to a real call from God, than to any literary qualification without it. Keep a pure ministry, and you will have a pure membership. The fall of the primitive church began with the clergy; and should we fall, our declension will begin here. It is better to have a pious, laborious, successful ministry, than to have wealth and ease without such a ministry.

"My dear brethren, I hope better things, though I thus speak. As a people, I hope we shall have a standing among the pious through a succession of ages. Unworthy as I am, I can look back with pleasure; and when faith gives me a glimpse of that sweet world above, I think all the little toil and sufferings that I have passed through are nothing. Eternity! O an eternity of felicity! Who would not bear the cross, and follow Jesus for a lot in that sweet world, where we shall dwell with the blessed Trinity, the holy angels, and the spirits of all the just made perfect through the blood of the Lamb.

"I bless God for what I have seen and felt; but I have often wept whilst looking back on my unprofitable life, and on my many defects; and I think, had I my time to live over again, I would strive more ardently to do good, and to live nearer to God. And soon, my dear brethren, I must leave you, and go the way of all flesh. I have lived long with you, and have seen a happy and prosperous half century. I love the Methodists, and hope they will prosper. I love Christians of every sect; and I pray that the world may be filled with the glory of God;—that false doctrines may be banished from the earth, and that the pure doctrines of the gospel may run and be glorified.

"Before I leave you, I wanted for a moment to look into the invisible world; but I am lost! Could we see the angelic host, and listen to the songs of the redeemed! Could we join that blood-bought company, and converse, with the patriarchs and prophets, and sages of the past, what rapture!—But one glimpse of our Lord Jesus Christ would outshine them all; for he only is worthy of all honour, and glory, and praise. We shall cast our crowns at his feet, and say, 'Not unto us, O Lord, not unto us, but unto thy name give glory.'

"My dear brethren, let us labour faithfully in scattering the good seed; let us do every thing in our power for the prosperity of Zion, and wait patiently for the great harvest day, when we shall all be gathered home, to be happy with the ever blessed Trinity, Father, Son, and Holy Spirit: to whom be glory, now, henceforth, and for ever. Amen."

At the close of this conference, Mr. Garrettson remarks, "Our dear brethren seem much engaged in the work, and I can truly say that I have sweet fellowship with them, and they treat me as a father.

"Monday 22. Bishops M'Kendree and Hedding accompanied me to Rhinebeck, and after spending several days pleasantly together, they took their departure on their way to the Genesee conference."

The following is the last entry I find in his journal. After remarking that he had preached in the mission chapel at Rhinebeck, he says,

"Monday 6. As I was appointed by the conference on a committee for the purpose of trying an unfortunate ——, and as my daughter wished to visit Union college, we prepared for the excursion, and on Tuesday evening we arrived safely at Dr. Nott's, where we were kindly received.

"Wednesday 8. I am pleasantly situated, feeling a pleasure in retirement. God is good to me."

For the purpose of exhibiting to the reader the prevailing disposition of his heart in his concluding days, I have thus minutely followed Mr. Garrettson through the last two years of his valuable life, giving his sentiments as recorded in his most retired moments, chiefly in his words. In the next chapter we shall follow him to his grave, and likewise present some general outlines of his character.

CHAPTER XIX.

Continued a Conference missionary—Instance of his affection—His last letter to Mrs. Garrettson—Attends Conference at Troy—His health and activity—Presentiment of his approaching dissolution—Visits New-York—His last sermon—His sickness, and death—His remains taken to Rhinebeck, and buried—His death a loss to the church—General outlines of his character—Simplicity his distinguishing feature—This gave him success in his ministry—Inspired him with persevering zeal—Induced him to forsake all for Christ's sake—Gave him liberal views—Attached him to his brethren—It shone in domestic life—In the order of his household, his hospitality, his placability, and in the pulpit—His perseverance—Veneration for the sacred Scriptures—Dependence on Divine aid—Variety and usefulness of his preaching—Infirmities common to man—His unblemished reputation for nearly fifty-two years—Was the oldest Methodist preacher—Concluding remark.

At the conference of 1826 Mr. Garrettson was continued a conference missionary, and he employed his time in his usual way, making occasional excursions to New-York and some other places, preaching as often as his strength would permit him. Wherever he came he was hailed as a messenger of peace, and as a father in the gospel, both by the preachers and people.

It was in the beginning of the winter of this year that I accompanied him to the city of Hudson, on an invitation from the brethren in that place, for the purpose of opening a new church. Having attended at Poughkeepsie for the purpose of dedicating a church recently built in that place, I went on board the steam boat which came along about 12 o'clock at night. I shall never forget the tender and affectionate manner in which he received me. He was in his birth, but hearing my voice, he addressed me by name, raised himself in his birth, affectionately squeezed my hand, expressing his gladness to see me. Indeed he always seemed revived whenever he came in company with his brethren in the ministry, whom he loved, I believe, "with a pure heart fervently." I have mentioned this circumstance merely to show how sincerely he loved his friends, as well as the readiness with which he obeyed the calls of his brethren to aid them in their work.

It was during one of his visits to the city of New-York, this year, that he sent the letter to Mrs. Garrettson, the last she ever received from him, of which the following is an extract:—

"Yesterday I spent mostly in prayer and conversation; to-day in reading, and this evening in writing. To-morrow I expect to be in the book room with the committee.

"I groan for perfect freedom. I have heard people talk of laying up a stock of grace; but, blessed and happy is that person who has a sufficiency from moment to moment, to keep him humble, innocent, and pure. We are every moment dependent upon God. I have no doubt but that retrospection on a long life spent in the service of God, with a continuance in piety, must be very consoling; but I know there is as great a necessity for watchfulness and perseverance as ever. The holy, blessed God knows our various weaknesses, and will in old age put beneath us his everlasting arms. O! to come near to the throne of grace, and touch the hem of his garment by faith, and have every stain washed away. O! to love God supremely."

In 1827 our conference convened at the city of Troy.

He attended its sessions with his usual diligence, and among other things supported a resolution, that there should be preaching at five o'clock in the morning, and cheerfully filled the first appointment himself. At this conference he was elected again as a delegate to the ensuing general conference, which was to be held in Pittsburgh, Pa., May 1, 1828. He did not, however, live to see the conference.

Notwithstanding his age, I believe none acquainted with him, who observed his healthful appearance and activity, thought him so near his end. After the close of the conference he persevered with his accustomed zeal and diligence in the discharge of his various duties, visiting his old friends, and preaching once or twice every sabbath. But though his family and friends flattered themselves that he might yet be spared some years to the church, it appears that he had a presentiment that his departure was at hand, and would often speak of it. Whether this arose from any direct impression upon his mind, or from feeling the natural decays of age, or from an impression which he received some years since, I cannot tell. I, however, often heard him observe,—I think he made the remark to me for the first time in the year 1813,— that being unwell a short time previously, he was calling on God, if it might be his will, to prolong his days; when he received for answer, that *fifteen years should be added to his life;* but he observed, at the same time, that he could not satisfy himself whether it meant fifteen years from that time, or so many years beyond the usual term of human life, "threescore years and ten." From whatever cause the impression proceeded, the sequel proves that his presentiment at this time was correct.

About the 20th of August, 1827, after dining with his family with great cheerfulness, and commending them to God in prayer, Mr. Garrettson left home for the city of New-York. On his arrival in the city he preached his last sermon in the Duane-street church, on the words of St. Peter, " But grow in grace," and then administered the sacrament of the Lord's supper to a large number of communicants. It was remarked by some who were present on that occasion, that Mr. Garrettson preached with unusual warmth and energy, a Divine unction attending the word. Thus this venerable servant of God closed his public labours in pressing upon his brethren the necessity of going forward in the "work of faith and labour of love," and in participating with them in "drinking of the fruit of the vine," in anticipation of drinking it anew with them in the kingdom of God.

Soon after he was violently seized with a disease called the *strangury*. Dr. Mott, a surgeon of established reputation in the city of New-York, was immediately called; but though his applications afforded a temporary relief, the disease was so obstinately fixed as to resist the power of all attempts to arrest its progress. To Mrs. Garrettson and his daughter the mournful tidings of his illness were speedily conveyed, and they hastened to the city to comfort him, and if possible to administer relief. But the hand of death had arrested him. I was absent from the city at the time he was taken ill. On my return, hearing of his illness and the nature of his disorder, it immediately came to my mind that "this sickness was unto death." As soon as convenient I repaired to the chamber where he was confined, and had a long conversation with him. He seemed to entertain but slender hopes of recovery, and observed, that should the disease be so far removed as to permit him to live a little longer, he should be a preacher all his days. Though on the first approach of the disease, which was of a most painful character, he manifested some little restlessness, as if nature struggled involuntarily to free itself from suffering, he soon bowed in humble submission to the Divine will, and evinced an unshaken confidence in the mercy of God through our Lord Jesus Christ.

In the conversation to which I have alluded, he unbosomed himself with great freedom, rehearsed the goodness of God, which had been so abundantly manifested to him through every period of his life; at the same time, as was usual with him, expressed himself in terms of the deepest self abasement. At one time he would express his admiration of the perfections of God, as manifested in creation, and more especially in the grand system of redemption, and then cry out with holy rapture, "I am filled with the perfect love of God." With much feeling and emphasis he said, "My hope is all founded in the infinite merits of the Lord Jesus; in this hope I enjoy unspeakable consolation." In this way he lingered, sometimes suffering exquisitely, for about five weeks. He did, indeed, pass through the furnace, but he came forth not only unhurt, but abundantly refined; and he died as he had lived, a witness of *perfect love*. Redemption was the theme of his contemplation through his sickness. Toward the last he became eager to depart—to *go home*.

The following account of some of the last days of Mr. Garrettson is from the pen of Miss Mary K. Garrettson, in a letter to the Rev. Richard Reece of England:—

"Dear and Rev. Sir,—Another memento of your kindness most forcibly reminds us of our obligations, and of the duty of giving you the interesting particulars of my blessed father's last illness and death; a duty which has been long delayed, for as often as it impressed itself on my mind, a sense of my inadequacy to the subject, and the pressure of my heavy bereavement, has most forcibly withheld me from the attempt.

"For several months before his death, my dear father seemed to feel, in an unusual manner, the uncertainty of his own existence; and an impression of the shortness of his stay, made him rather reluctantly consent to an election for delegate to the general conference. Our presiding elder, Mr. Scofield, has since informed us, that during his last visit *here*, papa took him to a little retreat in the garden, where he spent many of his hours in devotion, and after conversing on the affairs of the church, (which ever lay near his heart,) with the spirit of one ready to depart and be with Christ, he said he should not probably live to see the next conference. They then kneeled down and prayed together, when the power and presence of God were felt, said Mr. Scofield, in a manner never to be forgotten by me.

"On Friday, the 17th of August, my dear father left us in usual health, expecting to spend the sabbath in New-York, and to return the ensuing Monday or Tuesday. I can never forget the last day he spent at home,—a serenity and happiness marked his manner, and the purest love was reflected in all his actions. Our table was surrounded by friends. Some had recently arrived, and others were about to depart. A mingled sensation of pleasure at the coming, and regret at the parting guests, pervaded our minds;—but pleasure was predominant, for fancy painted futurity with the pencil of hope, and the regret we felt was just sufficient to soften her vivid colouring. But my dear father;—the heavenly expression of his countenance during that social meal I can never forget; and I find a mournful pleasure in recalling again and again the events of that last day of family enjoyment. After dinner we kneeled down, and he prayed with us in a manner unusually solemn, tender, and affecting. Almost every eye was suffused in tears:—we parted. The next sabbath was spent by him in the services of the sanctuary, in preaching and administering the sacrament. On Monday he underwent considerable fatigue, but spent the evening at Mr. Suckley's. He appeared to the family to be in unusual health and spirits, sat up beyond his customary hour, although it was his intention to take the six o'clock boat, and dine with us on the morrow. That night, however, he was seized with his last agonizing disorder, and after spending several days of intense pain and extreme danger, he consented to abandon the thought of returning home, and to send for mamma and me.

"On our arrival we were told that the crisis of his disorder had been favourably passed, and that, though lingering, there was every prospect of his ultimate recovery. But though we suffered our judgment to be led captive by our wishes even to the last, no hopes of that kind were implanted in his mind. I believe he knew and felt that his time of departure was at hand. His sufferings at times were unutterable; but through them all were manifested a resignation and fortitude which no agony could destroy. 'I shall be purified as by fire; I shall be made perfect through sufferings:—it is all right, all right; not a pain too much,' he would often say. Daily, and almost hourly, he was visited by some one or other of his brethren, who added much to his consolation during those seasons when the heart and the flesh fail, but when the religion of Christ is indescribably precious; (the recollection of their kind attentions will never pass from my mind;) and as he descended into the dark valley, his views of the grandeur and efficacy of the atonement became more and more enlarged. His disorder inclined him latterly to slumber, and he was often delirious; but even then the same subject was the theme of his discourse. Towards the last his strength was so much exhausted, that articulation became a painful effort; but he would often, in a languid feeble voice, say, 'I want to go home; I want to be with Jesus, I want to be with Jesus.' To a friend he said, a short time before his death, 'I feel the perfect love of God in my soul.' A day or two before his departure I heard him say, 'And I shall see Mr. Wesley too.' It appeared as if he was ruminating on the enjoyment of that world, upon the verge of which he then was;—enjoyments which he said a Christian could well understand, as they began in his heart before he was disembodied. His mind seemed employed with subjects for the sweetest feelings of love and adoration. When asked how he did, he would answer, 'I feel love and good will to all mankind,'—or, 'I see a beauty in all the works of God,'—forgetting that the infirmities of his body were the subject of the inquiry. He had resigned his wife and daughter into the hand of God, and so great was his desire to be with Christ, that parting with us was disarmed of its bitterness. His last sentence spoken, even in death, was, 'Holy, holy, holy, Lord God Almighty! Hallelujah! Hallelujah!' After that, though he lingered many hours, he could not speak articulately. Once only, clasping his hands, and raising his eyes to heaven, he uttered, 'Glory! glory!' Many petitions were offered around his dying bed, that he might be permitted to give his last testimony, but they were not granted. For myself, I felt it was not necessary. A holy and laborious life of more than fifty-two years bore ample testimony to the triumph of his soul over its last enemy.

"Never can I hope to give you more than a faint idea of the solemn yet glorious hour when the spirit achieved *that* last victory, and was ushered into the joy of the Lord. Encircled by his kind and affectionate friends, by his brethren and his sons in the gospel, my venerable father lay apparently unconscious of every thing that surrounded him. We *felt truly* that he was only leaving the church militant to join the church triumphant. Just as the period of his departure approached, one of the preachers broke forth into prayer;—prayer so elevated, so holy, that it seemed to wrap the hearers above all sublunary consideration, and as he commended the dying saint into the hands of God, he prayed that the mantle of the departing patriarch might rest on his surviving brethren. His prayer seemed answered;—a Divine influence pervaded the apartment;—two of the preachers almost sunk to the floor, under a glorious sense of His presence who filleth immensity. My dear mother, with clasped hands and streaming eyes, exclaimed, 'Yes, Lord! we give him up freely,—*freely give him* up to thee!'

"The spirit departed, leaving the body impressed with the sweetest expression of peace and tranquillity; an expression which it retained until the moment when it was shrowded from human observation. We could stand beside those dear remains, and imagine that their appearance of renewed youth and happiness was a pledge of that glorious resurrection, when death shall be swallowed up in victory, and the mortal put on immortality; and we could look on the grave as a sure and certain deposit, until that day when it shall give back its precious seed rejoicing."

Thus as a ripe shock of corn was he gathered into the garner of his God, in the 76th year of his age, and the 52d of his itinerant ministry. He ended his useful life and suffering at the house of his long tried friend, George Suckley, Esq., in the city of New-York, about 2 o'clock in the morning of the 26th of September, 1827.

His remains were taken to Rhinebeck, his late residence, accompanied by his bereaved widow and daughter, the writer, and several of the preachers on the New-York station, Mr. Suckley, and other friends. These had the mournful pleasure of following the lifeless body into that friendly enclosure, which had so often been enlivened by his presence while living, and while entertaining his friends with gospel simplicity and hospitality, and placed in that mansion which had been dedicated to God, and where God had so frequently honoured his servant with his peaceful presence.

On Friday, the 28th, a numerous circle of family connexions, friends, and neighbours, who seemed deeply affected with their loss, were addressed at the house of the deceased by the Rev. Thomas Burch. Afterwards the procession, which was long and solemn, slowly moved to the burying ground at Rhinebeck Flats, a distance of about two miles, where the funeral service was performed by the writer, and the corpse was deposited in the earth, to sleep till "the resurrection of the just and unjust." A discourse was immediately delivered to a deeply affected audience, who evinced by their conduct their respect for departed worth.

The next sabbath his funeral sermon was preached on these words: "Mark the perfect man, and behold the upright, for the end of that man is peace."

The following inscription is on his tombstone:—

Sacred
to
the memory of the
Rev. FREEBORN GARRETTSON,
an itinerant minister of the
Methodist Episcopal Church.
He commenced his itinerant ministry
in the year 1775.
In this work he continued until his death,
labouring with great diligence and success
in various parts of the
United States
and of
Nova Scotia.
He died in peace in the city of
New-York,
September 27, 1827,
in the 76th year of his age,
and 52d of his ministry.

"Mark the perfect man, and behold the upright, for the end of that man is peace," Psalm xxxvi, 37.

In the death of Mr. Garrettson the church militant was deprived of one of its most aged, most devoted, and successful ministers. From the commencement of his ministerial career to its termination, he seems to have pursued his object with untiring constancy and perseverance; and wherever he moved, the purity of his intentions and the uprightness of his deportment secured for him the confidence of all who feared God; while the holy unction which generally accompanied his public administrations, announced him as the commissioned messenger of God to a lost world.

This, I think, has been sufficiently manifest in the preceding pages. It is therefore unnecessary to add much more, as his private exercises and public labours have been exhibited as they in reality were in the various relations of life which he sustained.

I shall, however, in accordance with the general custom, endeavour to exhibit some general outlines of a character which the more I contemplate the more I admire— not so much on account of the brilliancy of talents which it unfolds, as on account of the noble, the *gospel simplicity*, which so conspicuously distinguished our departed father in the gospel of Christ.

Let no one suppose that in fixing on this as the distinguishing feature of his character, there is an intention to diminish his worth. Far otherwise. There is no intention either to diminish or to exalt, but to speak what I believe to be the truth in relation to him. When I say that he was eminently distinguished by *simplicity*, I mean that simplicity which is inseparably connected with a "conscience void of offence towards God and man," the effect of that Divine love in the heart which is always productive of a single and sincere desire to do good, to "glorify his God below, and find his way to heaven." If ever there was a man on earth devoid of subtlety, guile, or suspicion, FREEBORN GARRETTSON was that man. While his judgment was well matured by study, by habits of reflection, and a close attention to passing events, his heart was filled with that love which caused this prominent trait of his character to shine forth in all its loveliness, and will no doubt be recognised by all who knew him as his distinguishing peculiarity. No corroding suspicions disturbed the sweet repose which reigned in his breast. Until compelled by the irresistible language of facts, to denounce any one as insincere who professed to love the Lord Jesus, he embraced all such as "brethren beloved." Being honest and sincere himself, he could not indulge in a suspicious temper towards others. And if this heavenly disposition sometimes exposed him to the impositions of the cunning and the crafty, it happily relieved him from the vexations of imaginary evils, and the pain of "fearing where no fear was." And if we must err, as seems unavoidable in this fallible and changeable state, how much better is it to suffer the hand of charity to lead us astray, than to be tormented day and night by the evil forebodings of a restless disposition! From the demon of jealousy, and the evil genius of suspicion, it behoves us all to pray, "Good Lord, deliver us."

This, therefore, is so far from being a defect, that I humbly conceive that it ought to be reckoned among the cardinal virtues of a Christian. And this marked all his actions, pervaded his whole soul, and contributed to that pure enjoyment in which he so largely participated in the society of his friends.

It was no doubt this simple intention to please his God in all things which gave him such distinguished success in the ministry of the word. It may be fairly questioned whether any one minister in the Methodist Episcopal Church, or indeed in any other church during the same period, has been instrumental in the awakening and conversion of more sinners than Mr. Garrettson. This I think has been abundantly evinced in the preceding Memoir.

It was this simple desire to do good which inspired him with such a flaming ardour and such intrepid courage in the cause of his Divine Master. Neither the heat of the south, the cold of the north, nor the variable atmosphere of the more temperate clime; neither the dust and smoke of the city, the hill and dale of the country, nor the forests of the wilderness; neither riches nor poverty, ease nor luxury; neither frowns nor smiles, could dampen the ardour of his zeal, or quench the thirst he had for the salvation of immortal souls. Wherever he came, in whatever company, whether of the rich or the poor, in whatever climate, his theme was the same; it was "Jesus and him crucified;" declaring to all that he was not "ashamed of the gospel of Christ." This was the soul and main spring of all his actions; that which set him in motion, and which kept him moving in the circle of obedience to what he considered, and what the effect of his labours proved to be, a Divine call.

What else but a simple desire to do good to all men as he had opportunity, could have induced him to forsake all in early life, to persevere through "good and evil report," for upwards of fifty years, without fee or reward? For it may be observed here, that Mr. Garrettson, during the whole course of his ministry, never received any pecuniary recompense, or if at some times, through the solicitation of his friends, he received any, it was given either to necessitous individuals, or deposited with the funds of the conference. In this manner the patrimony he inherited from his ancestors was all expended, and it has often been observed, that for this sacrifice, so nobly and freely offered upon the altar of benevolence, he was rewarded "a hundred fold, even in this life." And after he came into the possession of a larger estate by his happy marriage, I have frequently heard him say, that the entire income of his property, after meeting his annual expenses, was devoted to charitable purposes. In pursuing this course, and making these sacrifices, what else, I say, could have moved him forward so steadily, and for so long a time, but a single desire to promote the glory of God in the salvation of souls?

It was the same principle which inspired him with that spirit of liberality towards other denominations of Christians by which he was characterized. Though Mr. Garrettson was sincerely and conscientiously attached to the church to which he belonged, firmly believed and faithfully defended its peculiarities, yet towards all others which he believed held fast the cardinal and distinguishing doctrines of the gospel, he exercised a spirit of charity, loving the good of every name, and rejoicing in every thing evangelical he could discover among them. Hence his residence was the resort of Christians and of Christian ministers of different denominations. While he could hold no fellowship with those who openly denied the proper Deity of Jesus Christ, and consequently set aside his atonement for the sins of the world, most cordially he gave the right hand of fellowship to all who "loved the Lord Jesus Christ in sincerity," and who believed and defended the grand cardinal truths of Christianity. However much they might differ from him in points of minor importance, if they held fast these great doctrines of God our Saviour, he embraced them as his brethren in the Lord. Here was a full display of that "love which thinketh no evil." As a proof of the truth of these remarks, the following anecdote is related of Mr. Garrettson, at the time he visited Providence, in Rhode Island:—

A member of Mr. Snow's church—Mr. Snow was either a Congregational or a Presbyterian minister—expressed some anxiety to know whether Mr. Garrettson meant to establish a Methodist church in Providence. Mr. Garrettson replied to this effect:—"Be assured, sir, that if I do, I shall not admit you." "Why would you not receive me," said the gentleman; "have you heard any thing to my disparagement?" "No, sir," said Mr. Garrettson; "I have heard nothing which would not entitle you to an honourable standing in any church; but ...re under a spiritual minister. I would rather add you ... take from Mr. Snow's church; and were I to to, th... church in this place, they should be gathered from raise ...

among those who were not privileged with such a ministry, or those who would not avail themselves of the privilege."

It was this same principle which attached him so affectionately to his brethren in the ministry, as well as to all the members of the church. Though, as before said, he loved and honoured all ministers of Christ, of whatever name, he manifested a very peculiar attachment to the ministers of the Methodist Episcopal Church. He never seemed so happy as when in their society. To those of them with whom he was intimate he would unbosom himself without reserve. His house was the free resort of all who could visit him, and they were entertained with all the hospitality and simplicity of primitive times. To his house, his table, and his heart, they always found a hearty welcome. Many happy hours of social intercourse, and of Christian conversation, has the writer enjoyed under that peaceful roof, the mention of which brings to mind so many endearing recollections.

This leads me to mention the manner in which this heavenly disposition displayed itself in domestic life. Here the beauty and excellence of religion shone in all its divine lustre and heavenly simplicity. I remember a few years since a conversation with a pious Presbyterian lady of the city of New-York, who was in habits of intimacy with Mrs. Garrettson, and who had recently returned from a visit to the family at Rhinebeck. She was expressing her great satisfaction at the admirable order which prevailed there; "I do not mean," said she, "the order of the farm or of the house, though this is indeed worthy of all praise; but I mean the *religious* order which prevails throughout every department; the orderly arrangement for family devotions, and the orderly manner in which the servants, and all attached to the household, attend to their *religious* as well as to their other duties." This was saying nothing more than what was strictly true. God indeed seemed abundantly to bless him in this respect. All about the farm, all his domestics, were moral, most of them religious, and they were generally members of the Methodist church. The example continually set before them, taught them the utility, as well as the indispensible duty, of an orderly and regular attendance to all the duties of the sanctuary, as also to their private and family devotions. In this circle, therefore, God reigned. Here he "commanded his blessing, even life for evermore." Every thing here was "sanctified by the word of God and prayer." Reading a portion of the sacred Scriptures, singing some verses of a hymn, and prayer, formed the family devotions of the evening and morning, and then every one went orderly to his business. If company remained, they might either retire to a room, or enjoy the benefits of society in the house, or, particularly in the summer season, in the pleasant walks in the garden, or under the shade of a delightful bower, or the foliage of the forest trees with which the mansion was surrounded. Wherever they went on this enclosure, peace and contentment smiled around, and produced a charm unknown to thoughtless and dissipated minds.

I am here reminded of a saying of the late lamented Bishop George. Speaking of Mr. Garrettson, he remarked, how agreeably disappointed he was in visiting him at his own house. Having only seen Mr. Garrettson occasionally at the general conference, and sometimes being under the necessity of differing from him on some points of ecclesiastical polity, the bishop had formed an idea that Mr. Garrettson was rather austere in his manners, and somewhat bigoted in his views; "but," said the bishop, "when I had the happiness of visiting him under his own roof, and of observing the pious order of his household, the hospitality of his disposition, the kindness and attention with which he treated his friends and visiters, all my prejudices were banished; and I now think that the worth of brother Garrettson has not been duly estimated."

What contributed much to his own comfort was the *placability* of his disposition, another inseparable companion of that divine simplicity which predominated in his heart. That he had enemies was not his fault. No one should have been his enemy. Neither had such any cause to fear him, because he would not have hurt them even if he could. While he fulfilled the Divine command in loving his friends, he also inherited the blessing of those who *bless and curse not, and who pray for those who despitefully use them*. On how many heads he has thus heaped "coals of fire," and by the influence of this love melted them into tenderness, and made them his friends, "that day" alone can declare; but I have heard it remarked, that if you wanted to obtain a special favour from Mr. Garrettson, you must do him some injury, for he was sure to repay it by an act of kindness. Not that he was insensible to injuries and insults. He felt them, and felt them keenly; but he well understood the difference between *feeling* an insult, and manifesting a suitable indignation at the conduct of the malevolent, and suffering the passion of revenge to linger in his bosom. While he wept over the miseries of the wicked, and commiserated the condition of those who might be actuated by private malice, or personal hostility, he bore them before the throne of grace in prayer, evincing the tenderest love to their persons, and the sincerest desire for the salvation of their souls. He thus exemplified the spirit which actuated his Divine Master, when he prayed, "Father, forgive them, for they know not what they do." I have known him take special pains to conciliate the good will of persons whom he feared he had wounded merely because he conscientiously differed from them in opinion, lest they might harbour the thought that he entertained unkind feelings towards them. He could, indeed, be reconciled to any thing but sin, and those dangerous errors which struck at the fundamental doctrines of Christ. To these enemies of God and man he showed no mercy.

To the same ardent thirst for the salvation of lost men may be attributed his zealous co-operation in all our benevolent institutions. He lived to see that Divine principle which thrust him out into his Lord's vineyard in the midst of obloquy and reproach, when the true disciples of Jesus were "as a speckled bird, and the birds round about" were against them, enlarged into an expansive benevolence; and so mightily had the word of God increased, and the number of disciples multiplied, that institutions of charity were springing up in every direction, to bless the world with an increase of light and knowledge. Mr. Garrettson watched the rise and progress of these institutions with strong and increasing interest. He aided their operations by contributing to their funds.

To the American Bible Society he became a life member. He assisted as one of the founders of the Missionary Society of the Methodist Episcopal Church, became first an annual contributor, afterwards a life member, and often stimulated others to become its supporters. To the Tract and Sunday School Societies he was a warm friend and faithful patron. And if at any time he did not answer the expectations of some in the frequency and the amount of his donations, it was because they knew not the multitude of calls which were made upon his bounty, nor the urgency with which they were pressed upon his attention. It being generally believed that he was rich in this world's goods, and well known that he was a friend to suffering humanity, all were ready to turn their attention to him for aid; and hence had he given according to each one's expectation, he would very soon have been a pauper himself, and thus been deprived of the means of "scattering abroad" the charities of a liberal mind. That he endeavoured conscientiously to "use his Lord's money," and to make to himself "friends of the mammon of unrighteousness," none will dispute who were acquainted with his manner of life.

If we view Mr. Garrettson as a minister of the Lord Jesus Christ, we shall behold the same disposition displaying itself on all occasions. Indeed so habitual was the impression on the minds of all with whom he was acquainted, of his deep sincerity, of the simple desire of his heart to ascertain and promulgate the truth as it is in Jesus, that however some might differ from him in his views, they could hardly resist the conviction which the force of this principle made on their hearts. And if it be the chief business of a minister of the sanctuary to carry a conviction to the hearts of sinners of the truths of the gospel, and to awaken within them a serious concern respecting the solemn realities of eternity; if the object of his mission be to point those "that mourn in Zion" to the "Lamb of God which taketh away the sin of the world;" if he should not cease his exhortations until he lead the penitent sinner to the blood of atonement, "which cleanseth from all unrighteousness," and until he *so believe as to receive the witness in himself that he is born of God;* if the end of his commission is to build up believers "in their most holy faith," and never let them rest until they are *filled with the perfect love of God;* if to accomplish these objects be the principal aim of the minister, then we may pronounce the Rev. FREEBORN GARRETTSON to have been a true minister of Jesus Christ. If it be the duty of a minister commissioned of God to "go into all the world, and preach the gospel to every creature," as far as his strength and opportunities will permit; and if in doing this he is to give evidence of his call to the work by preaching with all that zeal and pathos which distinguish men influenced by the Spirit of God, and having the worth of souls pressing upon their hearts; then did the subject of this memoir discharge his duty, and give the most substantial evidence of his Divine call to this holy and important work. His labour and diligence were great, and his success in winning souls to Christ was in proportion. Wherever he went he left the impressions of truth behind him. Sinners were made to feel their awful responsibility to God, while His people felt the "holy anointing," and often "shouted aloud for joy."

He held on his way. Whatever impediments were thrown in his path, they did not stop his progress. Having fixed his "single eye" on the "prize of his high calling" at the outset, he pursued it to the end of life. We have seen him renouncing ease, affluence, all those enjoyments which domestic felicity might afford, for the sake of winning souls to Christ. The church,—the *welfare of the church*,—occupied his private meditations and engaged his public labours. And he lived to see that church to which he belonged, and whose interests were identified with his own, increase from 3,148, the number in membership when he commenced his youthful and successful career in 1775, to 381,997, the number returned on the Minutes in 1827, the year in which he died; and the number of travelling preachers increase from 19 to 1,576. Well might he say, as he did in his Semi-centennial Sermon, "We shall hear of spiritual fathers and of their spiritual children blessing and praising God that they were ever sent out to traverse the mountains and valleys to call sinners to repentance." How many will rise up in that day and call him blessed, He only who numbers the hairs of our heads can tell.

But that which gave such efficiency to his labour in the gospel, was the "unction of the Holy One," which rested upon him. No man, I believe, was more deeply sensible of the indispensibleness of the Holy Spirit to enable the minister of Christ to succeed in his work, than Mr. Garrettson. Deriving all his doctrine and precepts from the pure fountain of Divine truth, the Holy Scriptures, he made these his daily study; and being deeply conscious that he must have the enlightening and sanctifying influences of the Holy Spirit, to enable him rightly to understand and apply these truths, he was assiduous in his addresses to the throne of grace, firmly believing that God would "give the Holy Spirit to them that ask him." The success, therefore, which accompanied his public labours, is not attributable to the force of human persuasion, or to the "words of man's wisdom," but to the "demonstration of the Spirit," which accompanied his word. Thus armed with the "sword of the Spirit," his word was "mighty, through God, to the pulling down the strong holds of Satan."

His action in the pulpit was not generally graceful, nor could he be pronounced eloquent, according to the usual definition of that word. On some occasions, however, he seemed inspired with an eloquence far surpassing all human attainments, when his words were accompanied with a gesticulation appropriate and striking, and which bespoke a soul filled "with glory and with God." On these occasions the congregation would be overwhelmed with a sense of the Divine presence, while tears and groans, prayer and praise, would sufficiently attest the power with which he spoke.

There was great variety in his preaching, both as to the manner and matter, which made his discourses always both entertaining and useful; and I believe he seldom wearied an audience with a dry detail of uninteresting matter, or with speculations which did not profit the hearer. His was the preaching of a man aiming to be *useful*, aspiring to be *good* instead of *great*, penetrating by the arrows of truth into the sinner's heart, and pouring the balm of consolation into the "wounded spirit." It was *deep, experimental*, and *practical*.

Such was the character of the Rev. Freeborn Garrettson. And if his name be not handed down to posterity as one of the *greatest* ministers with which the Methodist Episcopal Church has been favoured, he will unquestionably be ranked among the *best*, the most *devoted*, and the most *successful*.

Perhaps it might be expected that I should mention his imperfections and faults. That he was in every respect perfect, who will contend? But whatever defects he may have had, they were such as are inseparable from man, defects of the head, and not of the heart; natural, not moral. Were I to attempt to describe a perfect character, one that was free from the infirmities of human nature, I should not only render myself ridiculous, but prove myself destitute of that very virtue which was so estimable, and which shone so conspicuously in Mr. Garrettson,—I mean "godly simplicity and sincerity."

"To err is human." And that Mr. Garrettson was liable to err from the natural imperfection of his judgment, and therefore might have often been under mistakes in his estimation of men and things, needs neither an apology to admit, nor any false colouring to hide. This is common to men,—to the *best* of men. When therefore it is said that such a man had his infirmities, that he exhibited foibles, made mistakes, and erred in his judgment, we do but describe what is common to man, and say nothing to distinguish one human being from another. These sad marks of our original apostasy cleave alike to all, the wise and the unwise, the learned and the ignorant. But when we say of a man that, in the midst of these natural infirmities, with a thousand temptations from without to entice him from the path of obedience to his God, he held on his way,—that he triumphed over sin and Satan,—that he uniformly maintained an unspotted character,—that he lived and died in the fear and favour of God,—we describe a man that rose far above the efforts of human nature,— we behold a man in whom "dwelt the Spirit of the Holy One," and in whom is "magnified the grace of God." It is of such a one that I now speak. Human nature, however improved by education and reflection, is not competent to gain a victory over evil propensities, to subdue sinful habits and passions; but when renewed by the grace of God in Christ Jesus, it shines,—it triumphs, —and vanquishes every enemy to its peace and happiness.

For such a perfection, therefore, as exempts men from these inseparable infirmities of our nature, we plead not. But this I think I may affirm without any fear of contradiction, that among all the ministers of Jesus Christ during the period in which he lived, none maintained a more unblemished reputation, was more deeply and sincerely devoted to God, more successful in extending the Redeemer's kingdom among men, or more perfectly answered the end for which the Christian ministry was instituted. From the time of his conversion to God, in the 23d year of his age, until his death, in the 76th year of his age, under the protection of "the everlasting arms," the purity of his life, and the uprightness of his deportment, were never questioned, but acknowledged by all with whom he had intercourse; and for upwards of fifty-one years he appeared before the public as an ambassador of the Lord Jesus Christ, during which time the words of his lips gained the more credence from the unimpaired confidence which every one had in the integrity of his heart and the righteousness of his life. And when he sunk into the grave, he was the oldest travelling minister of that church, whose general economy he loved, whose doctrines he believed and preached, whose God and Saviour he adored, and served in "the fellowship of the gospel," and whose ramparts he left, after having defended them for more than fifty years, to take his seat in "that house not made with hands, eternal in the heavens, whose builder and maker is God."

Finally, in contemplating his character, we may take the text on which he so often delighted to preach, and which was selected as the foundation of his funeral discourse, and say, "Mark the perfect man, and behold the upright, for the end of that man is peace."

THE END.

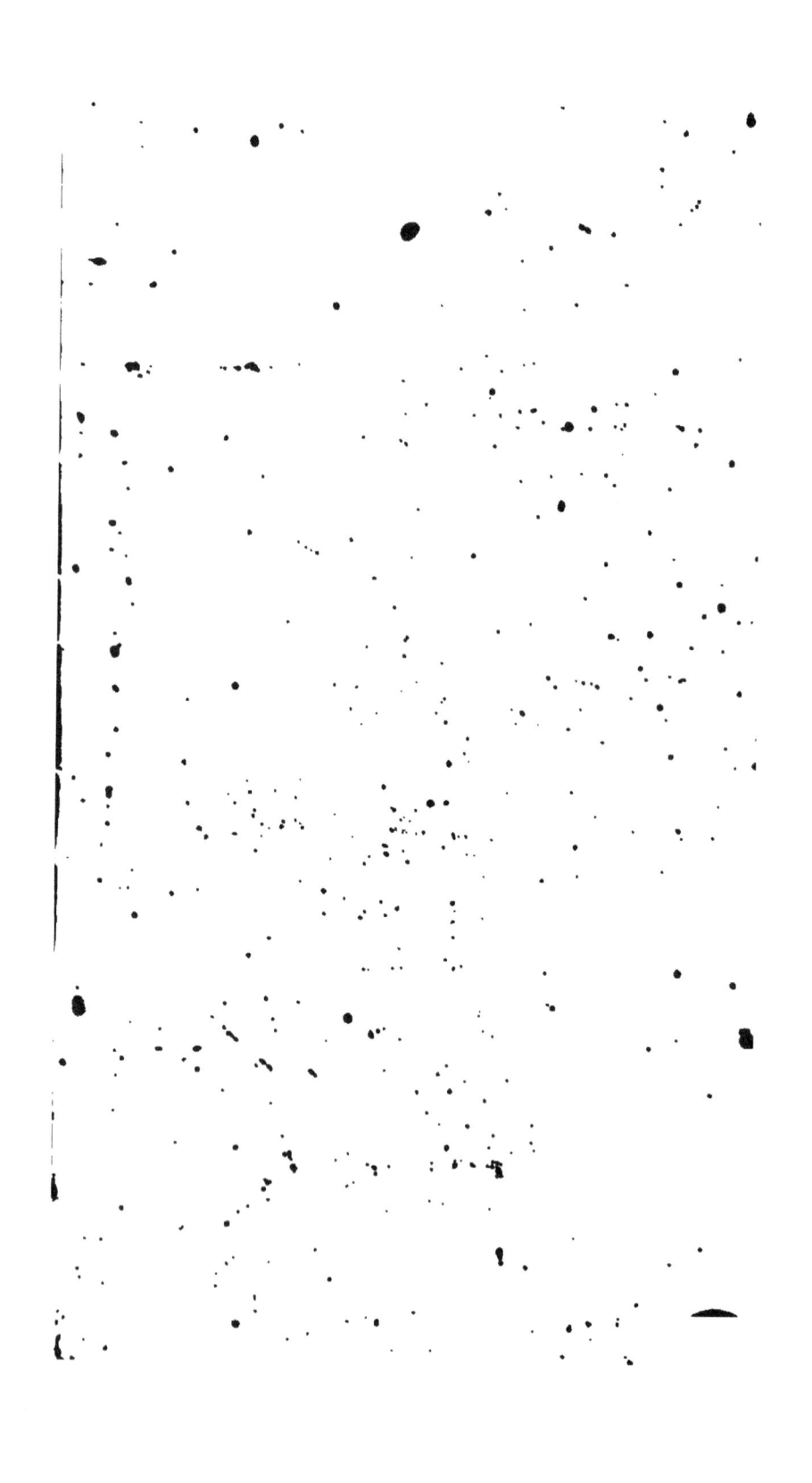

THE NEW YORK PUBLIC LIBRARY
REFERENCE DEPARTMENT

This book is under no circumstances to be taken from the Building

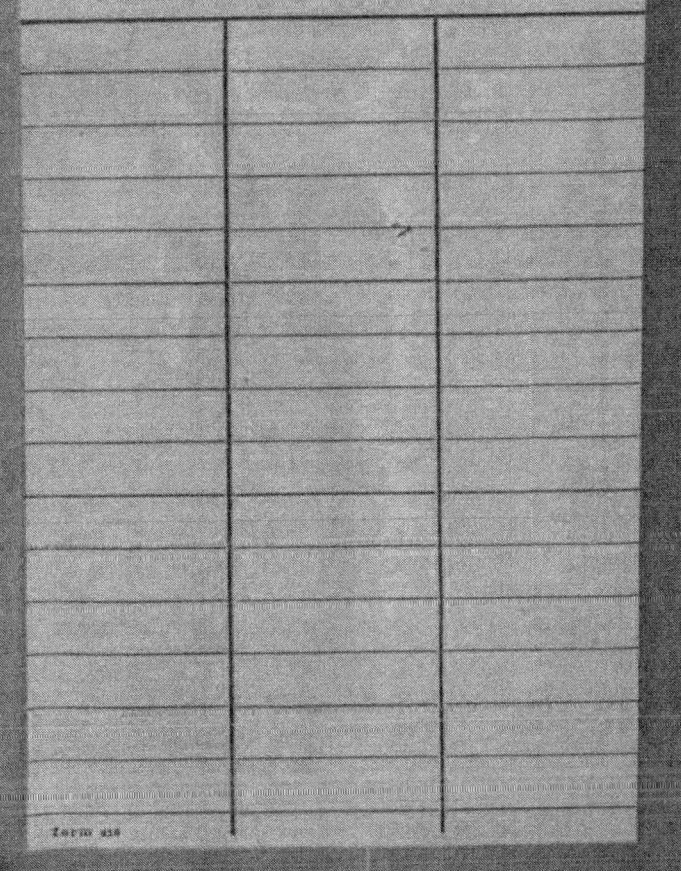

form 410

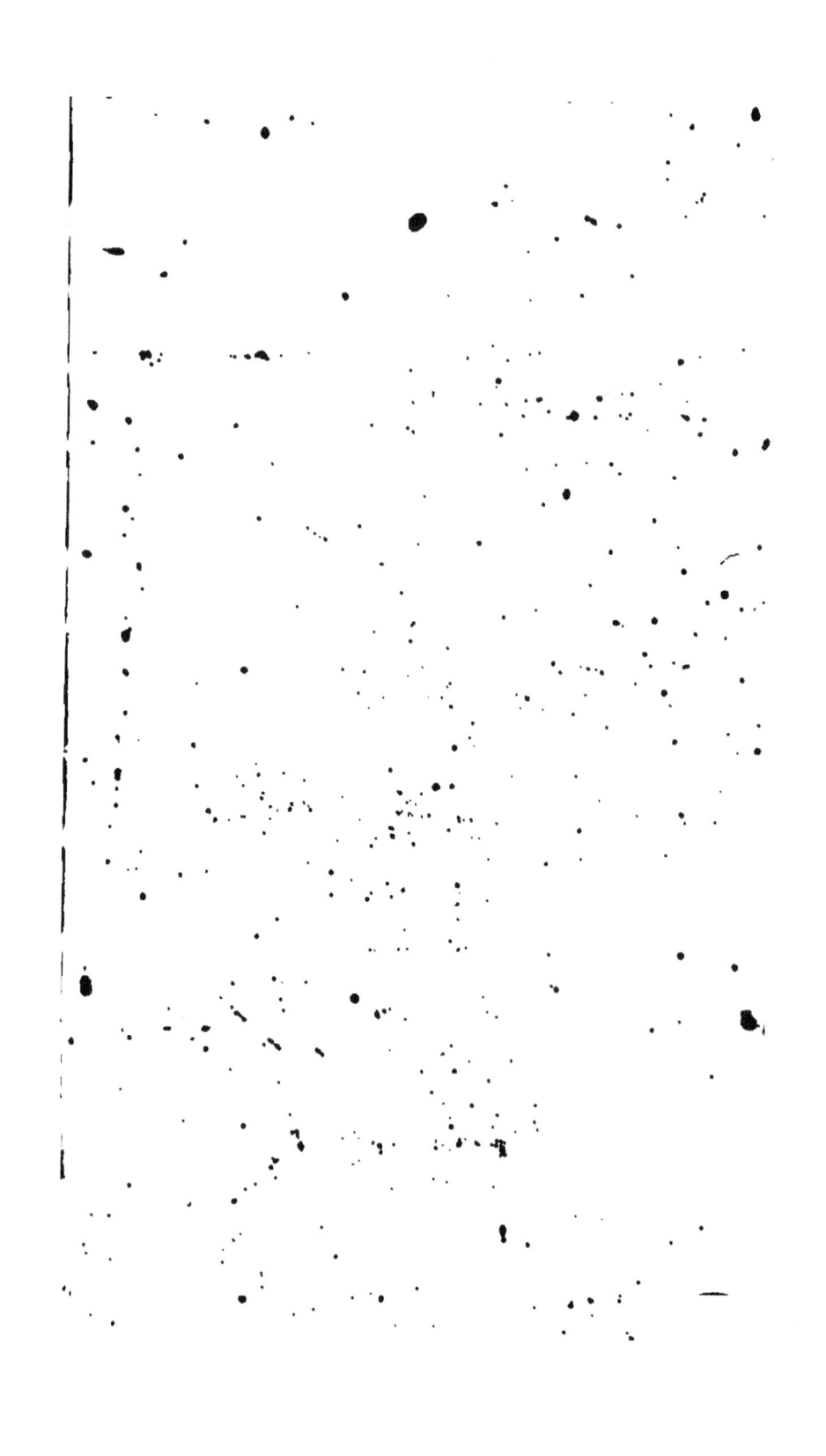

CPSIA information can be obtained
at www.ICGtesting.com
Printed in the USA
BVOW06s1256250917
495845BV00005B/55/P